The
Business Owner's
Guide
to
Personal
Finance

The Business Owner's
Guide
to
Personal Finance

*When Your Business
Is Your Paycheck*

Jill Andresky Fraser

BLOOMBERG PRESS

PRINCETON

Books are available for bulk purchases at special discounts. Special editions or book excerpts can also be created to specifications. For information, please write to: Special Markets Department, Bloomberg Press.

BLOOMBERG, BLOOMBERG NEWS, BLOOMBERG FINANCIAL MARKETS, OPEN BLOOMBERG, BLOOMBERG PERSONAL FINANCE, THE BLOOMBERG FORUM, COMPANY CONNECTION, COMPANY CONNEX, BLOOMBERG PRESS, BLOOMBERG PROFESSIONAL LIBRARY, BLOOMBERG PERSONAL BOOKSHELF, and BLOOMBERG SMALL BUSINESS are trademarks and service marks of Bloomberg L.P. All rights reserved.

This publication contains the author's opinions and is designed to provide accurate and authoritative information. It is sold with the understanding that the author, publisher, and Bloomberg L.P. are not engaged in rendering legal, accounting, investment-planning, or other professional advice. The reader should seek the services of a qualified professional for such advice; the author, publisher, and Bloomberg L.P. cannot be held responsible for any loss incurred as a result of specific investments or planning decisions made by the reader.

First edition published 2002
1 3 5 7 9 10 8 6 4 2

Library of Congress Cataloging-in-Publication Data

Fraser, Jill Andresky.
    The business owner's guide to personal finance : when your business is your paycheck /
Jill Andresky Fraser.-- 1st ed.
        p. cm.
    Includes bibliographical references and index.
    ISBN 1-57660-025-4 (alk. paper)
        1. Businesspeople--Finance, Personal. 2. Business enterprises--Finance.
3. Finance, Personal. I. Title.

    HG179 .F72 2002
    332.024'338--dc21

                                                                    2001043224

Edited by CHRISTINE MILES

Book Design by LAURIE LOHNE / DESIGN IT COMMUNICATIONS

For Lynne and Steve Andresky,

Ida Norkin Pinkwater, and Mary Andresky

Contents

Stage 1

Stage 2

Stage 3

Acknowledgments

IN MY CAREER AS A FINANCIAL journalist, I've been fortunate in many ways. But none seems more relevant to this project than the many years I've been privileged to work for *Inc.* magazine, which sets the gold standard for coverage of the vibrant and ever-changing entrepreneurial world. My colleagues there are an extraordinary bunch—as are our readers! I've learned from them all, but must single out a small group for my special thanks: George Gendron, an inspiring editor-in-chief; Karen Dillon; Evelyn Roth; Nancy Lyons; and Kascha Piotrzkowski. I'd also like to thank a good friend and former colleague, Jeffrey Seglin.

Within the Bloomberg organization, I have a number of talented and supportive colleagues to thank as well: Bill Inman, Steve Gittelson, Janet Bamford, and Jared Kieling. I must reserve a special note of gratitude, however, for Christine Miles, my insightful, resourceful, and endlessly encouraging editor on this book and many other writing projects (over the course of many years and quite a few magazines), as well as my first "boss" years ago at *Forbes* magazine and my dear friend for what has now been two decades. Without her help, this book would not exist. She is one of a kind.

I'm also grateful to the many entrepreneurs who shared their insights and experiences with me, both on and off the record. I'm well aware that personal finance is—first and foremost—personal and deeply appreciate their willingness to discuss with me some of the good and bad decisions they've made over the years. This book owes a great deal to their participation.

No project of this magnitude can be completed without one final set of thanks to my husband, Steve Fraser, and our two children, Max and Emma. They make everything possible.

Introduction

PERSONAL FINANCE. The words are so simple and familiar that the topic seems scarcely worth special attention, especially when compared to its counterpart in the business world, corporate finance. How many business owners have the spare time or energy to worry about personal finance (or many other personal matters) when they're struggling with the never-ending, simultaneously exhilarating and terrifying challenges of running a start-up, young, or fast-growing company?

Ask an entrepreneur about personal finance goals, and the answer is likely to run along lines like these: "Oh, I don't worry about that." Or "I worry about that, but I'm concentrating on landing new customers," or "raising cash for the company," or "hiring the right staffers." Or whatever. The specifics will differ, but the inattention is usually the same.

That's the too-busy-to-breathe approach. There's also the optimist's refrain—very common since entrepreneurs are a perpetually optimistic lot: "Why should I bother to think about personal finance? As soon as my company gets big enough"—or goes public, or gets sold, or otherwise achieves all the success that optimists dream of—"my family will have all the money we need for everything we'll ever want."

After having spent more than a decade as *Inc.* magazine's finance editor, I've become convinced that personal finance is one of the most frequently and dangerously overlooked issues for entrepreneurs. Without ever bothering to articulate it, most business owners have a personal finance strategy that boils down to two words: *my company*. Is there a back-up strategy, a set of plans to create a safety net that will safeguard their family's well-being in the event that their company's success takes years, doesn't ever happen, or is anything short of spectacular? Forget about it.

How risky is this approach? From where I'm sitting—after literally thousands of telephone calls, e-mails, letters, interviews, and meetings with entrepreneurs—I have become convinced that there must be a better way. In fact, many of the problems I hear about from small business owners, relating to their *company's* finances as well as their family's, often could have been minimized or avoided if they had devoted just a fraction of their time and savvy to the right kind of personal finance planning.

Does it seem a stretch to you that inattention to *personal* finances could have serious, negative consequences for one's company, not just for one's family? Then just let your mind wander through some scenarios that are, unfortunately, far too common in the entrepreneurial world. Do bankers keep nixing a growing company's credit line applications, or potential backers continuously pass on an investment deal, despite its apparently healthy business prospects? Odds are fairly strong that the owner's personal credit flaws or lack of family assets are a big part of the problem.

Was an entrepreneur forced to bring in investors—or maybe even sell off the venture—prematurely, at a fraction of the price the stock would someday be worth? More good companies than I care to recall have been forced to sell themselves at bargain-basement prices, whether in pieces or whole, for lack of an emergency savings nest egg, college-tuition fund, or retirement savings. Countless more have closed up shop because of their owners' failure to take sensible steps to "divorce-proof" their corporate, as well as their personal, finances.

When I talk about a "better way" for entrepreneurs, it's not the same personal finance path that works just fine for the rest of the world. Business owners, and their families, really *are* different from everyone else, which is why you need to adopt a comprehensive approach to personal finance that not only takes into account but actually aims to enhance the financial goals of your business. Following such a course, I am convinced, will not only safeguard your family's financial future but also increase your company's long-term prospects for success.

The pages that follow outline personal finance solutions that make sense for every entrepreneur. That's a bold statement, I realize. After all, there are as many types of entrepreneurs as there are kinds of companies. You may know a great deal or very little about the ways and whims of finance. You may be among those who fund their start-ups with credit cards, loans from family members or friends, venture capitalist investments, or alternative capital. You may pursue fast growth at all costs from day one of your operations, or you may instead aim to build profitability along a slow but steadier course.

Your ultimate goal may be a lucrative initial public offering or a merger with a large corporate partner, or you may dream instead of creating a long-lived, independent company to pass on to your children. You may wind up, as growing numbers of men and women do, as a "repeat entrepreneur" who starts multiple business ventures. (For some people, that means accumulating a string of successes; for others, attempting to learn from their failures.)

It sometimes seems as though the only thing entrepreneurs have in common is their passionate, deep commitment to building and running their companies. But that's not the case. Most encounter a fairly predictable set of financial problems. (I know, because I spend a good bit of my time diagnosing these problems and trying to help business owners solve them.) Their companies voraciously consume capital, especially in the early and fast-growth stages. Cash flow crises are inevitable, even for the most successful businesses.

It's no surprise, therefore, that for many small business owners, the effort involved in simply coping with day-to-day challenges can wreak havoc upon the family's finances. That dual obligation is another thing many entrepreneurs have in common.

But all that can change, starting right now, for business owners willing to follow the basic strategies outlined in this book. You can learn how to establish—and achieve—important personal priorities even while taking steps to cement the prospects for business success. Best of all, rather than struggling to fit your unique goals and lifestyle into everyone else's blueprint, you'll learn how entrepreneurs can take advantage of special personal finance opportunities, thanks to U.S. tax laws; changing credit, insurance, and investment possibilities; and the vibrancy of capital markets.

Each of the three major sections of this book (defined by an owner's needs at progressive growth stages of a company) is broken into articles outlining specific strategies, as you can see in the table of contents. But to help guide you through this book, across all stages of company growth, I've included a table of Hot Topics at right. Here you will find such subjects as Taxes, Savings, Retirement Planning, and much more, with page numbers of the related articles.

These personal finance strategies are not difficult, not nearly as difficult as creating and running a company. That's not to say that they won't require some of your time and energy and even, upon occasion, short-term sacrifices in the interests of long-term rewards. But most entrepreneurs have already proven themselves capable of devoting this, and much more, to their businesses. Your personal finances deserve this kind of attention from you as well. After all, there can be no better payoff for all your business

Hot Topic Index

savvy, risk-taking, and hard work than your opportunity to enjoy the fruits of entrepreneurial success.

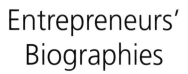

Entrepreneurs' Biographies

Aaron Cohen
Founder and chief executive officer
Concrete Inc., founded in 1996
New York City–based consulting firm that worked with large companies to develop Internet-based businesses. The company was partially sold and partially liquidated in 2001. *Prior experience:* After working as a management consultant, Cohen founded a series of Internet-related businesses, including GirlsOn Network, which he sold to Oxygen Media.

Bill Daugherty
Cofounder and co–chief executive officer
iWon.com, founded in 1999
Irvington, New York–based Internet portal that awards cash prizes to users
Prior experience: Formerly the senior vice president of business development for the National Basketball Association. Daugherty met Jonas Steinman, iWon's cofounder and co-CEO, on the first day of their freshman orientation at Harvard Business School.

Fran Greene
Founder, president, and chief executive officer
Cakes Across America, Inc., founded in 1992
Flagler Beach, Florida-based bakery network and delivery
system
Founder, president, and chief executive officer
SellWise, Inc., founded in 1989 (originally as an electronics distributorship)
Flagler Beach, Florida-based military subcontractor and
value-added repackager of electronics products
Prior experience: Greene spent almost twenty years with a
Fortune 500 company in positions that included marketing
representative, sales executive, and acting general manager.

Barbara B. Grogan
Founder, president, and chief executive officer
Western Industrial Contractors, Inc., founded in 1982
Denver, Colorado-based building contractor
Prior experience: Grogan's background includes an M.B.A.
and career stints as the executive director of a child-abuse-prevention program; chairman of her local chamber of
commerce; and chairman of the board of the Federal Reserve Bank, Kansas City–Denver Branch, for six years
(1989–95).

Holly Hitzemann
Founder and president
Holliken, Inc., founded in 1983
Albuquerque, New Mexico–based firm specializing in delivery of photographic stock imagery to the restaurant, hospitality, and direct-marketing industries
Prior experience: Trained as an M.B.A., Hitzemann worked
for defense contractors in the areas of technical writing
and proposal development, as well as for a marketing research firm that specialized in the restaurant and retail
industries.

Patrick McGovern
Founder and chairman
International Data Group (IDG), founded in 1964
Boston, Massachusetts-based global provider of information technology media, research, conferences, and events
Prior experience: While studying for a biophysics degree at MIT, he launched his career in publishing by working for the first U.S. computer magazine, *Computers and Automation,* where he eventually became associate publisher.

Ruth M. Owades
Founder and chief executive officer
Calyx & Corolla, founded in 1988
San Francisco, California-based catalog retailer of fresh flowers
Prior experience: After college and a Fulbright scholarship to study theater in France, she worked in marketing, earned an M.B.A., and founded her first company, Gardener's Eden (a catalog retailer of upscale gardening accessories), in 1979; she sold that company to Williams-Sonoma in 1982.

Lucille Roberts
Founder and president
Lucille Roberts Health Clubs, founded in 1969
New York City–based national chain of fitness centers
Prior experience: Roberts was a self-proclaimed "health nut" who worked as a school teacher and then as the retail buyer for a small shoe store while fantasizing about ways to open her own company.

Tom Stemberg

Founder, chairman, and chief executive officer
Staples, Inc., founded in 1986
Framingham, Massachusetts-based retailer of office supplies, business services, furniture, and technology
Prior experience: Armed with an M.B.A., Stemberg held various corporate management posts at Jewel's Star Market stores and First National Supermarkets, including the presidency of the Edwards-Finast division (where the formula was to cut costs, buy in volume, and slash prices).

Brian Sullivan

Practice managing partner, Global Financial Services
Heidrick & Struggles
Founder and chief executive officer
Sullivan & Co., founded in 1988 (and sold to Heidrick & Struggles in 1999)
New York City–based executive recruitment firm focused on financial services
Prior experience: Sullivan gained Wall Street expertise by working as an investment banker for Kidder Peabody and as the head of asset management for Revlon before spending two years learning the recruitment business at an existing firm.

Lillian Vernon

Founder and chief executive officer
Lillian Vernon Corp., founded in 1965
Rye, New York–based catalog and online retailer
Prior experience: Vernon launched her first forays into the mail-order business back in 1951, when she was pregnant with her first child and looking for a part-time job that could supplement the family's income.

Robert F. Young
Cofounder and chairman
Red Hat Inc., founded in 1993 as ACC Corp. (which merged with another company and changed its name to Red Hat in 1995)
Research Triangle Park, North Carolina–based technology company, whose products include the Red Hat Linux operating system
Prior experience: Canadian-born Young founded two computer rental and leasing companies before starting Red Hat's predecessor, ACC, out of his wife's sewing closet.

Y

ou are in the planning stages of making your company a reality. Or maybe you've just gotten it off the ground. At this critical start-up time you're in . . .

STAGE 1

Setting Reasonable Goals

During the start-up period, the most important personal priority for any entrepreneur should be financial self-protection.

WHEN MOST PEOPLE START their own companies, their sights are set firmly on the personal profits they *eventually* expect to earn. During the short term, they are prepared to make all kinds of financial sacrifices by taking on debt, spending the family's savings, and, usually, drastically reducing the size of their paychecks. They don't expect anything good to happen on the personal financial front, and for many business owners nothing does, at least not for quite a while.

But this strategy—which develops whenever entrepreneurs place their business's financial health way ahead of their family's—can create enormous difficulties during the start-up phase. I always tell start-up owners that there's a better way to approach this challenging period: by setting modest yet realistic goals for personal financial development that should occur *while* your new business venture takes root and, hopefully, grows. Sometimes people respond by arguing that they're too busy to think about anything other than their new business endeavor. But the owners that I stay in touch with usually concede, later on, that they should have made the time for their personal finances. It's simpler to avoid problems up front than to clear them up once your family situation is completely intertwined with your company's.

It's tough to predict how long this start-up period will last for you or any entrepreneurial company. But it should include some fairly predictable landmarks: developing a business plan (which hopefully will involve putting the plan on paper and testing your business model's assumptions); raising start-up capital (usually from your own savings or personal borrowing capabilities); setting up operations, either in a separate corporate facility or a home office; and launching your business.

During these and other early-stage events, your company will be a consumer—rather than producer—of cash. (In fact, if you are like many entrepreneurs, you will find that you have underestimated its start-up capital requirements on not one but a number of different occasions.) Cash flow patterns will be erratic, unpredictable, and all too often, negative.

This is where the notion of self-protection comes into play. No one is going to get rich during a company's start-up period; but entrepreneurs who do the right kind of personal financial planning should be able to make it through this period without severely handicapping the family's finances or significantly reducing its overall quality of life. Such planning helps founders position themselves and their families to start reaping the benefits of ownership as quickly as possible (in part because they won't find themselves distracted later on by the necessity of clearing up personal problems that can easily develop during a company's early growth).

An entrepreneur's personal financial goals during this period should focus on these central issues:

❑ **Controlling the family's financial exposure to the new venture** by setting reasonable limits to the founder's investment, whether through savings or debt. For every entrepreneur, the definition of *reasonable* will differ, but you'll know that you're stepping outside the safety zone if you contemplate extreme financing measures such as cashing in a retirement plan, wiping out the family's savings, or credit card charging at levels that could push you into personal bankruptcy if your business venture does not take off quickly. Before even launching your business, it pays to explore nonowner

Risk is in the eye of the beholder. Investing in ACC was the only solution I could see to reduce the virtual certainty of not meeting my financial objectives.

—ROBERT F. YOUNG

sources of start-up capital (see "Bootstrapping the Start-up," page 22, "Banking Basics," page 73, and "Friends-and-Family Financing," page 77) as well as to seek ways to limit the company's capital demands. For many entrepreneurs, the best way to be cost-effective is to headquarter a start-up at home (see page 27), but don't overlook "The Personal Benefits of Corporate Bartering" (page 81) when you are seeking other ways to keep your company's cash outlays low.

❑ **Limiting personal legal and tax liabilities** by selecting the right corporate structure, estate plan, and other safeguards early on. You'll find road maps to guide you through all of these essential issues throughout Stage One, but do pay special attention to "Incorporation Issues" (page 34), "Structuring Your Company's Stock" (page 38), and "Preparing Personal and Corporate Wills" (page 62).

❑ **Establishing a list of basic lifestyle priorities** that deserve your family's financial attention as much as your company does. This list may be short, but it should contain all those items too important to ignore: health insurance, life insurance, and emergency personal savings (all issues that are discussed in-depth among the Stage One strategies that follow).

❑ **Treating yourself professionally,** which means devoting as much attention to your own compensation package as you would to those of your employees. Many entrepreneurs worry about everything *except* themselves during the start-up phase and, as a result, they miss out on whatever small opportunities might exist to begin rewarding themselves—if only at a basic level—for their enormous sacrifices of time and energy. The strategies discussed in "Smart Owners Pay Themselves" (page 46) and "The Benefits of Bonuses" (page 49) will help ensure that you don't forget about yourself during this demanding period. (There's an added benefit to following the steps outlined in these sections: Prudent self-compensation can help you control your family's financial exposure to the company by allowing you to slowly rebuild personal savings and pay down credit card and other outstanding debt.)

❑ **Creating an early warning system** that will alert you if you diverge significantly from any of these early-stage personal financial goals. If you stick to the blueprint outlined in "Record-Keeping Rules: Save Everything!" (page 42), you'll be able to quickly and clearly detect warning signs. Some slippage will probably be unavoidable, but if you identify potential risks quickly, you should be able to strategize ways to minimize their consequences and repair damage as soon as possible.

Stage 1

Making a Savvy Transition

By planning ahead, company founders can reduce the personal finance risks of a switch from corporate to entrepreneurial life.

FOR ANYONE ACCUSTOMED TO the predictability of a regular paycheck and the security of a large-employer's benefit package, ownership of a start-up can be a harrowing experience. In most cases, owners and their families represent their company's only line of financial defense; when anything unexpectedly goes wrong—low sales, slow collections, rising costs—corporate survival usually depends upon their ability to make financial sacrifices large enough to withstand the cash flow crisis.

Some preparation can help ease potential pain. At the same time that would-be entrepreneurs are working on their business plans, researching the marketplace, and investigating their (admittedly limited) financing options, it is also essential for them to create a security net that can help protect their families during this transition period. There are several ways to do this:

❑ **Spend less and save everything you can** while your income is still relatively high and predictable. This strategy has two unbeatable advantages: The earlier you start, the better able you'll be to finance your new venture out of savings rather than more costly debt options. Also, cutting back prepares your family to cope with life on a reduced monthly paycheck, which will likely represent its new financial reality, at least for a while.

❑ **Stop using your personal credit cards and try to pay off any outstanding balances.** Besides reducing your monthly expenses (which is essential at a time when your income soon may become irregular), this precaution will leave you better prepared to rely upon your charge cards to help your company when no other financing is open to it.

❑ **Check your own (and your spouse's) credit reports to make certain that they are accurate and positive.** As a company owner, you must expect your personal financial history to be examined by any potential lender or investor before they will ever agree to back your business. If you've got a history of problems, it's worth taking some time early—*before* even trying to raise capital and, ideally, prior to the launch of your start-up—to clear them up. This should include correcting any errors that may exist in your credit report, paying off excessively large or old outstanding balances, and sending a letter of explanation (along with backup documentation) if there are extenuating circumstances or billing disputes involved with any of the problematic charges.

> *Have at least eighteen months' income in the bank, perhaps have another job and be able to start your new venture part-time, or have a working spouse with a good income and health benefits.*
>
> —FRAN GREENE

@ **Internet Guide:** To order a copy of your credit report, visit www.transunion.com, www.experian.com, or www. equifax.com. Any of these services will provide it to you free of charge if you reside within certain states (Colorado, Georgia, Maryland, Massachusetts, New Jersey, and Vermont) or if you have been turned down for credit within the past sixty days. Otherwise expect to pay a fee of up to $10.

Emotional Support

IF YOU TAKE THE TIME TO SET these financial plans in place, you'll go a long way toward sheltering your family against the risks inherent in any start-up. But when I recently visited a group of would-be entrepreneurs—all working on prelaunch activities with the help of some early-stage advisers—there was another type of planning that I recommended as well, which falls into the category of emotional support for their families.

Spouses and children pay a big price when a parent decides to start a business venture, and I've heard many types of complaints (about all those hours spent away from the family, increased financial pressures, insecurity, and much more). It just doesn't make sense to pretend that these problems won't arise or to try to wish them away. Instead, I urge would-be entrepreneurs and early-stage owners to figure out some way to include self-help family time in their regular schedules. This needn't be elaborate: You can plan to set aside a half-hour for complaints or problems, or something as simple as snuggle time after each week's Sunday dinner.

Or you can try an approach that one computer consultant recommended to me from personal experience: Keep a notebook in a prominent place in the living room and encourage all family members to write in it whenever they've got good feelings,

❑ **Get liquid.** Hopefully, you haven't invested every last dime that you've got in your company *before* it even opens its doors. (That's not to say that you may not eventually wind up investing everything.) It can be financially suicidal to launch a start-up if you've already exhausted all of your personal savings and borrowing capabilities. Once you've determined how much of the family's wealth, great or small, will go into the new venture, you need to restructure the rest of the household's assets with one goal in mind: to complaints, or anxieties to share. Then make certain that *everyone* takes the time to read it once each week.

"A lot of times, business owners complain that their families don't understand the problems that they face or the pressures they're under. But the truth is," she pointed out to me, "it's easy for us to lose sight of what's going on with our kids or our spouses. We forget about the pressures that *they're* experiencing, which are usually directly tied to the risks and challenges posed by our companies. These are our choices, but they have to live with them too."

Don't think of these notebooks—or other family-communications strategies—as simply places to vent negative feelings. So long as you're committed to the process of sharing, day in and day out, you'll be able to help your family members experience some of the thrills (and chills) connected with your life as an entrepreneur. One last point is emphasized by the computer consultant: "The best family communications take place on a two-way street. So don't act as though the only thing worth talking about is *your* company and the way it affects everybody in the family. Don't let yourself get so preoccupied with the entrepreneurial experience that you forget they've got important things worth sharing too!"

counterbalance the high risk and illiquidity of your entrepreneurial investment.

Do this by switching stock, bond, or mutual fund holdings to money-market funds or bank savings accounts. Since your goal is to keep your spare funds safe *and* completely accessible, you don't even want to choose a long-term bank certificate of deposit, which might tie up your money during a period when you need it for the company.

There are two exceptions to this rule:

❶ **Don't sell at a loss** simply in order to reposition your funds in more liquid and risk-free investments. You can always opt for this course in the event of a cash flow emergency, if you've got no other financing option.

❷ **There's no need to be this defensive** in your overall investment strategy if your family is well-heeled and you plan to invest only a small portion of its savings portfolio in the new venture.

Stage 1

Bootstrapping the Start-up

In order to protect your family's finances, look for ways to limit your early-stage investment in the company.

THE TYPICAL SCENARIO FOR A START-UP goes something like this: An entrepreneur empties the family's bank accounts, maxes out the credit cards, and otherwise stretches his or her family to its financial limits—all in the interest of getting the venture up and running while hanging on to equity and management control. But since the majority of new businesses either fail or stumble along without ever achieving any significant level of growth or profitability, it makes sense for even the most optimistic of founders to try to control their financial exposure and accompanying personal risk. Here's how:

❑ **Develop and test a full-scale business plan before launching the company.** New businesses can turn into sinkholes for money, especially when their owners don't at least attempt to accurately predict operating expenses or early-stage cash flow patterns. There are quite a few good business-planning software packages to steer you through this process, but if you need an expert's advice, good sources of free assistance include your local Small Business Administration office, a Small Business Development Center, or a branch of SCORE (the Service Corps of Retired Executives).

Tip: It pays to exert some self-discipline at this stage and iron out any kinks *before* you start operating and running through your own limited personal funds.

In order to control capital requirements during the start-up period, many entrepreneurial incubators recommend that would-be founders emerge from the business-planning process with a scheme for *slowly* unfolding the launch of the company, concentrating first on those operations that have the best chance of quickly generating positive cash flow. That helps control the hit to the family's finances while creating the possibility of funding growth internally.

❏ **Look for ways to raise outside capital rather than relying entirely on personal resources.** Once your business plan has been completed and tested, you may be in a position to raise seed capital from any of these sources: *economic development groups,* which often provide early-stage funds to entrepreneurs willing to locate their ventures in targeted cities or regions; *venture capital funds,* which increasingly are getting involved in seed-capital arrangements (although these tend to be limited to whatever industries are currently perceived as so "hot" that VCs see an advantage to jumping in early); and *prospective strategic partners,* which may include your new venture's likely suppliers or larger corporations that might benefit from your product or service.

Another possible source of early-stage funds is a *micro-*

loan—that is, a small loan to your company, which could range from hundreds of dollars to as much as $5,000 or $10,000. These are usually available from regional or community banks that have made a commitment to supporting start-ups in certain industries, minority- or female-owned ventures, or others on a short list of targeted business ventures (which might include companies operating in economically underdeveloped areas or those that are projected to generate large numbers of jobs for disadvantaged groups).

@ Internet Guide: While Web-surfing doesn't guarantee that you'll be able to access whatever start-up funds you're seeking, it can be a godsend when it comes to generating potential leads. Since new opportunities develop all the time, I often advise company owners to conduct keyword searches using a variety of capital terms, but it's also worth visiting comprehensive financing sites. One that I especially like is www.businessfinance.com, which provides great local leads to microloans, all kinds of government financing programs (including those sponsored by the SBA), and first-round equity financing sources.

❏ **Set personal limits and try hard to stick to them.** The basic idea is simple here: Be ready to apply the brakes before you bet your family's future on the fate of your company. There are various ways to do this. You could set a dollar limit to any business-related charges that you allow yourself to make on personal credit cards, or you could plan to use only a single family credit card for the company's early needs. (The safest course of action is to refuse to use a personal card for corporate matters, but that's a difficult rule to obey during the start-up stage, when you probably can't qualify for a corporate card.)

What you want to avoid is a situation in which you sign up for every possible credit card you can obtain and then charge yourself to each one's limit—beyond all reasonable hope of paying them back within your company's likely rate of progress. After all, if you destroy your personal credit rating, you will create havoc for both your family *and* your company.

That's what happened to one business owner who contacted me when she found herself in a seemingly inflexible bind: There was tremendous demand in her relatively remote location for her fledgling bookkeeping and clerical service. But she couldn't raise the capital to hire additional staffers or invest in necessary equipment because her credit record was plagued by late payments and excessively high debt loads. "My company is good and my business plan is strong, but it doesn't seem to matter!" she complained to me.

> *For Gardener's Eden I raised some private money and put in a fair amount myself. Also, I didn't take a salary for three years. Not everyone can make that commitment. I was very careful about cash flow and watched every penny that was spent.*
>
> —RUTH M. OWADES

Unfortunately, she was right. Given the extent of her credit problems (which dated back to a costly divorce that had left her in precarious shape), it was clear that she'd never find a backer to overlook them, no matter how good her business model was. I advised her to scale back to a more modest business plan, one that could be funded entirely through the company's cash flow; that allowed her to concentrate on cleaning up her personal financial picture before trying to develop the company's greater longer-term potential.

@ **Internet Guide:** For any entrepreneur forced to rely on credit cards as a business financing aid, it's essential to keep these costs as low as possible. Comparison shop for the best rates by visiting www.bankrate.com, a comprehensive site that allows you to fine-tune your search according to such factors as whether you tend to pay off or carry a balance, want frequent flier miles, or can benefit from a charge card rebate program.

Another good rule of thumb is that it's better to invest in your start-up only those dollars that you actually possess rather than those you can borrow (because borrowing ratchets up your personal exposure and often puts valuable assets at risk). Founders and early-stage owners are sometimes so eager to get started that they convince themselves that borrowing isn't risky, especially if personally backed loans will go toward the acquisition of hard assets, such as computers or office furniture.

But that's a mistake. I recently lunched with the co-founder of a short-lived Internet venture who had used his family's personal assets (which mainly meant the equity in his home) to support loans for tech-related acquisitions as well as business-development activities. "When something goes wrong with your company, especially in a period of economic downturn, it's incredible how quickly things can go bad and how bad they can get," he told me. "The vultures were out there. We had pieces of equipment that we had bought six months earlier for $15,000—but when we needed to sell them fast, they weren't even worth $1,000. It was a miracle that we managed to raise enough money from asset sales and receivables to pay off the loan without needing to tap into my personal assets."

That means it's preferable to use personal savings, an early-retirement package, or a job-severance payment rather than borrowing from your 401(k) plan or taking out a home equity loan or second mortgage. Don't hesitate to set limits if your family possesses any savings account worth preserving, such as a college savings nest egg, which might be tough to replace.

Starting Out at Home

Headquartering a start-up at home offers financial benefits but also poses risks for the founder's family.

ABOUT A HALF-MILLION COMPANIES get started in homes each year across the United States. By choice or financial necessity, some never relocate elsewhere; but for many others, home-based operations are a short-term management strategy that helps keep early-stage business expenses down to a minimum, until cash flow is strong enough to cover office rent and related costs. There are also time-management advantages to running a new company out of the home, which may be especially important if you've got young children or other pressing family considerations— or if you decide, as some fledgling entrepreneurs do, to start your company *before* leaving your current job.

Despite the obvious benefits of running a lean start-up, there are a number of potential personal financial problems that deserve careful attention if they are to be avoided. That's why I don't automatically advise this technique to would-be business owners. I warn them, instead, that there are risks they need to be aware of, which are especially pronounced on the personal financial front. If they proceed with a home-based operation, they need to plan accordingly.

Risk: Home-based businesses can qualify for attractive tax breaks, but they also increase the likelihood of federal and state tax audits for their owners.

Strategy: Since start-ups seldom generate much, if

anything, in the way of tax liability, there's no reason for you to be aggressive in the pursuit of tax deductions at this stage. That will help you control this audit risk. If you plan to deduct a proportion of your mortgage or rent payments and other home-related expenses, observe the letter of the law, which requires business owners to make this calculation according to whatever percentage of total square footage is used *entirely* for business purposes. In the event of a personal audit, it helps to keep documentation that will support your tax claim. This might include photographs of your business operations as well as a floor plan of the entire house that clearly details personal and corporate space.

> *To keep expenses down, I started the company in my home. It was a twelve-room house, and as the business expanded, it took over ten of the twelve rooms, leaving me with just a bedroom, a small sitting room, and a shared kitchen.*
>
> —PATRICK McGOVERN

A certified public accountant who's been a longtime resource for me boasts that he's never had a business-owning client lose an audit over a home-office issue. Here's his secret: He rigorously double-checks both their tax claims and the backup documentation every single year before filing a personal return. He takes a more conservative position on these deductions than he does with other write-offs that are less likely to raise red flags with the IRS or state tax authorities. "No exceptions," he told me. "No kinda, maybe, it feels like about half the house is the office. No way will I let them claim a bedroom as an office just because it's got a desk in it. Those are the tricks that can really trip you up." Then, to make certain that vital records don't get lost, he retains all home office documents in his files.

Risk: In their efforts to keep start-up costs to a minimum, many home-based entrepreneurs mistakenly assume that their family's insurance policies will cover the company automatically—which can result in denied claims or canceled coverage if fire, theft, flood, or damage occurs. I can't tell you how many problems I've heard about in cases where owners failed to focus on this insurance issue.

One owner, who distributed cosmetics out of her basement, lost thousands of dollars' worth of supplies, as well as an expensive computer and office furniture, in an electrical fire. When she filed her claim for business as well as personal losses, the insurer canceled her coverage for violating the fine print of its policy terms (which prohibited any commercial activities on insured premises) and refused to make any reimbursement at all. "I was shocked. But I was also stupid," she told me. "And I certainly paid the price for that."

Other typical policy prohibitions include commercial enterprises with employees, those involving on-site visits by customers or suppliers, or those requiring the installation of production-related equipment or other heavy machinery. If you can't understand the fine print in your policy's exclusion and coverage clauses, consult the insurer's customer service division or your broker before launching your home-based operation.

Strategy: Before setting up a start-up at home, entrepreneurs need to contact their insurance carriers to find out which type of business operations—if any at all—are covered under their existing home owners policy. In very simple circumstances (no employees or visits to the home from customers or suppliers, no business equipment except for some basics such as a computer and some file cabinets) there may be no need for additional coverage. But most home-based start-ups will be required by the family's carrier to purchase a special rider to guarantee adequate protection of business assets. The cost will vary, mainly in relation to the perceived risks your business runs and the replacement value of its hard assets. For a small-scale operation or start-up, your extra expenses may add up to less than $1,000.

Tip: In rare cases, when a start-up is perceived by insurers as unusually risky (perhaps because of complicated machinery or a large number of employees), founder-home owners may find themselves unable to purchase such a rider—or even to maintain their family's existing *personal* policy. If that happens, the only safe course of action is to relocate the business elsewhere, rather than expose the family's assets to financial hazards without shelter from home owners coverage.

Risk: Without creating the right paperwork structure, the owner of a home-based business may be personally liable for the corporation in a variety of unexpected and costly ways. These may include municipal fines if you fail to comply with local zoning laws, or all kinds of legal risks if you're operating at home as an unincorporated sole proprietor without personal protection from business creditors.

Strategy: Despite an owner's understandable desire to keep start-up costs low, a lawyer's assistance is essential at this stage. But these fees shouldn't cost you any more than you would expect to pay with any new venture (meaning no more than $1,000 or so for a simple start-up). First, as with any entrepreneurial venture, it makes sense to incorporate so as to minimize the family's legal and financial liabilities. Since personal and corporate affairs are easily muddled when business operations take place at home, careful record-keeping precautions are especially important in order to control the family's potential exposure (see "Record-Keeping Rules: Save Everything!" page 42).

Meanwhile, company founders need to investigate state and local regulations governing home-based businesses to make certain that they are not breaching zoning laws or corporate or residential real estate restrictions, which may carry with them significant penalties. Before starting business operations, it also pays to investigate essential services such as trash pickup and utility capabilities. Keep in mind that what's considered acceptable on the personal front may not be enough for a growing business. You may need to sign up for extra levels of service, rewire your home, or hire commercial carriers if that's possible in your neighborhood.

@ Internet Guide: For information about start-up strategies, special purchasing plans that can help keep costs low, and valuable links to government, legal, and other resources for home-based business owners, two sites are worth visiting: www.hoaa.com and www.gohome.com.

Stage 1

How Much Do You Need in Emergency Reserves?

During the start-up phase, it's especially important for you to create a nest egg that can protect your company as well as your family if unforeseen difficulties arise.

ALTHOUGH EVERYONE SHOULD have an emergency reserve fund, this precaution is especially essential during the period when a young company's cash flow patterns and capital demands may stress its owner's personal finances

Investment Strategy

WHEN IT COMES TO INVESTING your emergency nest egg, remember that you've already taken on all the risk your family can handle during this period, in the form of your start-up. So keep these funds in safe, highly liquid investment vehicles, such as a bank savings account, money market fund, or short-term certificate of deposit.

in unpredictable ways. Popular wisdom has it that an emergency savings account should cover three to six months of living expenses.

But early-stage entrepreneurs need to think about this issue in a completely different way than other people do. That's because it's both incredibly hard for business owners to set up and maintain an emergency fund but also absolutely essential that they figure out how to do so. I'm sympathetic to the quandary: At the same time that you're paying yourself very little (or nothing at all), you're the main source of growth capital for your company. Your family needs a security blanket too, but it's probably not clear to you (or to most new business owners) how to create one, given the many demands that already are being placed upon limited household resources.

During the years in which I've watched this phenomenon play itself out, I've developed some theories about ways that start-up owners can—and should—get around these roadblocks:

❶ **Start by calculating two months of personal living expenses.** Although that's not much of a safety zone, having that much of a cushion should buy you enough time to scramble around for other sources of income in a crisis.

❷ **Calculate three months of fixed operating expenses for your company**, as well as any variable monthly costs that you wouldn't be able to eliminate during a cash flow crunch. ❸ **By adding these two numbers together, you'll be able to set a reasonable target for your emergency reserve fund.** If your company operates at a high monthly tab, your savings goal might well turn out to be higher than an employed person's target (even assuming that six-month cushion they're aiming for!). But don't despair: You don't need to save the entire amount right away.

❹ **Instead, create backup reserves by signing up for a home equity line of credit** or personal credit line through your bank or credit card company. If you've already tapped out these sources, you may be able to convince a relative to guarantee an emergency credit line. Another option is to investigate whether your spouse's 401(k) plan permits loans in cases of family emergencies.

Looking backward, the thing that I regret most is that I didn't early on decide to set up automatic debit arrangements for both a corporate savings account and a personal savings account.

—HOLLY HITZEMANN

One caveat: These strategies will work *only* if you exert self-discipline and don't immediately draw down the funds to support nonemergency business activities.

❺ **With a backup reserve fund in place, aim to save something**—if only $25 or $50 each pay period—with the goal of creating a real savings account that will eventually free you from the necessity of relying upon credit in an emergency. Whenever your company closes an operating quarter in healthy condition, give yourself a savings boost by paying yourself a small bonus that you can invest directly in this account (see "The Benefits of Bonuses," page 49).

I've had highly favorable feedback from business owners who follow this five-part strategy to the letter. They respond to its realistic approach (relying on that credit reserve until the family can slowly but surely accumulate the household savings to replace it). Best of all, it works: While your emergency nest egg slowly transitions its way from a credit-based to a savings-based crisis-reserve fund, your family and company are both protected every step of the way.

Tip: When you're shopping around for a corporate line of credit (see "Banking Basics," page 73), be sure to mention to bankers that you'll want to switch your family's emergency savings fund to their bank, along with other services you sign up for. As this fund grows, it will become more of an enticement for prospective lenders.

@ Internet Guide: For quick (and free) comparison-shopping advice, visit www.bankrate.com, which provides leads to banks offering the best rates on a variety of savings vehicles. Up-to-date listings include telephone numbers as well as links to most banks' websites.

Stage 1

Incorporation Issues

By choosing the right corporate structure for your start-up, you can minimize your personal liability risks while improving your financial prospects in a variety of ways.

HOW'S THIS FOR SHOCKING? I was recently talking to a public accountant I've known for a long time who runs a financial-services consulting firm, frequently filling in as a chief-financial-officer-for-hire at fast-growing young companies.

And I learned, to my amazement, that he hadn't incorporated his own company for years—although he certainly must have been aware of the personal risks he ran in the event of a lawsuit from a disgruntled customer (which could have put his household's assets at risk). Fortunately, he never got hit by one of those lawsuits. But by the time he finally decided to incorporate, he needed to change his company's by then well-established name, because the one he'd been using was already taken.

Why do business people who *should* know better either overlook the self-protective act of incorporation or decide to opt for sole-proprietor status for their new ventures? I suspect this course seems appealing because it's simple and basically cost-free, at least in the short run. The truth is, I've been stunned over the years to find companies that have grown quite large—sometimes even into the seven-figure revenue range—without rectifying this error (and sometimes without even recognizing what kind of risks exist).

But a misguided choice here can have serious consequences for an owner's personal as well as the company's financial future. That's because corporate-status decisions fundamentally influence an owner's legal and tax liability, while also affecting the business's ability to bring in outside investors or, one day, to go public. Difficult as this may be to believe, investment bankers will sometimes go so far as to reject some private companies as potential clients because problems in their corporate status make them unacceptable for financing without a major overhaul.

Worst of all, it can be difficult and costly to make many kinds of switches from one incorporation form to another. So it pays to devote some attention to this issue early on (and probably to consult your legal or accounting advisers) before making any final decisions. Whole books have been written on this subject, but there's no reason to immerse yourself in every minute detail. For the owners of most start-ups, these are the important distinctions to keep in mind:

❏ **Sole proprietor status.** Although the easiest incorporation form, this choice has limited advantages. The good news is that there's only one round of taxation, since corporate income and losses are given what's known as "pass-through" treatment, meaning they're taxed only once, at the owner's personal level. But owners face unlimited personal liability for their company's debts, and they're also unable to claim a wide range of business deductions. The bottom line: It seldom makes sense for any start-up's founder to choose this corporate-entity form; if you have done so, investigate your other options and switch as soon as possible. (Fortunately, that's fairly simple to do.)

❏ **S corporation status.** As with sole proprietorships, S corps offer their owners tax-advantaged pass-through treatment, but they also offer another tremendous benefit: limited personal liability for business debts. This corporate form's only real disadvantage is its stock ownership limitations: S corps may have only up to seventy-five shareholders and one basic class of stock.

For most start-ups, the pros outweigh the cons here; but if you anticipate capital-intensive early growth (meaning the possibility of bringing aboard a large number of investors or creating multiple categories of stock), or you can envision a public stock offering in the relatively near future, it won't make sense to lock yourself into an S corp's restrictions.

If your long-term vision, on the other hand, centers on basically owning and running your company until you sell it and retire, an S structure is the way to go. (That's because these deals can be structured in tax-advantaged ways for purchasers, which is why S corps usually sell at higher valuation levels than comparable companies with other corporate status.)

Tip: Keep your eye on the calendar. If you want to elect S corporation status, you must do so by filing Form 2553 with the IRS before the 15th day of the 3rd month of your corporation's tax year. If you miss this deadline, your election won't go into effect until the following calendar year.

❑ **C corporation status.** Think of C corps as offering the flip side of an S corp's advantages and disadvantages. Their ownership rules are completely flexible: There are no limits to the number of shareholders a company can have or to the types of stock classes or voting arrangements that can be designed. Personal liability is limited for all owners. But the tax treatment of C corps is far less favorable than that of either S corps or sole proprietorships. That's because income gets taxed first at the corporate level and then again when it is paid to shareholders in the form of dividends. (Another tax downside: Business deductions stay at the corporate level, which means they cannot be claimed on an owner's personal tax return, the way they can with an S corp.) The bottom line: Since entrepreneurs will face a far bigger tax bite if they go this route, it makes sense to choose C corp status only if your growth strategy depends upon large-scale financings, a major strategic alliance with a large public corporation (which may want an equity stake in your company), or an early IPO.

❑ **Limited liability company status.** This is a relatively new option, but it's got some pluses worth considering. LLCs offer their owners personal liability protection as well as pass-through tax treatment; they also permit an unlimited number of so-called members (their term for shareholders) and a lot of flexibility in the ways that "membership" arrangements can be structured.

Why isn't every entrepreneur making this choice? LLCs have two big problems: There's a prohibitive cost attached to switching to this form of status if you've already incorporated as either a C or S corp. That means this choice only makes sense at the start-up phase or if switching from a sole proprietorship. And although limited liability companies can, in theory, go public, only a tiny number have done so, which can be a discouraging factor if venture capitalists and other professional investors are considering making an investment in your company. The bottom line: Unless your company is new and you know that you'll never consider an IPO, it's probably safest to choose another incorporation option instead.

Stage 1

Structuring Your Company's Stock

An owner's decisions during the start-up phase about how much stock to issue and how to value it will affect the family's finances as the company grows.

ENTREPRENEURS ARE NOTORIOUSLY terrible paper pushers, which means that all kinds of paperwork issues tend to get either ignored or rushed through, especially during the harried early days of a company's operation. With some matters, that's not really significant, because owners can catch up later on, once they can afford to hire administrative staff to keep track of corporate details. But there's one task too important to overlook during the start-up period: creating the right stock structure, which means one that will facilitate your company's growth while maximizing your own potential for longer-term financial gain.

It makes sense to address this issue, with some input

from an attorney specializing in small business, at the same time that you weigh the pros and cons of incorporation options. Unfortunately, there's no one-size-fits-all formula to steer you in the right direction. But these basic guidelines should prepare you for a well-informed discussion with your adviser:

❶ **How many shares will you authorize?** Think of this as the total size of your stock pool: It's the number of shares you will register with your secretary of state. If your startup's business model involves little or no outside investment capital, with growth financing coming mainly from yourself, bank loans or other debt vehicles, and internal funds, then there's no compelling reason to authorize a huge pool of shares. You might as well keep matters simple by authorizing a relatively small number, such as 1,000. If you're not certain, it probably makes sense to err on the high end by authorizing something closer to the maximum limit, which varies by state.

❷ **How many shares will you issue?** This sounds more complicated than it actually is. Out of the total pool of shares that have been authorized, your company can issue (meaning actually transfer ownership of) as few or as many shares as you like. Realistically speaking, this is the number that determines who's controlling the company. If a founder authorizes 5,000 shares but decides to issue only 1,000 of them entirely to himself, then he currently owns 100 percent of the company, regardless of all those other shares that have been authorized but not issued.

Here again, entrepreneurs should probably be guided by their long-term intentions. If they know with a fair degree of certainty that they intend to seek outside investments or to use equity as a recruitment and compensation tool once they are ready to hire key personnel, then it makes sense to issue only a portion of the stock that they have authorized. Owners who are concerned about maintaining majority control of their outstanding shares can eliminate risks by initially issuing themselves a bloc that represents more than 50 percent of all authorized shares; another alternative is simply to issue themselves more stock whenever they issue shares to anyone else.

Keep in mind: In this matter, as with so many other entrepreneurial challenges, simplicity can be a virtue. There's a lot to be said for following the approach recommended to me by one owner, who runs a sporting goods manufacturing firm that has managed to log impressive growth for several years now without bringing in any outside investors: He has issued himself 100 shares of stock, despite the fact that a much larger pool of shares has been authorized. "If nobody else owns any shares, why do I need any more for now? I can always give myself some more later on," he says.

> *We initially raised $100 million in cash and media equivalents, which meant that we were able to pay ourselves a salary from the beginning and also to establish a good set of medical benefits for our employees. Benefits can make a big difference when you're in a competitive hiring field.*
>
> — BILL DAUGHERTY

❸ **How do you price the shares?** Don't get confused here. The decision that you make has nothing to do with the real-world value of your company or its future growth potential. It is purely a matter of personal finance: Depending on the state in which you reside, your pricing decision may reduce your family's tax bite when you sell your shares (whether through a public offering, outright company sale, or other transfer of ownership); the right choice may also help you limit the estate tax consequences if you decide to gift shares to family members as part of an estate-planning strategy.

Local tax laws should guide your thinking. So look to

Keep It Simple

YOU MAY NEED TO REVISIT this issue at a later date if you switch growth strategies (and find yourself in need of more stock shares to satisfy prospective investors than you've authorized), or get heavily involved in estate planning, or bring aboard a venture capital or other private equity firm (which may dictate its own terms for stock authorization and issuance). Winning approval for corporate changes should not be difficult as long as you've kept your capitalization structure clean by following the proper procedures when it comes to state registration, tax filings, and related matters.

your attorney for help when you weigh your various choices, which run the gamut from pricing your own shares at no-par (meaning no stated value, which has its own advantages in keeping personal-accounting tasks simple) or at a par value calculated according to your initial investment in the company. The bottom line: Whatever decision you make will have no impact on how you price shares at any later point in your company's growth and development—regardless of the reason why you're pricing them and the timing of this activity. That's because your stock's share price is a moving target: Even if you decide to sell stock to a friend or family member sometime very soon after this initial process of authorizing and issuing it, the price will be determined by the company's fair-market value at *that* time, which may need to be determined by a valuations professional.

Record-Keeping Rules: Save Everything!

To make certain that you don't miss out on any personal financial opportunities, start building a simple, maintainable paperwork trail from day one of owning your company.

TO ANYONE LACKING OBSESSIVE personality traits—and that may well include you—it might come as a surprise to realize how important careful record keeping can be for entrepreneurs for maximizing their profit potential and minimizing their personal risks.

You may find it difficult to accept that anything really matters during the intense, start-up phase besides attracting customers and building sales. But paperwork glitches or omissions often fuel real problems for even the fastest-growing business ventures. These can take many different forms. On the corporate end, your company may find itself unable to claim valuable tax write-offs, or wind up on the losing end of an audit because it cannot document legitimate business expenses. As for the family's finances, I've seen business owners whose credit ratings plummeted even while their companies grew because they were unable to maintain the distinction between their personal and business credit activities.

That's why record keeping is worth paying attention to, especially at this early stage. As your company grows and, hopefully, becomes more successful, you'll benefit by staying on top of these matters. Record-keeping issues can get quite complicated, especially when transactions have both personal and business implications (as when, for example, your family owns a building or piece of equipment that your company leases). In such cases, don't hesitate to involve your accounting and legal professionals on both the corporate and household fronts in developing a paperwork system that keeps up with your company's growth.

Here's some good news. During your company's early stages, you should be able to handle these tasks by yourself, so long as you live by business's golden rule: Retain everything. (Granted, that's a slight exaggeration. But the closer you can get to this goal, the better off you'll likely wind up, financially speaking.)

Here's a simple system that works:

❶ **Set up three accordion files.** Do this annually, labeling one "Family," one "Company," and one "Hybrid," for matters that relate to both. During the early ownership period, the Family and Hybrid files should be sufficient to handle each year's *personal* paperwork, including receipts, bank statements, monthly credit card bills, and other current documentation. Paper clip related records together for easy reference as the year progresses. The records in these files may be transferred elsewhere (into tax-related or long-term files) by the end of each year.

❷ **Keep the company's records separate.** This is a good discipline to establish—regardless of which type of corporate status you choose—because it reduces the potential for misunderstandings about where your personal finances end and those of the company begin. That's especially important at tax time and when appealing to prospective lenders or backers. Ask your accountant for a decision if you're confused about which kind of records to keep in the family's or the company's files.

A good rule of thumb: If receipts or paperwork are related to a *corporate* account (such as a credit card or credit line in the company's name, rather than your own), then they belong at the office, whether or not you were the person who signed for them or used them.

❸ Sort through your personal files quarterly. The end of each quarter is the time to organize all receipts related to tax deductions that you plan to claim in April. But don't stop there. As you look through the records of business-related expenses that you've paid for with personal funds (many of which you've probably already forgotten about!), you may be able to develop a plan to guarantee your reimbursement, if only at some point in the future.

Do this by totaling each operating quarter's expenses; then draft a simple promissory note between yourself and the company stating that you are owed that sum in return for expenses, which you can then document in an attachment to the note. When drafting this document, keep its payment date open, while stating that no interest charges will be attached to the loan. Then save copies of this document in both the Company and the Family files. Plan to repay yourself as soon as the company's cash flow becomes stable enough to support it.

I recommend a similar strategy if a cash flow crunch forces you to skip a paycheck or invest additional personal funds in the company (see "Should You Rely on Personal Funds in Corporate Crises?" page 53). Proper accounting procedures will require you to disclose outstanding obligations like these in your financial reports, especially those that are sent to any lenders or investors your company may have. But don't make this finance-reporting judgment on your own. Provide your accountant with the most up-to-date numbers relating to the company's debt to you as its owner; then rely upon his or her advice about how and when to disclose the debt.

❹ Be prepared to protect yourself in the event of an audit. Save each year's tax-related receipts, other business-related personal documentation, and a copy of your key banking and credit card records in a large, annual file that you store along with a copy of your personal tax return. Make certain that these files will be accessible if you need them.

How long should you save them? If you've got the storage space, it pays to hold onto these records indefinitely, since business owners never can fully anticipate what kind of information they might need to track down during their companies' lifetimes. If that's not possible, store them for at least seven years, which should offer adequate protection from federal and state tax audits.

❺ Keep long-term personal records separately, with the most important documents stored in a safe-deposit box. As your family's liabilities and, hopefully, its assets grow, this set of records will become more elaborate. You'll need individual files, for example, for each investment account. You may decide to rely upon a computer software package to help keep track of these matters as they become more complex.

There's no single software program that works best for all business owners. Plenty of people have told me that they managed just fine with a basic system such as Quicken, especially while their investments and savings were relatively small-scale. When I'm asked for referrals, I usually urge entrepreneurs to consult their accountants, since there may be quirks in their personal (or business) situations that necessitate a more specialized or sophisticated software approach.

Don't get too bogged down with this investment-record-keeping issue, at least for now. During your company's start-up and early-growth stages, most of your important long-term records will probably relate to your new venture. As corporate documents, therefore, they should more appropriately be kept in the company's files or at your accountant's or attorney's office.

At home, meanwhile, you'll probably be able to manage perfectly well with one long-term "Important Papers" file (rather than a software program). Just keep this accessible to the family at all times.

Smart Owners Pay Themselves

Despite the difficulties, there are ways that entrepreneurs can—and should—pay themselves a salary during the start-up phase.

IT'S AN AGE-OLD STORY: NO MATTER how much money they were earning in their previous lives as employees, many business owners live without a salary during their companies' early days. In some cases, such abstinence can last a year or even longer as founders wait for their companies to achieve key breakthroughs in revenue growth, cash flow, or profitability before they feel comfortable taking money out of the business. Their families, meanwhile, often pay a significant financial toll along the way. Emotional pressures mount for everyone—especially for the early-stage entrepreneur.

As one entrepreneur wrote to me recently from the home-based office in which she runs a fledgling import operation, "Nobody understands why I gave up a very good paycheck to try something like this, which is making life so much harder for all of us. Even I wonder about it sometimes, because I'm putting in so many more hours at my job—without being able to pay myself anything in return!"

I worry when I hear such comments. Anxieties about a

forgone paycheck—or guilt toward family members who must make do with less, much less—can sap founders of the self-confidence, optimism, and high levels of energy that are nothing short of essential when it comes to getting a young company past all the initial hurdles it inevitably faces. The self-compensation issue is a tough one during this stage. From the perspective of many early entrepreneurs, skipping a salary is simply another way that they can help to capitalize growth activities—not all that dissimilar to investing their personal savings or relying on personal credit cards to pay business bills during a period in which their companies lack sufficient revenue streams or other financing prospects. For business owners whose spouses earn sufficient income to cover their families' monthly expenses, the no-paycheck choice may not be a bad one, *so long as it is viewed as a strictly short-term strategy.*

From the beginning, I paid myself a very small salary which grew as the profit dollars grew. I found that by doing this I wasn't tempted to hire someone else to do the same job.

—FRAN GREENE

But there's another philosophy worth considering here. If a start-up is *not* required to pay its owner a salary, even a token one, it is not operating under normal business conditions, and therefore its business plan and cash flow model are not being truly tested. I find this *business* justification for an owner's self-compensation truly compelling. After all, if they're not required to pay their owners, many companies can struggle along with limited cash flow resources for years, never achieving real viability but never quite going under—as their owners fall farther and farther behind the earnings they might have achieved as paid employees elsewhere.

Given that risk, some small business experts and even

experienced entrepreneurs go so far as to argue that a new venture is not ready to begin operations unless it is prepared to pay its owner a regular salary, the same way that there are plans to pay for business supplies, office space, utility bills, and other essential business matters. That position may strike you as too inflexible. So here's a compromise strategy:

❑ **As early as possible—ideally, before the company even begins operations, but if not then, soon—figure out a minimum salary that makes sense for you.** Then pay yourself this amount regularly, without second-guessing all the other ways that the company could invest this money instead. Don't expect this early paycheck to bear any relationship to your previous earnings or the salaries that other, more established entrepreneurs earn in your industry. It should be calculated according to (1) your predictions about what salary the start-up's cash flow can support and (2) your assessment of your family's essential financial needs and how much, if anything, you must be able to contribute to monthly income.

❑ **Do some family bonding about the self-compensation dilemma** you've been grappling with. Rather than just expecting their families to grin and bear it, I always urge owners to talk about the paycheck issue with older children as well as their spouses. Don't hide your own conflicted feelings—by sharing them, you'll win emotional support that will strengthen you during these tough early days.

❑ **Remember, this is temporary.** At the same time that you establish your bare-bones salary, take a long-term view by developing a set of reasonable goals that the company must achieve in order to handle a bigger owner's paycheck. Write these down so that you don't lose sight of them or allow corporate priorities to overshadow your self-improvement objectives. If you're too close to this issue to be able to view it dispassionately, consult the company's accountant or attorney for advice.

No Salary Now?

WHAT IF YOU ARE ABSOLUTELY CERTAIN that there's no way your start-up could support even a tiny, token salary for you? That's OK for now. But reexamine this issue at the end of every operating quarter, with the goal of starting to pay yourself something as soon as it becomes feasible. Cash flow conditions change rapidly at young businesses, and you don't want your personal financial development to lag too far behind your company's.

❑ **Examine your self-compensation progress every six months during this early stage.** If it seems stymied, there may well be something worth correcting in your growth model; you may also need to solve cash flow problems (perhaps by addressing accounts receivable or payable problems or tightening inventory controls).

Stage 1

The Benefits of Bonuses

Through the judicious use of bonuses, start-up owners can help ease their family's financial discomfort and take steps to erase personal problems early.

WHEN VIEWED STRICTLY FROM a personal vantage point, there aren't many opportunities worth boasting about during the start-up phase, when entrepreneurs generally find themselves forced to make all kinds of financial sacrifices in order to get their ventures running. But if used correctly, self-bonuses can be used to help protect the family's finances without overtaxing the fledgling company's resources. That makes them, at least potentially, one of the most important tools in a start-up owner's management arsenal.

When I talk to owners about the right—and wrong—ways to think about self-bonuses, I emphasize to them that these financial rewards at the start-up stage have little in common with the payments they once might have received from an employer. That shouldn't really be too surprising. At larger or publicly traded companies, bonuses tend to be a matter of formal corporate policy: There are usually strict guidelines about when they can be paid and who is eligible to receive them, as well as a fixed set of business goals that must be achieved.

When you're running your own company—especially a small, fledgling venture—there aren't any rules like that to worry about. Unless you've got an independent board of directors (unlikely) or an active major shareholder, no one is going to look over your shoulder and try to second-guess whatever decision you make about paying yourself a bonus. You don't have to wait for an extraordinarily successful operating quarter, the end of your fiscal year, or any other date on the calendar. All you need to do is be certain, in your own mind at least, that the company can afford some type of extra compensation.

From the IRS's point of view, there's no difference between a bonus and a regular paycheck: When you pay income tax on April 15, that tax is calculated against total compensation, which includes bonuses and salary. In the real world, however, a bonus and a paycheck *are* different in some key respects. If you pay yourself a paycheck (and I do hope that you've made this choice), it's a fixed sum that you can count on receiving at regular intervals, usually weekly or biweekly. There's nothing regular or fixed about a bonus. It's an extra financial reward that can be as big or as little as you decide to make it and can happen once, more than once, or many times a year.

I recently received an inquiry from a start-up owner in a highly competitive Web-development niche. He was paying himself a token paycheck but had been forced to pay his single, key staffer a significantly higher salary in order to woo her away from a larger and better-established company. Now that the start-up had won some customers and started generating positive cash flow, this entrepreneur felt as though he could afford to pay an occasional bonus—but he wondered whether he needed to pay one to his employee as well as himself. He didn't want to, which wasn't too surprising. After all, it was his family that was making the big financial sacrifice tied to his truly tiny paycheck.

As I explained to him, this is a call that every owner must decide individually. In this case, since his employee already was earning a salary that was comparable to what the rest of the industry would pay, I'd expect that a bonus wouldn't be necessary to keep her on board. If that assumption was accurate, I told him that I'd recommend that he pay himself the entire bonus pool that the company could afford. But if he feared that headhunters were calling and the employee would consider moving, splitting the bonus with her would certainly help.

Careful timing is the secret to successful use of any bonus strategy. While it makes sense for business owners to be looking for self-bonus opportunities from a new venture's launch onward, such payments can jeopardize a start-up's growth prospects if they drain cash from its coffers at any precarious juncture. One common example of this for growth-oriented companies is a period in which sales have accelerated—which may ratchet up costs connected to payroll, supply purchases, or production—but billings and collections have yet to catch up, which results in a cash crunch.

So, caution is essential. Pay yourself a small bonus only after any operating quarter in which cash flow is positive *and* projections seem good for the following quarter. One exception: If monthly results are unusually robust (perhaps because you've just collected a payment from a large order or cluster of outstanding bills), the company may be able to support an earlier-than-expected bonus payment.

When corporate cash is tight but your personal needs are great, it can be tough to decide just how much to pay yourself in a bonus. The biggest mistake start-up owners can make is to decide on the amount by how much they think they need. The only safe course of action is to backtrack from the company's current financial results to whatever payment can be supported from cash flow.

Don't blow your bonus on a weekend vacation or other ephemeral self-reward. An entrepreneur's occasional bonus payments should be used to help accomplish more important objectives, such as reducing the family's credit card debt, adding to its emergency savings nest egg, or otherwise repairing personal financial problems. Keep in mind: Since the start-up phase is unpredictable and full of cash flow challenges, you may later on find yourself reinvesting your bonus payments—plus much more—in the company's growth efforts. So during this early entrepreneurial period, it pays to use any bonuses to bolster your personal stability, which will better position you to support your new venture for as long as it may take to get off the ground.

Stage 1

Should You Rely on Personal Funds in Corporate Crises?

Here's how to protect your family's finances when unexpected business developments disrupt your own salary payments or require additional infusions of personal cash.

IT MAKES SENSE FOR A BUSINESS OWNER to pay a small self-salary from the first—or early—days of the company's operations. But it would be unrealistic to assume that a young company will always be able to pay that salary, month after month, with all the overwhelming challenges of growth.

This early, entrepreneurial period is simply too unpredictable to guarantee such fiscal regularity, given the multiplicity of ways that cash flow can be jeopardized within a fledgling venture with skimpy financing, a developing revenue stream, and a yet-to-be-tested receivables system. One business owner who runs a small and still-struggling independent bookstore recently said about her salary, "In theory, [I get paid] fifty-two weeks a year—in reality, maybe half the time. But at least I'm trying."

Some business owners, maybe even the majority of them, adopt a fatalistic approach and respond to cash flow difficulties during the start-up phase by forgoing a salary entirely. Or they behave as this bookstore owner does: simply skipping their own paychecks whenever cash is tight. In some cases, they go one step further, using their personal funds to meet pressing obligations to suppliers, employees, or others.

But I believe that each of these approaches is problematic. They involve unnecessary self-sacrifice, and as entrepreneurs all too often decide to do, they place the company's interests far ahead of the family's. That's why I urged the bookstore owner to adopt a different course.

> *Protecting my investment in Red Hat was always the first priority. Having said that, I am not suggesting that you should allow yourself to suffer personal bankruptcy in the event of the failure of your enterprise.*
>
> —ROBERT F. YOUNG

Here's the strategy that I prefer. During any pay period when your company cannot afford to give you your paycheck (or requires you to make even a small additional infusion of personal funds), document the lapse through a promissory note that states the full amount of the payment skipped as well as the fact that this sum was owed to you as payment for full employment during the period. Treat this as seriously as any other corporate document. This promissory note should also briefly explain that you, as owner of the company, *loaned* it this sum in order to help meet current operating expenses, under the condition that the loan be repaid in full, at an unspecified future date, with no interest attached to the outstanding debt.

At times when you're documenting not a skipped salary but an extraordinary contribution of personal funds, this promissory note should detail the sum you paid (whether to the company itself or directly to specific creditors) and, in full detail, which corporate expenses it covered.

There are several advantages to following this course:

❶ **Once the loans are documented, business owners increase the likelihood that they will one day receive the personal compensation** that they—and their families—deserve. The loans should be repaid as soon as cash flow restabilizes for at least one fiscal quarter. If too many loans accumulate for the outstanding debt to be reimbursed all at one time, don't simply forget about it. Instead, the outstanding balance can and should be paid off gradually (so that it doesn't siphon off all those internal funds that could also be used to pay for growth-oriented activities).

❷ **Having the IOUs on paper minimizes future complications,** which may occur if investors or lenders later get involved with the company. I've seen a number of instances in which owners tried to pay themselves what they considered to be past-due compensation or reimbursements but lacked the documentation to prove their case. That gave investors the opportunity they wanted to challenge payments to the owner, saying that they preferred to see the funds invested in corporate growth activities.

Keep in mind: A common mistake business owners make is to assume that they will be able to compensate themselves for past salary sacrifices simply by paying themselves some large bonuses at the end of healthy years. But once outside backers get involved, this becomes much more difficult to carry off, since backers seldom view owners' compensation as a high priority for corporate funds, especially when compared to growth-oriented expenditures. When a paper trail of promissory notes exists, it creates a clear-cut financial obligation that is more difficult to ignore.

❸ **In a worst-case scenario, if your young company tanks and ends up in bankruptcy court,** the promissory notes might give you some legal status along with the company's other creditors and suppliers, whether assets and cash are disbursed by a judge or a future payment plan is developed.

A Blueprint for the Note

IF YOU EMPLOY A COMPTROLLER or chief financial officer, that person should sign the note on behalf of the company. But if your early-stage venture lacks such a finance staffer, there's no problem with your signing the note twice, as both the lender and the corporate borrower. It's a good idea to have the note notarized or at least witnessed by someone other than a family member. Keep the note in the same set of files in which you retain all other essential corporate documents. You may even want to send a copy to your company's attorney or accountant.

Don't expect miracles. Your compensation-related loan won't carry the same weight as bank debt in a bankruptcy situation. But if a corporate reorganization or liquidation occurs, you can expect to receive at least partial payment if sufficient funds are available.

Cost-cutting tip: Since this transaction is simple and legally binding, there's no need to spend extra funds hiring an attorney to draft the promissory note. You should be able to find a useful fill-in-the-blanks loan form at an office supply or stationery retailer.

Stage I

Simple Ways to Provide a Health Care Benefit

While your business is young, the best way to protect your family without overloading the company's cash flow is to obtain benefit coverage through other existing plans rather than setting up one of your own.

COMPANIES TYPICALLY OVERLOOK benefits in the start-up phase. That's not surprising: They're costly, and most fledgling entrepreneurs need to invest all the cash they can raise (whether from their personal savings, current operations, or early-stage investors) in business-related opportunities.

Yet benefits deserve some up-front attention by new business owners for one simple reason: The failure to guarantee at least a minimum level of protection can put a founder's family at financial risk as few other lapses can.

Fortunately, bare-bones benefit coverage should be achievable for *any* entrepreneur. What minimal level of coverage can be considered adequate for an early-stage company? While various enhancements might be appealing, medical insurance is usually the main essential for a business owner's family. (Life insurance can and should also be an important element in an owner's security blanket, but it's up to you whether you purchase it the same way any other individual would or through an arrangement with your business: See page 66, "Life Insurance Protection for Your Family.")

Here's what I tell start-up owners when they call me with questions about health care coverage, which is often exorbitantly expensive when purchased directly by a company that is either tiny or young (meaning less than three years old, the longevity that many insurers insist upon in order for a company to qualify for a more reasonable rate structure). Check out *all* your other options before signing up.

If you can buy medical coverage for your family through any of the following three methods, consider this shopping decision a no-brainer:

❑ **A spouse's benefit plan.** Larger and better-established companies usually offer their staffers the opportunity to sign up for family coverage at lower premiums than any small start-up can qualify for. If your spouse can buy this coverage for you and the rest of the family, use that option. It doesn't make financial sense to set up your own, costly corporate plan when there are so many other demands on your new venture's limited capital resources. There's another advantage to going this route: Large-company plans often also include enhancements such as vision care, prescription drug discounts, or dental coverage, which are typically unobtainable by small or young companies at any price.

❑ **A former employer's plan.** If you, like growing numbers of entrepreneurs, have left the large-corporation world to run your own company, you may be able to retain your previous medical benefits at your own expense. You just need to act quickly: You'll have to sign up for coverage through your employer's benefits office within 60 days of leaving the payroll.

This type of health care coverage, which lasts for as long as you want it and can pay for it—up to 18 months in total—is provided under a federal law known as COBRA (shorthand for the Consolidated Omnibus Budget Reconciliation Act of 1985). You're eligible to participate under a variety of conditions, which include leaving your former job to become self-employed or losing your job for any reason other than "gross misconduct." The only exception: an employer with fewer than twenty employees is exempt from COBRA rules.

Some corporate refugees shy away from COBRA coverage because they experience "sticker shock" when they see how much they'll be expected to pay each month. (Premiums do increase from the fees you previously paid as a full-time employee, because ex-staffers are expected to pay the full share of their medical coverage, without any subsidies from their former employer.) But this is an option worth exploring by entrepreneurs who don't qualify for spousal coverage, because it will likely be cheaper—and undoubtedly be more comprehensive—than any health care plan a start-up could afford.

> *I had a benefits program in place as soon as I started my company, back in 1988. Basically, the company paid for everyone's COBRA benefits, including my own, for about a year.*
>
> —BRIAN SULLIVAN

One caveat: After your eligibility to participate in COBRA expires, your former employer's insurance carrier may offer you a scaled-down version of your original health care plan. But by that point, you and your company may be able to qualify for a better deal elsewhere. So do some comparison shopping before signing up for an extension.

❏ **Any group plan that will accept your family or company.** Here's where you might have to do some digging, but the financial savings—and peace of mind—that you can achieve should be worth the extra effort. What you basically need to look for is any large organization that offers its members the ability to buy into a pooled group health insurance plan. (Although this will probably be more expensive than either spousal or COBRA coverage, it still should offer your family better protection at a lower cost than any plan your young company can purchase on its own.) Your local chamber of commerce, trade association, or other business groups may offer such insurance coverage either to your family or to your company. The downside: The availability of these plans differs widely, and business owners in states or large cities that are less desirable to insurance carriers may not be able to track down a plan that will cover them.

Tax tip: If your company pays for this plan and it's structured as an S corporation, partnership, or sole proprietorship, be aware that you (and other owners) will owe income taxes on the value of this benefit.

A Do-It-Yourself Strategy

If you cannot come up with a good group-based option, consider banding together with some other small companies to create your own insurance buyers' pool. You'll probably need an insurance agent's help if you try this, but don't let that discourage you. If you can achieve a critical mass (ideally, more than fifty participants, including all owners, family members, and employees), you should be able to cut health care costs even without the involvement of a larger organization. Such a plan may even be able to qualify for some extras such as prescription drug coverage or a drug-discount plan.

What If Your Employees Complain?

If hiring conditions are tight, you don't want to find yourself losing qualified employees to other companies that offer health care benefits you can't yet afford. So here's how to keep your staffers happy if you opt for one of the cost-saving strategies outlined above:

❏ **Encourage them to sign up for a spouse's plan too.** If they do—and your company's cash flow can afford it—consider paying them a small quarterly bonus to help sub-

sidize their premium costs. This will probably still be a
bargain, compared to the costs of setting up your own
plan when the company is too small to qualify for attractive rates. What about staffers who don't qualify for
spousal coverage? You might earn some brownie points by
paying them the same bonus anyway (and encouraging
them to use the funds to shop for a health care plan
themselves).

❑ **Share information.** In a start-up situation, it's essential
to direct cash flow to growth-related activities. If you feel
you can't afford to set up a corporate benefit plan yet,
explain to your employees how they'll gain in the future
from the company's investment decisions today. And give
them some sense of when they can hope for corporate
health care coverage to become a realistic and more affordable option.

❑ **Keep your promises.** You'll end up antagonizing—
and maybe even losing—key staffers if you string them
along with visions of employee benefits that never materi-
alize. By the time your company transitions to Stage Two of
growth, make this a priority (see "Bringing Medical Benefits In-House," page 114).

Stage 1

Preparing Personal and Corporate Wills

Effective estate planning for owners of start-ups considers the company's finances as well as the family's.

FOR MOST PEOPLE, ESTATE PLANNING becomes a complex matter only after they accumulate significant wealth and extensive personal obligations. That's not the case, though, for entrepreneurs. During the early stages of ownership—when your assets and earnings are probably limited, or maybe even nonexistent—estate planning is worthy of your time and attention. That's because the only way that you can fully protect your family's financial future in the event of your unexpected death is by developing well-coordinated business *and* personal plans.

The Personal Plan

This part is relatively straightforward. As the owner of a start-up or young company, you need:

❑ **Life insurance** (as discussed later in "Life Insurance Protection for Your Family," page 66, and "Business-Oriented Life Insurance," page 69). The safest course of action will involve both family-oriented and business-oriented policies.

❑ **A will** that spells out your intended disposal of corporate, as well as personal, assets. This document should also include a designated guardian for minor children. For those entrepreneurs whose financial situations are complicated (perhaps because of precarious business conditions, or personal debt arrangements that intricately tie their family's finances to their companies), I usually recommend including a written recommendation about a financial adviser who can guide their spouse on business-related issues. Depending on your particular circumstances, a good choice here might be your corporate lawyer or accountant, a trusted professional colleague, or a business-savvy relative.

Caveat: Many people keep the only copy of their wills in a safe-deposit box. But this can be a time-consuming mistake, since some states, such as New York, require the contents of these boxes to be sealed for a period after the owner's death. Avoid problems by keeping a copy of your will in a safe place at home as well as at your attorney's office.

The Company Plan

Here's where matters get a little more complicated, although the potential payoff should compensate for the extra planning time involved. First, you need to ask yourself one vital question: Is there a possibility that your fledgling venture could survive without you, and if not, does the company possess *any* assets of value at all?

❑ **If the company could survive,** then you need to prepare for this in every way possible. That will certainly involve some type of business-oriented life insurance policy, since your company's survival prospects will be greatly enhanced by the availability of liquid funds during the precarious transition phase your death would cause.

You'll also want to think about succession planning. Depending on the particulars of your own situation, this might involve making certain that your spouse or another family member is closely enough involved in business operations to be qualified to take over after your death. Or you might prepare a key manager or other staffer for stepping into this new role. If you can't identify any promising successor within your family or employee base, then your next course of action should be planning for the likely sale of your company.

Whichever strategy works best, you should lay out your succession plan in a detailed document that accompanies your personal will. This document should explain the proposed change of management and/or ownership as well as any financing strategies that you may have

> *During the period while we were waiting to see if we would succeed in raising the capital we needed, I focused on some estate-planning issues. If I had waited to do this until the company was up and running, I would have never had the time to think about it.*
>
> —BILL DAUGHERTY

set in place through corporate-oriented insurance policies.

The bottom line: Although entrepreneurs may be emotionally attached to their new ventures, the governing principle in planning for your company's survival or sale should be the potential payoff for your beneficiaries. So it makes sense to involve spouses or older children in these contingency plans, to make certain that they'll be equipped with the knowledge necessary to carry them out successfully.

❑ **If your company cannot go on without you, but it possesses some assets of value,** then you need to plan differently. What I advise owners to do in such cases is to prepare a written guide that will accompany their personal wills. Its objective is to spell out the most profitable ways for heirs to dispose of these corporate assets.

Make this a comprehensive guide that includes the following: a detailed list of all assets worth selling (which may include customer lists, intellectual property, or certain business operations as well as equipment, inventory, furnishings, or real estate); assessments of the fair-market value for these assets; and suggestions about prospective buyers, whenever possible.

Don't make the mistake of assuming that just because *you* know all the players in your industry or other obvious potential buyers for key assets, your beneficiaries, accountant, or attorney will share the same knowledge. Be thorough when preparing the document that accompanies your will; then update it regularly as asset values or your suggestions about prospective buyers change.

@ **Internet Guide:** While many aspects of succession planning can be challenging for the owner of a privately held company, there's plenty of help available through the World Wide Web. To get a sense of your options, conduct a keyword search for *succession planning;* you'll come up with links to organizations that specialize in this activity, as well as some useful checklists and guides and descriptions of up-to-date software.

Life Insurance Protection for Your Family

A well-structured life insurance policy is a low-cost safeguard worth setting in place from the first day of your company's operation.

ENTREPRENEURS THINK THEY ARE going to live forever. That's one reason they overlook life insurance, especially in the early stages of building their businesses. They also assume that their families don't really need any type of income-replacement guarantee at a time when their salaries are next to nonexistent and their companies have little or no intrinsic value.

Don't let yourself make these mistakes. Running a start-up without some type of life insurance safeguard means taking a huge financial gamble. Owners' personal finances are much more precarious during the early ownership years than would be the case if they were working for a corporate employer.

Imagine what would happen if you died unexpectedly, before your company had achieved a level of success that could pay off your family's early investment in the business. Your spouse and children would be hit—hard—by a double whammy: the loss of all your future earnings as well as their past cash infusions into the company (unless it somehow manages to survive without you). They might also struggle to find ways to pay off personal debt tied to your company's start-up and early-stage growth costs. I've spoken to widowed spouses whose credit ratings have been ravaged by the process. Imagine how difficult all that would be. But a family's prospects for managing without any cushion from a life insurance policy may be tougher still. That's because many families also suffer after entrepreneurs' deaths from their failure to have invested in anything *other* than the company. In many cases there were no college savings, no retirement savings, and little home equity. There may even be a second mortgage on the house.

Don't delude yourself into believing that worst-case scenarios like this one never happen. I also frequently warn business owners about another dangerous fallacy: the belief that insurance is unnecessary because heirs can run the business without them—or simply sell it off at a handsome profit. While this does happen sometimes, it's much more likely that a small or young company will be too fragile to survive its founder's death.

There's a better way to proceed. With some forethought and planning, these financial risks can be reduced or eliminated with a life insurance policy that names your spouse (and perhaps your children as well) as beneficiaries, with the goal of paying off their debts in the event of your unexpected death. If your company's cash flow is strong enough, the company should be responsible for paying these premiums. But if not, make it a high priority to figure out how your family can cover this cost on its own.

One caveat: You can't count on a corporate tax deduction to make this expense more palatable; tax regulations don't permit companies to write off policy fees when the owner (or the company) are beneficiaries. To get around that, consider paying yourself a bonus to help cover your premium costs—you'll owe income taxes on this as an additional form of compensation, but at least the bonus will be tax deductible for your company.

The good news is, this is relatively straightforward. Keeping the cost of this policy low is of paramount importance. So it makes sense to purchase a *term* life policy in whatever amount adds up to your desired death benefit.

Term policies make better sense for early-stage entrepreneurs than do cash value policies because *cash values* combine a death benefit with a long-term savings component, usually concentrated in mutual funds or similar investments. Since you are already heavily invested in the equity market through your ownership of what hopefully will turn into a fast-growing business, an investment-oriented life insurance policy is inappropriate and unnecessary, especially during your cash-strapped start-up stage.

Ignore what you read in personal finance magazines or general-audience insurance guides. The families of business owners need to calculate their insurance needs differently from the rest of the world, following this checklist:

❑ **Immediate cash needs.** This should include three to six months' worth of living expenses, anticipated funeral costs, paying off all credit card and other outstanding bills, and any expected taxes during the current year.

❑ **Asset replacement.** This should cover the total amount of all family investments in the company (including the amount necessary to pay off any personal credit lines or home equity loans).

❑ **Long-term financial needs.** Ideally, this should include the expenses of paying off your home mortgage, your children's education, and, if necessary, your spouse's career training or upgrading. But this is where a term-life policy might get too pricey for a fledgling entrepreneur's family to handle. If so, try to cover at least two to three years' worth of lost salary. Don't calculate this according to your most recent earnings as a start-up entrepreneur, which are probably unrealistically low! Instead try to estimate how much you could have earned in a traditional corporate setting.

Don't just sign up for this policy and forget about it. The death benefit, or face value, of your term policy should be reevaluated each year at renewal time, since your family's financial situation may change quite significantly, depending on the company's growth pattern and level of success.

@ Internet Guide: The easiest way to comparison shop for a low-cost life insurance policy is through the Internet, by contacting an insurance brokerage that handles products from multiple carriers. Reliable sites include www.quotesmith.com, www.directquote.com, and www.insweb.com.

Stage I

Business-Oriented Life Insurance

Well-planned life insurance policies can also achieve personal financial goals indirectly, if you name the right business contacts as beneficiaries.

AFTER YOU'VE SET IN PLACE your family-oriented life insurance policy, there are two types of company-oriented policies that you also should consider during the start-up phase:

❶ **one that names *lenders or investors* as beneficiaries,** with the intention of repaying their investments in the company if your untimely death eliminates the company's prospects; and

❷ **one that names *high-level employees* as beneficiaries,** in such a way that they would have enough cash to buy out your family's ownership stake or the company's assets from your heirs if this course seems advisable.

Could your family benefit (at least indirectly) from either one of these policies, or maybe even both of them? What I usually tell start-up owners is that the answer depends on a number of different factors. If your personal life insurance policy carries such a high death benefit that your surviving spouse would be able to pay off company-related debt while also taking care of the family (and achieving whatever personal financial goals are important to both of you, such as paying for college for the kids), then these additional types of insurance may not be necessary. That might also be the case if your spouse has a high-paying, secure corporate job and could handle whatever financial challenges might arise in the event of your unexpected death. Such policies might also be unnecessary if your start-up hasn't required you to take on significant personal debt, or if it contains highly marketable assets that would easily be disposed of if your heirs inherited the company but wanted or needed to sell.

After I spell out these options for people, I usually make one final point. Most start-up owners don't fall into these categories. Unless you're very certain that your overall situation contains no hidden risks for your family if something happened to you, it's better to consider one or both of these precautionary measures.

How to Structure a Policy That Benefits Backers

This should be a relatively simple matter, because so many lenders and experienced investors already insist on what's known as key-man life insurance before putting any of their own funds at risk. Basically, key-man coverage relies on a term life policy that pays backers a death benefit if the owner (or any other personnel essential to the company's operations) dies before they can earn their anticipated reward from the business.

In most cases, lenders or investors dictate exactly how

much coverage they require and perhaps even which insurance carrier they want to provide it. Typically, the company will be expected to bear this expense (which is tax deductible as a business operating expense since neither the company nor the owner is a beneficiary). If cash flow is particularly tight, investors or lenders may help subsidize the premium's cost.

The bottom line: Despite the added expense, such insurance policies provide an extra level of comfort for an entrepreneur's family, who might otherwise find it difficult or impossible to repay business loans that are backed by the founder's guarantee. If a less experienced investor or lender (perhaps a relative or friend) fails to suggest setting this type of insurance safeguard in place, it pays to propose it.

But do keep in mind that this strategy can't be used to guarantee the payoff of credit card debt or home equity loans, both of which often also represent significant forms of household indebtedness tied to the company's operations. If your family is vulnerable on either or both of these debt fronts, I can't emphasize strongly enough how important it is to make sure that your personal life insurance policy is large enough to cover repayment.

> *I'd advise people to take, right from the beginning, 10 percent of your paycheck and send it off to a mutual fund or some kind of safe investment. And buy yourself a life insurance policy.*
>
> —HOLLY HITZEMANN

How to Structure a Policy That Benefits Employees

Setting up an insurance policy that supports an employee's stock or asset purchase after a founder's death can make good sense for both the company and its owner's family (see "Preparing Personal and Corporate Wills," page 62). This strategy keeps the business alive while also channeling additional funds to the founder's beneficiaries. There are two major, if often overlooked, advantages to using insurance in this way:

❑ An insurance policy's death benefit guarantees that the sale of your company won't be stymied for lack of an interested buyer with ready cash. (After all, it's not always possible for an employee without significant savings to borrow the capital necessary to finance a company purchase.)

❑ Because you can choose whatever policy and coverage level seems most appropriate, according to your own assessment of your company's value, this can be a way of influencing the terms of a prospective sale, sparing family members negotiations they may not be qualified to handle.

Tip: Just as with key-man insurance, look for a term life policy with the death benefit pegged to whatever seems a fair-market value for the business's stock. Policy premiums should be paid by the company, so long as your employee signs some type of contract promising to use the funds to pay for a stock purchase in the event of your death. These fees should also be tax deductible for the corporation. A lawyer's assistance is helpful here. What you want to avoid is a situation in which your employee receives a benefit tied to your death and then *doesn't* use the money in a manner that will help your family achieve its own important goals. Reevaluate the policy's face value each year, to make certain that coverage levels keep up with corporate growth.

Banking Basics

***When your company is too small or young to
attract a banker's attention, look for ways to make
your situation more appealing by shopping for
personal as well as corporate financial services.***

ALTHOUGH THERE'S PROBABLY NO higher priority than the
necessity to raise capital, banks—the most desirable source
of funds—are usually unwilling to take a gamble on a start-
up. What makes matters even tougher for new and small
business owners is a trend that I've witnessed a number of
times during the past decade: Whenever the nation's economy or the investment markets show signs of a downturn,
bankers typically respond by clamping down on credit
opportunities for entrepreneurs. Their financing standards become more stringent than ever, and rates go up.
Many financial institutions reduce or eliminate their exposure to this marketplace.

Given these financing realities, you'll need to develop
a well-planned strategy to get a banker to take notice.
Rather than relying on a scattershot method—applying
to every bank in town and hoping that someone will
decide to give your company a break—it pays to rethink
your entire shopping approach for the financial services
that your household, as well as your business, needs to
consume.

At a time when many of us have become accustomed to
comparison shopping for the lowest fees and highest rates
of return, it may be tough for company founders to adjust
to a different balance of power in which bankers, rather

than customers, control key decisions. You'll be far better off spending more for financial services in the short run if, in return, you manage to start building a banking relationship for your young company that will one day lead to a credit line and other valuable sources of support.

Your first look should be at the bank where you're already doing your personal banking. You won't be able to deal with someone at the consumer end, but if you've already built up a relationship there, ask for a good referral to a small-business loan officer. If you don't have this type of personal contact, the bank's customer service department should be able to point you in the right direction.

Although this is the right place to start, don't be discouraged if you find yourself dead-ending quickly. The prospect of losing you as a customer simply may not be enough to bring your present bank around to a lending mood. After all, many financial institutions that do a great job with consumer accounts have little interest in small-business lending—and even if yours does, it may not have any lending experience in your company's industry. If a quick phone call or face-to-face meeting indicates that you're not likely to win corporate loan approval from the bank where you write your personal checks, the next step is simple: take your show on the road.

If you decide to adopt this approach, you'll find that it takes some careful preparation in order to achieve your desired result. Here's a strategy that I recommend:

❶ **Draw up a complete list of all the financial services that your household currently consumes.** At the very least, this should include all checking and savings accounts held by family members; you should also list any bank-issued credit cards, as well as mutual funds, certificates of deposit, retirement accounts, mortgages, and other outstanding loans. Remember: Many of these could be potential sources of income for your new bank if you agree to switch them to its management. That could help make your personal/corporate package more appealing.

❷ Create a separate list that details your company's current list of financial services. This list may only include a corporate checking and savings account, but—here again—both will represent safe sources of revenue for the bank, as opposed to a credit arrangement, which will seem riskier, especially when the bank has no history with you or your company. If you haven't yet launched your start-up, try to project this accurately, not optimistically.

❸ Also make some realistic projections of the company's wish list of anticipated services. Here's where you should detail the size of your desired credit line or any other type of business loan that you might need. Don't be shortsighted in making this list. Once your company moves beyond the start-up phase and its cash flow becomes stronger, you may well want to set up a full-scale cash management system or some type of retirement account. These can be lucrative for your bankers!

❹ Research your local banking options. Consult other entrepreneurs, as well as your company's attorney and accountant, to get a sense of which banks in your region tend to be more interested in serving the small business community. For young or small entrepreneurial companies, independent community banks are often the best, although least glamorous, option; to find out about local banks, you can do an online search at a website maintained by the Independent Community Bankers of America (www.icba.org) or call them at 888-500-5538.

Don't set your sights too high: Until your company moves into Stage Three of development—true profitability and business maturity—it's unlikely that any of the nation's large money-center banks will offer much promise. Once you've developed a short list of realistic possibilities, you'll need to investigate their full range of services to make certain that they can offer your family and your company everything you'll need.

❺ Comparison shop with your short-term needs (and longer-term goals) in mind. The only way to conduct this kind of search is to carry out a full-scale discussion with any banking officer willing to give you the time. Be prepared: Quite a few of them won't be.

Since your goal at this stage is relationship building, pay attention to all those intangibles that could wind up making a big difference along the way: Do you feel any kind of personal rapport with the officer who would be handling your business? Will one person be responsible for serving your family's as well as your company's needs (and if bureaucratic procedures prevent that, does the bank take other steps to make certain that your total banking package will be well-coordinated)? Do your prospective loan officer and the bank display a good understanding of the dynamics of your industry?

Most important, of course, is the bank's willingness to discuss your business financing goals. Even if you can't qualify for a corporate credit line right away—and you probably can't—you should look for a loan officer who agrees, at least in principle, that the bank will be amenable to this once your company has met certain financial objectives or established a good customer profile.

Stage 1

Friends-and-Family Financing

Here are four ways to protect important personal relationships (as well as your family's financial stability) when raising investment funds from friends and relatives.

FEW NEW VENTURES CAN RAISE capital from professional investors or lenders during the initial stage, which leaves entrepreneurs with limited fund-raising options beyond their personal savings, charge cards, and the household's credit line. Still, some fortunate companies can attract early-round investments from well-heeled people who are closely connected to the founder. These are generally parents and siblings or lifelong friends, but corporate-refugees-turned-owners also sometimes can woo start-up investments from their former business associates.

The advantage to bringing in such investors at this stage is very simple: There aren't any other sources. In all but the least capital intensive of new ventures, it's usually preferable for an entrepreneur to share early financial risks with others, while reserving a personal savings-and-credit cushion in case the company winds up requiring unexpected infusions of cash. If that's the case with your business, you'll have an easier time establishing a savings-based rather than a credit-based emergency nest egg, which, of course, is desirable for any owner.

But there's one big disadvantage to F&F financings: They can be highly combustible and create waves of unforeseen problems for a young company and its owner. Here are some safeguards worth considering for various types of risks.

Risk: Close relationships can be damaged if unexpected financial problems occur (which is practically a predictable occurrence in a start-up). One owner of a small and still precarious publishing venture confessed to me that she had ruined her family's Thanksgiving get-togethers because of bad feelings between her and an uncle who had invested in her business some years ago without yet earning the quick payoff that he had counted on. "I blame myself," she told me. "In my heart of hearts, I must have known that he didn't really understand the nature of investing in an entrepreneurial company like mine—but I was so desperate for the funds that I didn't allow myself to focus on that. And now my whole family is suffering as a result."

> *If you borrow money from friends or family, you must pay it back or you will damage your relationship ... and the only fair way is with interest.*
>
> —FRAN GREENE

Strategy: Business owners face a special obligation to warn early-stage investors of the high potential for loss when they're getting involved for personal rather than professional reasons. One way to hedge everyone's bet is to offer F&F backers a combined debt-and-equity deal (so that they can have the security of principal and interest payments plus the potential for a longer-term reward). If the deal still goes under, this overly generous approach may help reduce the potential for remorse and resentment.

Risk: Inexperienced investors can easily become confused about what they are "getting" in return for their money—which can create huge difficulties for business owners when the company finally is ready to bring professional investors aboard. The kinds of issues that tend to breed confusion and stall later financings include equity terms (people may not understand whether they're receiving stock, options, or something else altogether), ownership percentage levels, and interest rate calculations.

Strategy: Keep your start-up's capitalization structure clear-cut by hiring an attorney to draft all early-stage stock or loan deals; then retain copies of all documentation. If your new venture has an independent board of directors, make sure that it signs off on each deal.

Caveat: No matter how much your company needs the money, avoid making personal guarantees to use your household assets to back up F&F loans (since these may limit your ability to qualify for bank loans later and meanwhile cause incalculable damage to the family's finances).

Risk: Having too many family-and-friend backers can scare off professional investors, who will fear unwanted interference in business operations. I hear over and over again about investment bankers or private equity investors walking away from promising entrepreneurial ventures because they were afraid that family-and-friend investors— especially the in-your-face, hyperenthusiastic types—were walking time bombs.

Strategy: Here's where you will really need your negotiation skills if you're going to finesse this issue in a way that keeps everyone happy. Remember that all sources of money are not the same—even at this early stage—and if you're relying on an old Cub Scout buddy or your Aunt Mabel, they need to understand that they *cannot* be involved in the company's growth activities or decision-making processes. On the other hand, if you can raise start-up funds from business colleagues with relevant experience in your industry or in other entrepreneurial ventures, you'll increase the company's future financing prospects by signing them up as board members or informal advisers.

Above All, Communicate

Do YOU WANT TO KNOW the secret to keeping F&F investors happy (and out of management's hair during difficult periods when you'll all have more than enough to worry about)? It's good communication. Treat them the way a banker or venture capitalist would expect to be treated by a business owner. That means sharing key financial results *in writing* at reasonable intervals—either quarterly, semiannually, or annually, depending on your backer's desires and your company's capabilities. When unexpected favorable developments take place, give your investors a call. Don't try to hide bad news. Instead, try to put it in perspective so that they'll understand your well-considered response and the overall impact on the company.

But don't convey the wrong message along with your financial results. You want to make certain that your friends and family members understand that you are *reporting* results, not discussing or debating them. They are not your employees, board members, or strategic partners, and it's essential to make certain that they understand this *before* any funds exchange hands. And if they can't or won't accept these boundaries, put an end to your financing relationship quickly.

One business owner, a small custom manufacturer, told me that he returned an investment from his brother just three months after accepting it. Although he needed to take out a home equity loan in order to raise the cash for the refund, he considered this far preferable to the daily phone calls filled with words of advice that his brother, a doctor, couldn't stop himself from making. In the end, he had probably protected his company from all kinds of future problems and undoubtedly safeguarded his relations with his sibling.

Stage 1

The Personal Benefits of Corporate Bartering

Techniques that reduce your start-up's demand for cash also help limit your family's financial exposure.

BARTERING IS AN OFTEN-OVERLOOKED STRATEGY that can help ease the capital crunch at companies too young or too risky to qualify for sources of nonowner financing. In its simplest terms, a bartered deal is one in which two companies swap products or services of equivalent value. There's no cash involved on either end, which is a big plus for a start-up struggling to pay for rent or other operating expenses. Whenever you can reduce your company's cash outlays, that's good news for your family, since it also reduces the potential strain upon personal savings and credit.

Unless your company operates in an extremely small or unusual market niche, I'm convinced that this strategy will work for you. I've talked to an amazingly diverse group of businesses over the years that have turned successfully to barter deals when they hit a brick wall in their search for bank credit or investor capital. Surprisingly enough, service companies—which often have the toughest time raising capital since they possess so few assets that can serve as collateral—may find themselves the most desirable to bartering partners, especially when their expertise includes valuable business skills such as advertising, marketing, administrative services, accounting, or computer consulting.

Thanks to some innovations in traditional bartering arrangements, there are a number of ways that these deals can help entrepreneurs shelter their family's finances:

❑ **Bartering networks** exist in many states and major cities, which eliminates the need for owners to track down their own partners for two-party transactions. Instead, network members earn barter credits whenever anyone within the organization wants whatever they have to offer. If you participate in such a network, you can spend any credits your company earns on a long list of goods and services offered through the network (which might include whatever corporate services your business needs—computer equipment, office furniture, even airline tickets or hotel rooms).

❑ **Bartering lines of credit** are another great alternative, especially for companies that can't qualify for a traditional bank credit line. They work like this: Bartering networks make an assessment of how much demand there will likely be for a company's offerings and then assign it a barter-credit limit, which allows the owner to "buy" goods and services from any of the organization's members—even before other businesses select their goods or services for "purchase." For start-ups in a fast-growth mode, whose heavy initial expenditures might otherwise have to be paid for with the owner's personal credit cards, this feature can be especially valuable.

One caveat: Bartering deals won't eliminate *all* demands on your company's cash flow, since there are tax implications in any swapping arrangement. Specifically, these transactions are treated, for tax purposes, as though they had been conducted in cash. So, for example, if your marketing company prepared an ad campaign that it valued at $1,000 for a bartering partner, that $1,000 would be added to all other corporate revenue when calculating taxable income.

That's another reason why it makes sense for start-ups

How to Check Out a Network

THE BEST WAY TO FIND A BARTER NETWORK in your region is to search through the Internet, using the keyword *barter*. You'll likely come up with a number of possibilities; then check them out by doing the following:

❑ Investigate their list of members, as well as the types of goods and services that they can provide. There's no point in signing up if you can't satisfy many of your company's needs through the organization.

❑ Compare the range of possible barter transactions offered by each organization, as well as their backup services (including the preparation of tax filings and other documentation). If you plan to barter only occasionally, you might be satisfied with a small, plain-vanilla operation. But if your company's needs are significant, you'll want to make certain that you choose an organization that includes credit-line opportunities.

❑ Check out each group's credentials through the Better Business Bureau, the State Attorney General's office, and any consumer protection agency that might exist. Look for customers complaining about glitches, sloppy paperwork, or that they weren't able to choose among the full range of bartered services that they had been promised. Also check customer references (especially from businesses in your industry); these should be provided by any barter service that you're investigating.

Expect to pay an annual membership fee as well as a small charge whenever you conduct a transaction. (An annual tax report should be provided to you at no additional expense.) There may be additional charges attached to special services, such as your company's involvement in a credit line arrangement.

to conduct these transactions through a large-scale organization rather than informally. Most networks handle the tax-related paperwork for their members at the end of each calendar year, so that the only thing entrepreneurs need to worry about is paying Uncle Sam (as well as any state and local taxes that may be due, based on their location).

Stage 1

The Self-Test

It's important to upgrade your personal financial goals as soon as your company's growth can support some improvements. Here's how to tell when the time is right.

DURING THE START-UP PHASE, an entrepreneur's personal goals and accomplishments should, by necessity, be fairly conservative. I've made that point throughout my discussion of Stage One recommended strategies and really cannot emphasize it enough. The notion of self-protection— rather than self-reward or self-denial—should be an achievable compromise strategy for most start-up owners. But personal gratifications are inevitably limited during this early period, when the bulk of a business owner's resources and energies must be channeled into getting the company off the ground.

That's why it makes sense for entrepreneurs to *redesign* their personal financial activities by moving beyond Stage One strategies just as soon as their companies have progressed past the start-up phase. Each new venture progresses at its own pace, which means that it's simply not possible to attach a fixed timetable to Stage One, something along the lines of "Eighteen months after you launch your company, you'll be ready to award yourself a raise and open up a mutual fund investment account." I wish that the entrepreneurial process were that predictable! Some business owners are able to move through the start-up phase quickly and relatively painlessly; for others, its challenges and risks get prolonged—in some cases, so prolonged that their start-up experiences drive them back to the corporate world.

Before you can be certain you're ready to move on to the next stage of financial planning, which I outline in the Stage Two discussions that follow, you need to evaluate your progress on both the corporate and personal fronts (and perhaps even patch up some problems). This self-test should help you:

The Company's Achievements

❑ **How stable is cash flow?** Signs of stability include a *positive* cash flow balance, as well as the owner's *ability to predict* with a fair degree of confidence how much cash will move into and out of the company's coffers each month. In most cases, these can be achieved only after the company has either set up an internal system to handle billing, collections, and payables, or outsourced these responsibilities to specialized firms.

❑ **How long has it been since your company's most recent cash flow crisis?** In young and fast-growing business ventures, there's a difference between cash short-falls—which are inevitable and can usually be surmounted by stalling on payables or relying on credit—and cash flow crises, which require owners to raise additional capital from personal or outside resources in order to keep their companies afloat. Until a start-up achieves at least two consecutive business quarters without experiencing such a crisis (and can predict positive cash flow for the next two quarters), your self-compensation will remain vulnerable, and your family's ability to save and invest will be limited or nonexistent. You won't be ready to explore the investment and compensation strategies spelled out in Stage Two (such as "Giving Yourself a Raise," page 107, or "Creating an Investment Portfolio," page 154) until you're sure that the company's cash flow has truly stabilized.

❑ **How reliable is your financial reporting system?** This is an essential but often overlooked issue for any start-up. Until a business owner bites the bullet and sets up an internal accounting system that accurately tracks results and facilitates budgeting, cost control, and business-planning projections, there is no way of knowing how much progress the start-up really has made.

Keep in mind: The consequences can be damaging if you rely on misguided information and decide to attempt the more aggressive risk/reward strategies outlined in Stage Two (or even later, in Stage Three) at a time when your company's finances really cannot support such additional demands. One early-stage owner, a former real estate broker who set up a commercial real estate management firm, relied on excessively rosy projections that convinced him that he was ready to purchase the company's headquarters as a personal investment.

"The crazy thing was," he later told me, "I didn't realize that my company was *especially* vulnerable in a market downturn—which is completely inevitable in a cyclical market like real estate—because it was so young and the client base was so small. I should have kept my salary low and invested all my spare funds in marketing efforts to build up my client list while the market was strong. Instead, I made matters worse by investing personal funds in more real estate." When commercial conditions slumped, he lost a few key clients and found that the company couldn't afford to pay him enough rent to cover the family's loan obligations tied to the property.

"Fortunately, I was finally able to bring in a business tenant to help cover some of my costs—but I learned a lesson the hard way," he recalled, "and I sold that property as soon as it became possible to basically recoup my investment."

Here's my basic message: Don't upgrade your personal financial activities until you're sure your company is ready. And if there's any ambiguity about what its financial reports are (and are not) telling you, consult your accountant.

Personal Achievements

❏ **How stable is your family's financial picture?** The best measure of this consists of the family's ability to keep its living expenses within total monthly income (or close enough so that occasional bonuses from the start-up can help it catch up quickly and restore a balanced situation). There should be stability at this end, as well as within the start-up, before any entrepreneur is ready to move to Stage Two strategies.

How can you tell if you've gotten to this point? The best indicator is simple: At the end of each month, is there some cash to spare in your personal checking account, or do you find yourself inching into overdraft as the end of each month approaches? Have you bounced any checks recently? Have you gotten hit by late-payment fees, which are another good sign that your monthly expenses outweigh your income?

❏ **What does an analysis of personal credit card debt reveal?** If the family and the company both have relied so heavily on a founder's charge cards that these outstanding obligations are teetering at dangerous levels, then this debt must be reduced before any personal financial upgrades can occur. What's dangerous? You know the answer here: If your personal debt levels are so high that you can't afford to pay down a part of the outstanding principle as well as the total financing charges each month on every single credit card bill, you're in trouble here. Don't even think about a Stage Two upgrade until you clean up the credit scene.

❑ **Have you taken steps to limit your household's personal exposure to the company?** Here again, entrepreneurs should only consider accelerating their personal goals and strategies once they've been able to set up a basic safety net that will shelter their family, regardless of the demands and risks of a young, growing business. I've laid out a good blueprint for accomplishing this goal (see "How Much Do You Need in Emergency Reserves?," page 31). Don't try to move beyond this point until you and your family carry out those important recommendations.

Entrepreneurial Insights

THROUGHOUT THIS SECTION, I've described the Stage One strategies that I'm convinced can best help start-up owners and early-stage entrepreneurs achieve the right kind of personal financial goals (which are modest but sustainable—and won't disrupt their company's all-important growth activities). If you follow the blueprints that I've laid out, you should be able to avoid common pitfalls, minimize your household's financial risks, and lay the right groundwork for your family's future.

I believe in these strategies. It's undeniable, however, that there are as many different ways to handle your personal finances as there are to run a fast-growing company. To give you a flavor of some of this variety, I've asked a number of well-known and successful entrepreneurs to share their secrets. Their company affiliations and biographies are listed on pages 7–11. Here's what they had to report about the personal challenges that they faced—as well as the strategies that they relied upon—during the early stages of their companies' development. (For later-stage "Entrepreneurial Insights" into personal financial planning, see page 191.)

SELF-FUNDING THE START-UP

❏ **Lillian Vernon**

"I started my business with $2,000 of wedding gift money. While it wasn't debt from a bank loan, it was all I had to begin my married life. I used the money to place an advertisement in Seventeen *magazine and to buy the two products that launched my mail-order business.*

"Once my business started to grow, I reinvested my profits, balanced my cash flow, spent wisely, and avoided taking out a loan until 1983, thirty-two years after I filled my first order. Because I wasn't used to debt, I repaid this well before its due date. Today, I am proud to report that Lillian Vernon Corporation is a $287 million debt-free company."

❏ **Robert F. Young**

"Prior to starting my companies, I had an emergency nest egg, some college savings accounts, and retirement savings. Upon starting the business, I treated the business itself as my savings account, my nest egg, and my daughters' college education fund. It was both highly motivating and caused me to concentrate on the mission at hand to know that there was no safety net. I knew that if I succeeded, I would multiply the value of my savings many times more than the best-performing mutual fund could do—and if I failed, I would get to start over from scratch.

"Risk is in the eye of the beholder. If you really believe in the venture you are starting, then it is less risky than giving your money to some institution run by people you don't know investing in businesses you have no control over.

"Personally, I did not see investing in ACC Corp., which was the original name of Red Hat Inc., as risky. Risky in my mind was investing my limited resources in a mutual fund promising a 5 percent to 10 percent annual return. At that rate of return,

my savings would not grow fast enough to put my daughters through college or provide my wife and me with sufficient retirement savings. Investing in ACC was the only solution I could see to reduce the virtual certainty of not meeting my financial objectives."

❑ **Ruth M. Owades**

"Entrepreneurship has changed dramatically in the last ten years. There is much less personal risk today, because there's so much venture capital money involved. When I started my first company, Gardener's Eden, there was some venture capital money around, but it was mainly for technology companies, not specialty retailing.

"For Gardener's Eden I raised some private money and put in a fair amount myself. Also, I didn't take a salary for three years. Not everyone can make that commitment. When Williams-Sonoma bought Gardener's Eden they were impressed that I had made such a large personal commitment and that the company was running so efficiently. I was very careful about cash flow and watched every penny that was spent.

"By the time I founded Calyx & Corolla, the venture world was more open and I had a successful track record. Though offered venture capital, I turned it down. It occurred to me that since VCs were so eager to invest in my new company, I probably didn't need their money. So I decided to raise the funds privately. In just three months I was able to raise $3 million from angel investors and keep a large equity stake for myself. I paid myself a salary, though not an exorbitant one, and hired stellar industry professionals as my key executives.

"The entrepreneurial world is changing so rapidly that it's hard to anticipate where things are going. An attorney advised me that whether or not I used venture capital, the guidelines VCs use were valuable: (1) Would you bet on this person? (2) Is the concept unique? and (3) Has the individual entrepreneur personally "bet the ranch" on the venture? Is *he/she willing to work to the utmost for its success? If you're not willing to put your own money in, you're not making a personal commitment.*

"So you need to think about how much you're willing to risk on your idea. If that makes you uncomfortable or you have responsibilities which don't allow total commitment, maybe it's not right for you."

❏ Barbara B. Grogan

"There were times when my company was growing substantially but all of my net worth was at risk. I don't care whether your company is large or small—sometimes that's going to happen, especially in the fast-changing global economy we're all operating in.

"Here are the rules of engagement that we call Free Enterprise: You have the ability to succeed, and you have the ability to fail. You can't have one without the other—they virtually cannot be decoupled. If you don't want the risk, you cannot be an entrepreneur.

"That said, I never brought in any outside investors. In part, that's because I felt very comfortable betting my own farm but never wanted to bet anyone else's on my business. Over the years, I've relied on bank debt and retained earnings to fund our growth. That's impacted my personal financial decisions. Because I never chose to liquidate any part of my corporate holdings, I've relied instead on a long-term self-compensation strategy that allowed me to gradually diversify my own assets. That's been the right decision for me."

❏ Fran Greene

"If you want to be approved for a small business loan, you must sign over the rights to your home, money, and personal items—generally at 2-plus points over prime. If you have no established business credit, you will have to give personal guarantees. If you borrow money from friends or family, you must pay it back or you will damage your relationship ... and

the only fair way is with interest. Pray that you or a member of your family doesn't become ill, because you won't have medical coverage—it's just not affordable when you're putting everything you can into your new venture.

"The only way around the above pitfalls is to have at least eighteen months' income in the bank, perhaps have another job and be able to start your new venture part-time, or have a working spouse with a good income and health benefits.

"I believe that today's entrepreneur must be aware and must go forward with eyes wide open. If the pitfalls are clearly marked and have been planned for and the real world is in focus, the chance of success is increased a thousand times."

SELF-COMPENSATION STRATEGIES

❏ Fran Greene

"From the beginning, I paid myself a very small salary, which grew as the profit dollars grew. I found that by doing this I wasn't tempted to hire someone else to do the same job.

"I'd like to say that I found ways to protect everything I had accumulated while working for someone else for so many years, but I don't believe that people have their cake and become entrepreneurs too. A new business, its owner, and the fruits of the owner's history will become one, which means that you will inevitably take on personal risks from your new venture."

❏ Brian Sullivan

"I was very strict when it came to self-compensation matters during my company's early stages of growth. Since the search business is a deal business, I knew that cash flow could be erratic. So I decided to pay myself a salary only when the company had enough cash in the bank to cover one month's worth of expenses and also had two months' worth of receivables on the books. That meant I probably paid myself six months out of twelve in the beginning.

"I stuck to those guidelines religiously, probably for a good five years. I was always aggressively focused on the company's growth and felt that my long-term compensation would be tied to that. In the short run, I just accepted the fact that there wasn't really any way to shelter my personal finances while maintaining that aggressive focus on growth."

❏ Lillian Vernon

"When I started my mail-order business in 1951, my major concern was keeping costs down, staying out of debt, and having a steady cash flow to grow my company. I made it a priority to put my profits back into my business so my company would be financially sound.

"During the early years in business, I gave myself very little compensation in terms of salary. My primary motivation was to help supplement my family's income, because I was expecting my first child at the time. I never dreamed that $32,000 worth of orders would pour in before the end of that first year.

"I established a small salary for myself, working from my kitchen table and entirely on my own. When my business grew too large for my home, I moved to a storefront and hired only part-time workers, so mine was the only full-time salary."

❏ Holly Hitzemann

"In hindsight, this is what I would recommend to any entrepreneur: Pay yourself a salary right from the beginning, or as quickly as you can. I didn't do that as soon as I should have. If you are working for Procter & Gamble and earning $200,000 and then you set up your dream business—whatever it is, even if it's a dry cleaning operation—aim to pay yourself a salary of at least $3,000 or $4,000 a month. If you can't accomplish that within six months, get out and go back to

P&G. There's something wrong with your business idea. Maybe you need to figure out a new kind of company to operate, or maybe you just belong in the corporate world after all.

"Now, let's say you're able to pay yourself that salary. I'd advise people to take, right from the beginning, 10 percent of your paycheck and send it off to a mutual fund or some kind of safe investment. And buy yourself a life insurance policy. I'd recommend choosing a policy that has a cash value as well as a death benefit. That's what I did. If you're in a financial crisis, you can always cash it in if you absolutely need to. It's another line of personal defense. So long as that's all you can afford to do, that's OK. Stop there."

❑ **Patrick McGovern**

"During the first three years from the launch of IDG, I did not pay myself a salary. My personal funds were used for over 99 percent of the working capital of IDG, so it did not seem appropriate for me to be investing additional funds in the company for the purpose of paying myself a salary.

"I began paying myself in the fourth year when the business turned consistently profitable. At that point, I took a salary that was just large enough to meet my living costs for the next two years, until the profitability of the company allowed me to begin to take bonuses based upon above-plan achievements in profit."

❑ **Aaron Cohen**

"When a company founder is considering whether or not to take a salary, it can seem very noble to forgo one. But I didn't make that choice. I paid myself very much less than the market would have paid me, but I did take a salary. I think that's very important to do right from the beginning. Entrepreneurial companies need to face up to the discipline of paying all their employees."

LIMITING EXPENDITURES

❑ **Lucille Roberts**

"When I started my first health club, my husband and I had some funds, but we also needed to rely upon our family members and friends. My parents and his parents both gave us loans. We didn't sign any kind of promissory note—our relatives wouldn't have dreamed of that.

"But in retrospect, I think we should have. You don't want to take advantage of your relatives. My mother-in-law I paid right away. But it was only many, many years later that I remembered I'd never paid my mother back. I'd bought her a house and done many other things, but I'd forgotten that loan. She didn't care, but I said to her, 'No, I'm paying you back.'

"When you're running a start-up, you do whatever it takes to get things going. These situations can be funny—but only in retrospect. For example, I couldn't afford to hire someone to paint the trim at our first club, which was in Manhattan, so I had a painting party for all my friends. Then I got someone I knew to give me a very good deal on carpeting. But when the carpeting arrived, it didn't match the paint, so we had to paint it again."

❑ **Patrick McGovern**

"To keep expenses down, I started the company in my home. It was a twelve-room house, and as the business expanded, it took over ten of the twelve rooms, leaving me with just a bedroom, a small sitting room, and a shared kitchen. At the end of the second year, the business took over all the rooms, and I had to move across the street to a small apartment. In 1967, when the business began to make money, it moved to a regular office building a few blocks away, and I was able to move back into my house."

BUILDING A BENEFIT BLANKET

❏ Bill Daugherty

"In many ways, I've been very fortunate. We initially raised $100 million in cash and media equivalents, which meant that during our start-up phase my cofounder and I have gone through a different set of experiences than many entrepreneurs do. We were entering an industry in which we needed to get very big very quickly. If we didn't, we knew that we might as well go home.

"Our success in financing meant that we were able to pay ourselves a salary from the beginning and also to establish a good set of medical benefits for our employees. Benefits can make a big difference when you're in a competitive hiring field. I have three children. If a start-up company had come to me and said, "We don't have any kind of benefits," that wouldn't have been too attractive a proposition. iWon.com has hired nearly 200 employees in less than a year—we wanted to be able to attract the best."

❏ Aaron Cohen

"Concrete was started with a seed round of financing that seems very modest by today's standards. But it gave us enough capital to be able to do things like offer a good benefit plan to our employees right from the beginning.

"We were able to provide very good health care coverage, and we paid 75 percent of an employee's premium costs. When we set this benefit in place, I wasn't thinking about myself—I could have continued to get coverage through my wife's employer—but I knew that it would help us be more competitive when it came to hiring and retaining qualified people.

"We also set up a 401(k) plan early on. A lot of business owners don't realize that it's not very expensive to do this.

We couldn't afford to match our employees' contributions, but at least we were able to encourage them to save for their futures."

❏ Brian Sullivan

"I had a benefits program in place as soon as I started my company, back in 1988. I had two employees and very quickly ended up with ten. It wasn't very elaborate: Basically, the company paid for everyone's COBRA benefits, including my own, for about a year. We were all coming from other jobs, and that allowed us to hold on to the same health-insurance coverage we had had.

"That was expensive, but it was also simple to handle since it basically just involved writing some checks. It was the only way that we could be at least minimally competitive in the job market. It sent out the signal that we were for real.

"Then, as it got close for those COBRA benefits to expire—because people could only hold onto them for eighteen months—we set up an in-house insurance plan. By that point, the company was established well enough for us to be able to administer it internally. And we were growing so successfully that we could afford it."

❏ Patrick McGovern

"IDG began offering a medical plan in its first year of existence, so I was able to stop my personal payments to Blue Cross and switch to the company medical plan instead. But other benefits—such as life insurance, disability insurance, and our employee stock ownership plan—came only after the company became consistently profitable."

COPING WITH CASH FLOW CRISES

❑ **Holly Hitzemann**

"Looking backward, the thing that I regret most is that I didn't early on decide to set up automatic-debit arrangements for both a corporate savings account and a personal savings account. I could have even started them out at as little as $50 a month. But I would have accomplished two very important things: (1) setting aside business funds that could have been used to support future growth and (2) setting aside personal funds that could have helped protect my family in the event of an emergency.

"You don't take your personal risks seriously when you start up a company. But if you don't have large secondary savings, anything can wipe you out—a serious illness, the need to take care of aging parents, a child's college tuition bills. Think about that. A smart kid, $35,000 a year in tuition, and it could all be gone if you didn't take steps to prepare yourself. If all that you invest in is your company's growth and not your family's financial stability, you could lose it all so quickly. I saw it all in my own family when we faced a serious illness. The risks are overwhelming."

❑ **Robert F. Young**

"On a couple of occasions we did not have the short-term funds to cover payroll. I was the first staff member whose check would be delayed in those situations. On several occasions, I made infusions of personal capital that were not unexpected but rather were predicted by our cash flow planning. I didn't worry about protecting my non–Red Hat personal finances. Protecting my investment in the company was always the first priority.

"You must think of your investment in the company as the most important part of your personal finances—the one that

you most need to protect. If risk avoidance is a priority, don't become an entrepreneur. If you are determined to succeed, you should do everything and anything to ensure the success of your enterprise.

"Having said that, I am not suggesting that you should allow yourself to suffer personal bankruptcy in the event of the failure of your enterprise. Don't allow your liabilities to exceed your assets to the extent that you cannot recover without declaring personal bankruptcy.

"But should your enterprise fail, you will suffer a personal financial setback. If you are not prepared to suffer this, you should not begin the enterprise."

LONG-TERM PLANNING

❏ Bill Daugherty

"There's one thing I did that I would recommend to anyone getting ready to start a company. During the period while we were waiting to see if we would succeed in raising the capital we needed, I focused on some estate-planning issues. My wife is an estate-and-trust attorney, so she had the expertise to steer me in the right direction.

"Our thinking was that this was the right time to gift away some of the stock—which we put into trusts for our children and some other things—because it wasn't worth anything, so the tax consequences were minimal. If our business plan succeeds, that stock should one day become very valuable.

"If I had waited to do this until the company was up and running, I would have never had the time to think about it. Life has been a blur for us since we launched iWon.com. That was my one window of opportunity. And I would bet that many entrepreneurs have a moment like that, while they're still in *the planning stages or they're waiting for approval on a business loan or seed-capital investment that's going to help them really get the company going. From my own experience, it was therapeutic to be able to concentrate on those estate-planning issues and stop obsessing about the capital."*

Your company's cash flow has stabilized, and it's on a clear path to profitability. A growing number of customers are signing on. Welcome to. . .

STAGE

2

A New Round
of Goal Setting

*Once your young company achieves stability, it's
time to begin sharing the rewards of ownership
while pursuing your family's other personal
financial objectives.*

MOST ENTREPRENEURIAL VENTURES can support enhancements in their founder's lifestyle and personal financial
condition as soon as they progress from the start-up phase
to Stage Two, a period of stable growth and, hopefully, the
movement toward and achievement of increasing profitability. But it takes careful planning to strike a healthy balance between corporate and personal development during
this challenging period.

As a Stage Two entrepreneur, you need to avoid two
common, and costly, blunders. On the one hand, if you
continue to invest all of the family's resources (as well as
the internal cash flow generated by your young company)
in growth activities, you may find yourself sacrificing much
more than is necessary to build a profitable business, subjecting your spouse and children to an excessive degree of
risk and discomfort. But if you place your personal priorities too far ahead of the company's needs, you may rob it
of essential capital and scare off potential lenders and

backers, since such choices indicate a lack of confidence in the business's future.

So the key to personal financial success during this period is moderation. Your personal financial objectives and activities should be upgraded, but only as far as makes sense within the larger horizon set by your company's current condition and growth strategy. The following guidelines should help you set appropriate Stage Two goals.

Develop a Family Budget That Moves Beyond Subsistence

During start-up, most founders have little choice but to cut personal costs down to the basics and to postpone all nonessential expenditures. While this still isn't the right time to add luxuries, the household's monthly budget is ready now to sustain a higher comfort level, as well as some initial investments for the family.

Tip: This new budget, combined with projections about corporate cash flow and capital requirements, should help you make modest but significant improvements in your compensation package (see "Giving Yourself a Raise," page 107).

> *Until a company is profitable, any bank line of credit requires the founder's signature. If you default, it's your house, your car, your savings. Get your personal signature off the line of credit as soon as possible!*
>
> —RUTH M. OWADES

Establish Three Personal Priorities to Achieve While Building Your Company

One of the great advantages of Stage Two stability is that an entrepreneur can begin to devote *a little attention* to the family's financial needs, without fearing that the new venture could unravel at any moment. The operative words here are *a little attention.* Since any founder's time and energy still will be monopolized by the business, personal goals need to be focused and manageable.

> *We've set ourselves the goal that in a year or less we want to reduce our outstanding personal debt (nonmortgage) by 50 percent. In another year after that, we want to eliminate it entirely. We're making huge payments and going through a lot of pain in the short-term.*
>
> —HOLLY HITZEMANN

That's why it makes sense to choose three personal financial goals. (A variety of possibilities, among them "Creating an Investment Portfolio," page 154; "Saving for Your Children's College," page 160; and "Retirement Planning: Make Moves Now," page 165, will be discussed throughout this chapter, as well as action plans that will help achieve them.) Rank these in the order of importance to your family, since your company's current stage of development, cash flow patterns, and capital demands may not permit you to concentrate on all three at the same time.

Look for Tax-Advantaged Ways for Your Company to Improve Your Personal Lifestyle

There's no doubt that privately held businesses can offer their owners a wide range of perquisites; but the company's financial condition must be strong enough to support their expense. It's time to investigate the less costly of these options, which should certainly include instituting a corporate benefit package that will protect your family while improving your ability to recruit and retain high-quality staffers. (See "Bringing Medical Benefits In-House," page 114; "Should You Add Disability Insurance?" page 119; and, as mentioned earlier, "Retirement Planning: Make Moves Now," page 165.)

Don't Lose Sight of Your Earlier Defensive Goals

It *always* makes sense for owners to look for ways to reduce their financial exposure to their growing companies and to diversify assets (see "Diversifying Your Investments," page 147). During Stage Two, this becomes more possible.

Evaluate Your Progress Regularly

You should assess your personal financial achievements on an annual or semiannual basis, ideally around the same time that you're updating your company's business plan and progress. These reality checks will help guarantee that you're maintaining a commitment to personal improvement along with corporate growth. In addition they'll give you the opportunity to readjust your objectives during this period, if the company's growth pattern reveals that your goal setting was either too conservative or unrealistically demanding.

Stage 2

Giving Yourself a Raise

When the volatility of the start-up phase is behind you and you want to improve your pay, watch out for the personal tax risks.

ONCE CASH FLOW AND OPERATIONS have stabilized, it's only natural for entrepreneurs to look for ways to raise their self-compensation. After all, for many people, Stage Two offers the first real opportunity to draw a decent, regular paycheck (although probably one that is still way below what they could command as a corporate employee).

That's the good news. But here's the rub: As compensation levels for owners—and the profitability of their companies—improve, the risk of personal tax audits by both the IRS and state regulators steadily increases. After discussing this issue with small business accounting experts for years now, I'm convinced that few personal finance challenges carry with them the same high risk/high reward potential as an owner's raise does. It's also an issue that's fraught with emotion. Owners have described to me heated arguments that they've had with spouses—and sometimes also with accountants—over whether it was their companies or their families that were more deserving of some extra cash.

You need, therefore, to devote careful attention to settling salary matters as your company continues to expand. But first, some essential background. This issue can't be resolved without considering some factors tied to your company's corporate structure.

C Corporations

The owners of C corporations face an audit risk if tax authorities believe that their salary levels are too high. That's because all salary payments (including those to an owner) are considered a tax-deductible business expense; an owner's paycheck gets taxed only once, on the personal tax return. If the IRS or its state counterpart decides that an entrepreneur's salary is larger than is justifiable given the size of the company or its industry norms, then an auditor might argue that some part of the paycheck was really a dividend payment instead.

Here's why that matters: Dividend payments are subject to double taxation, first at the corporate level and then at the individual level. That could add up to a hefty bill if a reclassified salary results in an overdue tax notice, back-interest charges, and possible penalties.

If you decide to give yourself a raise, you'll want to take

steps to protect yourself against these audit risks. Keep careful personal records that document the following:

❑ The extent of your unique contribution to your company, including a rough estimate of hours worked, including weekends, holidays, and out-of-the-office activities. The objective of this contemporaneous record is to convince an outsider who might be examining the company at some point in the future that you earned every bit of your current salary, if not more.

❑ The decision-making process behind your salary, including any research conducted to determine industry averages and other relevant norms. If anyone other than you was involved in determining your pay, such as a board of directors or the company's accountant or attorney, retain records that support this as well.

S Corporations

The owners of S corporations face an audit risk that is exactly the opposite of that of a C corp. Tax authorities can get upset if you're paying yourself a salary that seems much too low, especially if you then supplement your paycheck with a generous dividend payment whenever corporate results are strong. (They'll also get upset if you seem to leave money unnecessarily within the company's coffers. But in a fast-growth situation, that accusation should be simple to refute.)

Here's the problem: All salaries, including an owner's, are subject to FICA and Medicare taxes, which between them add up to a 15.3 percent charge. Dividend payments are subject to neither tax (and unlike the situation at a C corporation, there's also no hit from double taxation). An entrepreneur's risk here is of getting a dividend payment reclassified as regular salary, complete with an overdue-tax bill.

To protect yourself against this type of audit challenge, take one simple precaution: Pay yourself at least enough to meet the FICA threshold for taxable income, which in 2001 was $76,200. (Double-check this threshold with your accountant. It gets adjusted for inflation, and you'll want to keep up with changes.) This will greatly reduce your chances of being pursued, since the most you could be accused of escaping is the Medicare tax, which is levied at 2.9 percent in total against salaries, no matter how high they go.

❏ **How much is too much?** What if you're genuinely worried about paying yourself too much, even if cash flow seems to support it? Then you may be best off drafting a memorandum to your files that explains your reasons for caution. (These may include the cyclical nature of your business, anxieties about certain client or supplier relationships, or something along those lines.) To protect yourself against possible tax problems, pay yourself a bonus—rather than a dividend—when financial results seem to warrant it. This type of payment will be subject to the same tax treatment as your paycheck and won't generate suspicion.

Stage 2

Start to Think about Perks

Consider adding some affordable personal benefits that can qualify as deductible business expenses.

THE QUESTION OF WHETHER TO provide yourself with some of the perquisites of ownership can be tough to resolve. During the early stages of building a company, there are so many other demands on finances that it may seem inappropriate to spend money in ways that will better the owner's personal life rather than boost corporate growth prospects. Concerns about possible IRS audits can also be off-putting. As a result, many founders abstain from all corporate perks, delaying what might amount to significant benefits for themselves and their families for far longer than necessary.

While it doesn't make sense to fritter away large amounts of cash, most Stage Two owners can successfully navigate a course somewhere down the middle. The secret is simple: Consider only those perks that carry tax-deductible status *and* a bottom line—meaning an after-deduction price tag—that a growth-oriented company can easily afford. Some good examples of owner benefits to avoid because of their non-tax-deductible status: country or social club dues; reimbursement of commuting expenses (since permissible limits are low and the tax rules are too complicated for you to spend time worrying about them); membership in an off-site athletic facility; and clothing allowances (all that qualifies for a tax break is protective equipment or uniforms that wouldn't be worn outside of work).

Also keep in mind: If you're the owner of more than 2 percent of the stock of an S corporation (or a partnership or sole proprietorship), adding fringes at this stage may be less appealing than for owners of C corps. That's because, as with health insurance, the cost of many fringes is considered taxable income for these owners. The tax rules can get downright arcane here. I'd suggest contacting your accountant if you fall into this category. There are a few fringes that provide partial tax benefits for S corp owners, sole proprietors, or partners: Their costs are exempted from employment taxes. But you'll probably need some help figuring out whether that's enough of a tax incentive to make them manageable for you right now.

It pays to consult your corporate accountant for a complete list of acceptable business deductions. The criterion that commonly gets bandied about is "ordinary, necessary, and reasonable"—which can cover a pretty broad category of expenses, so long as you don't go overboard and do keep very good records in case the deduction gets challenged in a federal or state tax audit.

The kinds of perks that will probably work best for you during Stage Two are those that combine personal and corporate services. Then it's up to your company to deduct whatever portion of your expenses can be justified as relating to business activities. Some to consider:

Promotion Expenses and Business Entertainment

This is one of the likeliest areas to generate questions from the IRS, but that's no reason to overlook its potential, so long as your record-keeping system is strong (see "Record-Keeping Rules: Save Everything!" page 42).

Don't miss out on any opportunities: Travel and other outside-the-home activities, such as restaurant dining, are obvious candidates. But home-entertaining costs can also qualify, so long as those attending your events are either employees or business connections. I've spoken to business owners who made heavy use of this deduction—safeguarding it with meticulous tax-oriented records—in entrepreneurial ventures that depended heavily on their personal networking to woo potential clients, investors, or even new hires.

One caveat: If other guests were also in attendance, you'll only be able to deduct the appropriate portion of these costs. Don't pooh-pooh this rule: If the IRS decides to audit your overaggressive write-offs regarding home entertainment, it wouldn't be unheard-of for a tax agent to interview your guest list about matters such as who else was in attendance and was business ever discussed.

A Company Car

This is a natural for any owner, whether of a C corp, S corp, or any other business entity, although the tax rules that govern this deduction are, not surprisingly, complex. If you use your car, as you probably will, for both personal and corporate activities, you'll need to keep a usage log that will help determine at the end of the year what percentage of overall expenses will qualify as a deductible business expense. You may be able to get away with just claiming this deduction on Part IV of your Schedule C or Part III of Schedule C-EZ, but that's only the case if you're claiming the standard mileage rate, which is set by the IRS and adjusted annually. If you're not—or if you're required for any other reason to file IRS form 4562, "Depreciation and Amortization"—you'll need to complete Part V of this form as well.

To some degree, you're on the honor system here, since it's unlikely that the IRS will go back and double-check the validity of each of your log entries. But in the interests of accuracy, it helps to write down the date of each business-oriented drive, your destination, your round-trip mileage, and some details, including whom you met or what the business purpose of the day's trip was. Ask your accountant to help you sort through the pros and cons of the various methods you can rely upon when calculating your deduction; you'll also need to file a separate IRS Form 4562 when claiming this tax benefit.

Advisory Services

During the early stages of the company's growth, it makes sense to use the same attorney and accountant to handle both corporate and personal matters. Their fees, of course, are entirely tax deductible as related to business issues, but they're not supposed to be deductible when the conversation turns purely personal.

Obviously, that's tough to pinpoint, which means, realistically speaking, that owners should be able to take advantage of some flexibility here. Don't abuse the system: It does make sense to segregate some portion of your legal and accounting expenses when calculating how much to deduct at tax time. But you've probably got room to maneuver.

What if you've decided to hire a financial planner as well? If you invite the planner to attend a larger brainstorming session with your corporate attorney or accountant, you might be able to justify deducting a portion of this fee; you can't deduct anything relating to purely personal conversations.

Stage 2

Bringing Medical Benefits In-House

It's now time to start creating a corporate benefit package whose main feature is health care coverage.

FOR OWNERS WHO HAVE LEARNED to make do with barebones benefits or none at all, it may seem tempting to skip this topic and continue to channel all spare cash into growth-related activities. But there are several important reasons why it makes sense to start investing in a good benefit package once your company enters Stage Two of its development. I think that's the case even if you're an S corp owner, partner, or sole proprietor and will be taxed on the value of in-house medical benefits.

Here's one major reason: In tight labor markets—or

whenever you're competing for highly skilled employees—benefits can tip the balance when it comes to recruitment and retention efforts. "I could do without it—after all, I've managed just fine for a few years now," the owner of a software-development firm told me. (The fact that he and his wife were still in their early thirties and didn't have any children undoubtedly made it easier for them to "rough it" this way.) The trouble was, as his company pursued profitable growth by moving increasingly in the direction of high-end custom projects, this CEO found himself forced to bring more and more of his software designers in-house (rather than relying on a broad network of interchangeable independent contractors who could easily handle less complicated jobs). To compete for top talent, he needed a strong compensation package, including health care coverage, which is pretty basic at larger and better-established companies.

I've spoken to many business owners who told me that they had made or were contemplating the transition to in-house medical benefits for workforce reasons alone; generalizing from these conversations, this decision appears to happen most frequently when companies are dependent upon staffers with technical or financial expertise. Just as important, of course, is the fact that a transition is a huge step in restoring your family to the personal financial stability that you temporarily sacrificed when you launched your start-up.

Eventually, so long as your company continues to grow and become more profitable, its health package and other corporate benefits will become a source of personal reward for you, because you'll be able to choose plans that provide your family with exactly the security blanket it needs. (See "The Medical Savings Account Alternative," page 217; "The Case for Setting Up a 401(k) Plan," page 221; "Broadening the Benefit Blanket," page 226; and "Ways to Enhance Your Company's Retirement Plan," page 231.) But even at this stage, while your cash flow and insurance purchasing options are limited, there are still plenty of advantages for you as well as for your employees. One more point: Well-planned health care packages also qualify for valuable tax breaks, which means that there's a business justification behind setting these up as well.

Although I'm a big supporter of making this switch as soon as your company is securely anchored in Stage Two, there's a financial reality that cannot be overlooked: Health coverage is expensive for any business, and that's especially true for a small or young one. While its cost should not be as prohibitive for entrepreneurs at this stage of growth as it is at start-up, financial pressures significantly limit your options for now, no matter how lavish a policy you might like to set in place.

That said, here are two alternatives worth considering. Whichever one you choose should provide you and your employees with a decent level of coverage at a cost that won't break the bank.

Comparison Shop among HMO Plans

With an insurance agent's assistance, see if your company can afford HMO coverage. In order to make it appealing, you'll probably want to price a plan in which the business pays 75 percent to 100 percent of an individual's premium fees. If cash flow can handle it, you may also want to partially subsidize the cost of family coverage.

With the tax deduction that comes with this (because it relates to all employees), the company may be able to afford more here than you might first imagine possible. Ask your corporate accountant to work through some possible scenarios.

Cost-saving tip: Although they're desirable, benefit enhancements such as prescription drug coverage, dental plans, and vision care will really add up, so they're not worth adding at this stage.

Consider a Traditional Indemnity Plan with a High Deductible

Because HMO prices have been rising (along with discontent over the quality of some managed-care plans), high-deductible indemnity plans have become increasingly appealing to small businesses. The logic behind it is fairly simple: You're providing your family, as well as your employees, with so-called catastrophe coverage—protecting them against the kind of large-scale medical expenses that could devastate many families' finances—while assuming that they can manage to handle smaller costs on their own.

Opting for a high deductible (typically between $2,000 and $4,000 for a covered family) is a great way of keeping the company's premium costs low. Once your company grows into Stage Three, you may want to expand this type of plan into a medical savings account (see page 217). Corporate cash flow may be able to support the entire cost of this cut-rate coverage, which will help make the plan more appealing to staffers who might otherwise protest the unusual deductible levels. It's worth emphasizing that this type of coverage *can* be appealing in its own regard, since it's usually structured around a traditional indemnity plan, which means that people can choose their own physicians.

A Compromise Worth Considering

As your company's cash flow continues to improve, you might decide to supplement your high-deductible plan with a small annual bonus (ranging, for example, anywhere up to $1,000 per employee) and explicitly describe this as a health-care supplement. Do some in-house public relations campaigning to make certain that your employees recognize this as the valuable bonus it is.

The logic behind this move is simple: For many people, especially your younger and healthier staffers, this extra payment will probably cover most, if not all, of their medical expenses. That means it shouldn't really matter to them if the policy's deductible is sky-high; for all intents and purposes, the company is covering their health care costs by giving them a bonus to help pay their doctor bills.

This should work pretty well when it comes to making the high-deductible policy palatable to staffers so long as the company can't afford anything better. But it's worth pointing out that there are corporate advantages as well: The payment of this "health-care supplement" will be tax deductible, like any other form of compensation and legitimate business-operating expenses, which should keep costs under control.

Tip: It's up to you to decide whether to provide a supplement like this for all employees or simply to reserve it for key managers, including yourself. Since it's a bonus, not a formal part of the company's health care plan, there's no need to fear charges of discrimination, whichever policy you decide to adopt. But don't make any guarantees, especially in writing. Since cash flow may become erratic during Stage Two (and you're probably facing a wide range of demands on your still-limited capital funds), you'll want to keep your options open for discontinuing or reducing this bonus during years when it seems excessively costly.

One final twist: Bonuses also can be used to help *owners* cover the personal tax bite associated with this or other health care benefits in S corps, sole proprietorships, or partnerships.

Stage 2

Should You Add Disability Insurance?

As your income becomes more predictable, disability insurance can help protect against unexpected disruptions.

IN AN IDEAL BUSINESS WORLD, we all would be covered by insurance policies that guaranteed us financial security if an illness or other disability prevented us from working. But reality falls short of this ideal. Disability insurance is expensive, often difficult to obtain, and far from comprehensive in the protection that it can offer.

These unfortunate realities have convinced me to adopt a position that is at odds with the advice most personal finance experts recommend. I tell owners who ask that there's little point in worrying about disability coverage during their companies' start-up and early-growth phases. That may strike you as excessively risky, but here's my thinking: You probably couldn't qualify for it anyway—and even if you could, you certainly could not afford the cost while your new venture is gobbling up most or all of your funds.

There's another reason why I'm convinced this approach makes sense: Disability insurance protects your salary, but since owners' compensation is usually low, sporadic, or nonexistent during Stage One, that protection won't be worth much to your family. You're better off using your funds in other, more productive ways, whether this means building an emergency nest egg or investing in corporate growth-related activities.

The situation for Stage Two owners, however, is different. Once corporate cash flow and your paycheck become more regular, the problems surrounding disability insurance can and should be overcome. That's not to say that you'll ever be able to find the perfect disability policy. The best coverage you can hope for will pay you no more than 60 percent of your income if you're unable to work. And some policies offer a good bit less.

But by now, you should be earning a paycheck that's worth protecting. And given the fact that, at best, you've invested most of your savings in your young company— and, at worst, you've invested *everything*, plus taken on all kinds of debt to support its growth activities—each level of personal financial protection that you can layer into your family's security blanket can help.

The major question to resolve is whether to purchase your disability policy through your company or as an individual. Each option has its pros and its cons:

Corporate Coverage

Like any type of group insurance plan, this can be easier to obtain than an individual policy (for which you'll probably have to undergo a comprehensive medical examination and submit multiple years' personal tax returns to validate your earnings history). Surprisingly enough, it's usually easier to get coverage as a company, rather than as an individual, even if you're running a one-person operation. Whatever the size of your own business, if your personal medical history or age might raise red flags, it's probably not even worth wasting your time to shop as an individual.

There are other pluses to corporate plans: Policy premiums are tax deductible for your business, which should be appealing now that it is approaching profitability. But since group plans cover all employees, your total expenses will likely wind up much higher than if you had just purchased the policy for yourself. Obviously, the more people who are covered, the more costs go up. But bigger policies can bring with them some economies of scale. Meanwhile, in order to keep total costs under control, most corporate disability policies are fairly minimal in their coverage levels. You may want to price a variety of options and work through some after-tax comparisons with your accountant's assistance.

The cost factor may be enough to discourage you from buying disability coverage through your company instead of as an individual. But if you're still weighing both options, there is one more downside worth considering here. If you've set up a company plan, which means that it's your corporation that pays the premiums, *and* you receive disability payments at some point in the future, you will have to pay personal income tax on all benefits. If you pay the premiums yourself through an individual plan, you won't owe any taxes. Only you can decide how significant that tax risk may be. Are you young and healthy? Then a long-term *possible* personal liability may not loom large, compared to the immediate corporate tax benefits from setting up a company plan.

Individual Coverage
For owners who can afford to pay for this type of policy from personal funds, it's probably the better choice, since it allows them to fine-tune their coverage to whatever best suits their needs. Expect an individual policy to be pricey, especially if you opt for a relatively short waiting period— 30 or 60 days—before disability benefits start to be paid. You can keep costs lower by pushing the waiting period out 120 or 180 days, but that's not recommended unless you've got fairly sizable household savings. Meanwhile, although you won't be able to deduct the policy's premiums from your personal taxes, you also will not face a tax liability if you receive payments.

A Shopping Guide

YOU WANT TO KEEP THE COST of your disability coverage as low as possible. After all, with a little luck, this is one benefit you'll never need to receive. But low cost isn't the only feature worth considering. Look for:

❏ Policies that are guaranteed to be renewable and noncancelable (so long as you continue paying the premiums) until age 65.

❏ A waiver of premiums in the event that you become disabled and start receiving benefits. Expect to start paying premiums again once the period of disability ends.

❏ A favorable definition of disability, which usually means one that permits you to start receiving benefits whenever you cannot perform your "usual work" as opposed to any type of job at all.

❏ An automatic cost-of-living increase to make certain that your potential benefits keep up with inflation.

A Compromise Strategy

You might want to consider setting up a tax-advantaged group plan that will provide a basic level of coverage for you and all employees, then purchase a supplemental individual policy that will "wrap" an added level of financial protection for you personally around that of the group plan. This will spread the cost between your company and your family while raising safeguards around your earnings.

Tip: If the company's cash flow is strong, it can pay you an annual bonus that helps cover the wrap policy's premiums. Don't go this route, though, without weighing the tax consequences on both ends: The company will be able to deduct the bonus as another form of compensation (which is a legitimate business operating expense), but you will be liable for personal taxes on it, like all other compensation. To ease that personal tax hit, you may want to increase the size of the insurance-related bonus the company pays you to cover your anticipated tax liability as well as policy fees.

@ **Internet Guide:** Whether you're looking for a corporate or individual policy, it's fairly simple to do some comparison shopping through the World Wide Web. One site worth visiting is www.linea.com, which provides policy quotes as well as useful educational information.

Stage 2

Taking Your Personal Cues from Your Company

Your individualized approach to financial-planning issues should be shaped by your company's growth trajectory and realistic long-term prospects.

ONE OF THE BIGGEST REASONS why business owners cannot, and should not, follow a cookie-cutter approach to financial planning is that there's no single mold for an entrepreneurial venture. Some new companies prove to be enormously (or unpredictably) capital-intensive, forcing their founders to live with financial sacrifices for years. Others quickly stabilize, generating lavish cash flows and, along with them, all kinds of personal rewards. Some grow to be very big very fast, while others ... well, they just don't.

The point is, once you learn to listen to your company—which boils down to analyzing its growth pattern and potential, as well as the present and future lifestyles that these can support for your family—you will be able to fine-tune the right financial plan for your household. Few founders can accomplish this complex task during the start-up phase. Their companies are simply too new and untested. But by Stage Two, once revenue, cash flow, and capital patterns have time to reveal themselves, it makes sense to conduct some corporate self-analysis.

> *Buy only what you absolutely need for the growth of your company, and don't spend your profits on personal luxuries.*
>
> —LILLIAN VERNON

The questions below should help you evaluate your corporate and personal prospects.

Does it now appear likely that your company will quickly reach $5 million to $10 million in sales, with future growth achievable beyond that point?
Here's why this threshold is significant: Experienced investors, especially private equity funds and venture capitalists, probably won't take your company seriously as an investment candidate until it reaches this level. Then they'll want to be convinced that their infusions of capital will help your growth accelerate even further—probably to a level of at least $50 million to $100 million in sales.

The bottom line: Most entrepreneurial companies don't fit this profile—although it can be difficult to remember this fact, since fast-growth businesses often monopolize the small business coverage in the media. If yours doesn't, then you need to pay extra attention to limiting your family's financial exposure to your young venture. That's because you'll likely find yourself with few opportunities to attract outside investors (other than, perhaps, small-scale angel investors). You cannot count on them to bail you out if you've overborrowed or dangerously reduced the family's savings accounts in order to get your company off the ground. Your company's realistic cash flow prospects should define the household's financial-planning activities.

Have you already brought in professional investors, and with their help, does an initial public offering or company sale seem likely within the next two to three years?

One way that the dot-com mania of the late 1990s changed the entrepreneurial community is that owners can frequently tell—before even opening their company's doors—how strong or weak their capital-raising prospects will prove to be. If you're on a super-fast IPO track, you'll likely have raised a large round of venture capital financing either during start-up or by early Stage Two without any advice from this book. If you haven't, don't delude yourself. You're probably a candidate for the same advice just offered above, and your company's needs will continue to shape your personal planning.

The bottom line: If your company has raised a significant stake from professional investors and you anticipate raising more before you can carry out your liquidity strategy, you've got financial opportunities but also some risks to avoid. Reduce or eliminate credit card and other personal debt, pay yourself a decent salary, and also start diversifying your household assets. But you can't be too greedy, because there are plenty of eyes watching you. If professional investors believe that you're taking too much money out of your business today, they'll fear your lack of long-term commitment. Ironically enough, an owner without external financing prospects needn't worry about that particular problem.

In the cold light of day, does it now seem as though your company's growth prospects are stalled at a level too limited to help you achieve your personal goals?

Be ruthless when you answer this question. Some company ideas are good but not good enough, and they can limp along for quite awhile before their owners throw in the towel. If you're in this situation and spot it early enough— meaning, by Stage Two—there still may be time for you to change strategies and improve your long-term development prospects and short-term cash flow. Perhaps you need to revise your marketing approach, reposition your business in a more lucrative niche, or even consider making a small strategic acquisition that could boost your company's prospects.

The bottom line: The one mistake you want to avoid is, as they say, throwing good money after bad. Many companies are founded on flawed business plans and their prospects cannot be improved, at least not with the limited financial resources that their owners can bring to the effort. If your Stage Two self-evaluation tells you that this venture won't earn you your pot of gold, consider selling it (or at least trying to liquidate your main assets) or closing it down, before your personal financial problems exacerbate. Don't be discouraged if you need to try again. Many successful entrepreneurs learned crucial lessons from business failures.

Find a Mentor

Although it's always helpful to be able to consult entrepreneurial peers, mentors, or CEO coaches, they become especially useful for owners once growth presents personal as well as corporate opportunities.

A HOT NEW TREND SWEEPING the small business community has convinced growing numbers of fledgling entrepreneurs to seek out peer advisers (who themselves have usually been through starting up and running a fast-growing business, often more than once). One popular way to sign up is through a free or low-cost mentoring program, which might be offered through your chamber of commerce or trade association. Owners who don't have this type of local option can consider hiring a CEO coach, preferably one with an entrepreneurial pedigree. In either case, the appeal can be irresistible: Peer advisers promise to be available by telephone, e-mail, or in person whenever an entrepreneur needs help with the kind of thorny problem that only another business owner could understand. And you often won't owe them anything except your gratitude in return, compared to the hefty fees you might pay to a management consultant.

Unfortunately, most of these mentoring relationships confine themselves to "strictly business" matters, such as evaluating different growth strategies, marketing campaigns, or financing options. What a wasted opportunity! The truth is, anyone who has been through the entrepreneurial process—from start-up to successful operation and profitability—also has insights for you into the complex and ever-changing personal challenges that owners find themselves confronting as their businesses develop.

If you open the door to this type of interaction with an entrepreneurial mentor, I suspect that you'll find the results to be endlessly rewarding. One company founder, whose business operated in a thriving but high-stress niche in the entertainment sector, confessed to me that he now devoted most of his "gab sessions" with his mentor to personal issues, after having originally started the relationship to steer him through a particularly thorny set of problems relating to his own—versus his employees'—benefit needs.

For quite awhile, they spent most of their sessions talking about CEO compensation matters. "You wouldn't think it could be possible," he confided, "but I used to feel very guilty and anxious anytime I would pay myself anything that even remotely resembled adequate compensation for all the time I put in at the office and working at home. It got to the point where it didn't even feel worth it for me to pay myself an extra bonus when we had a great quarter and the company could afford it, because I had such a strong set of negative reactions. I almost felt like I didn't want the money! You'd never think about talking an issue like that over with a therapist—I mean, it wasn't as though I was going through a serious emotional problem—but I really needed some advice from a person who could identify with my anxieties. My peer mentor played that role for me and eventually helped me to establish some very formal guidelines about CEO bonuses, which helped make this more of a business and less of a personal decision."

For Stage Two entrepreneurs who can get formal or informal peer advisory relationships, here are some issues well worth exploring:

How—and when—should I begin to change the way I think about my compensation?
Most experienced entrepreneurs have very strong opinions

on this subject and should be able to provide some thought-provoking feedback, especially if you share with them the current recommendations of your accountant, attorney, and other corporate advisers. I've heard about a number of different instances in which mentors advised— actually, I should say ordered—entrepreneurs to start paying themselves a paycheck, or to give themselves a raise, in cases where the owner was excessively nervous about cash flow consequences.

Let me emphasize, though, that the best mentoring relationships involve confidence-swapping on both ends rather than simply the passing on of advice. Ask your mentor how he or she has handled personal compensation decisions in the past, as well as about mistakes that would have been resolved differently in hindsight.

How should I handle *specific* problems in which my family's priorities clash with corporate-growth needs?
No matter how resolved you are to do anything it takes to get your company on its feet, circumstances will arise in which you need to make painful financial choices—perhaps with a fair amount of pressure coming from family members who are fed up with short-term sacrifices. If you feel enough trust in your peer counselor to confide your problems here, you'll probably receive more useful advice than you could get from either a corporate adviser or your shrink. If your relationship with your adviser is strong, you'll probably hear about a few problems that were navigated by his family as well.

How can I steer my way past investment prospects that present themselves to me without conveying the wrong impression about my business?
When your company is still in the start-up phase, this question might seem esoteric. But as soon as you've begun to establish a presence in your small business community,

you'll likely begin to feel overwhelmed by the *other* entrepreneurs who begin to pursue you as an investor, as well as all those stockbrokers, financial planners, and others who start beating down your door! At a time when you'll be very conscious of conveying an image of success for your young company, you may feel susceptible to these sales pitches. Look to your mentor for guidance about how to say no without feeling or looking like a failure.

What about this nagging worry I've got about...?
(You can fill in the blank here.) By the time most entrepreneurs move beyond the start-up phase, it's rare to find a business owner who hasn't made at least one personal financial maneuver that produces middle-of-the-night anxiety attacks.

These are the kind of issues that I get e-mails or frantic telephone calls about: personal credit card bills that get maxed out for the company in times when cash flow is tight, funds borrowed from college savings or retirement plans, and all kinds of other risky maneuvers. In one terrible instance recently, I heard from an owner who had already tapped out her personal emergency funds, so she had now started delaying payroll tax contributions in order to keep her precarious company limping along. It's not unusual for an entrepreneur to hide these problems (at least, from everyone other than a spouse), because they represent an over-the-top risk that an accountant or attorney would never consider acceptable.

You may have such anxieties yourself, or maybe you're exaggerating potential problems. The point is, you'll never know unless you discuss them with a person who's faced down similar make-or-break crises and survived to tell the tale. Your peer adviser is the perfect confidante. Someone who agrees that you've got a significant personal financial problem may also be able to steer you toward a workable solution.

Improving Your Debt Profile

Congratulations! You finally should be able to start shifting the burdens of business borrowing from your family to your company.

WHEN YOUR COMPANY ENTERS Stage Two—with a stabilized cash flow, a proven revenue stream, and presumably a growing network of customers, suppliers, and other business contacts—corporate credit options should begin to improve. Unfortunately, many entrepreneurs wait far too long to take advantage of these new opportunities, or they don't even realize that they exist. Here's a two-pronged, proactive approach to reducing your personal exposure:

❶ **Switch as quickly as possible from personal to corporate cards.** To increase your company's chances of getting approved during a still-early period of growth, try applying to credit card issuers who already have covered your family (assuming, that is, that you've built up a good record of prompt payments).

Tip: Whether you've ever relied on an American Express card in the past, AmEx is another good place to start, because it has been aggressively pursuing small business customers and offers a variety of options that may help your company qualify on its own. Although you'll need to pay off your outstanding balance each month—which may limit your borrowing activities—using this card will help you build a corporate credit history and, hopefully, branch out at a later point.

❷ **Reduce your level of personal backing.** With lines of credit, your goal will be somewhat different than with credit cards. Getting a loan in your company's name isn't exactly the problem: Most entrepreneurs can achieve that once they move out of the start-up phase, so long as they sign a *personal* guarantee to back up that loan with whatever assets the family possesses. Your objective during Stage Two should be to look for ways to reduce those guarantees—ideally, what you want is for your *company* to begin assuming the responsibility for supporting its own level of borrowing.

How to Loosen Restrictions of an Existing Bank Loan

Be prepared: You'll face a tough set of hurdles and will undoubtedly need to come up with corporate assets to replace personal ones if you hope to keep a current loan in place. Fortunately, some banks will consider customer contracts or accounts receivable as adequate backing for a short-term loan, although hard assets such as equipment or commercial real estate will always be preferable.

The key to overcoming obstacles at this stage will be the quality of your working relationship with your loan officer. If you've got a good history as a banking customer, you should be able to approach him or her with a request to start diminishing your household's exposure to the company's debt. Be proactive here. If you wait for your loan officer to initiate this conversation, you'll be waiting for a very long time!

If your loan officer is amenable to working out a plan—or, at the very least, is willing to spell out exactly what objectives your business needs to achieve in order to get to that point—you'll know that you're on the right track. If your concerns are brushed aside, or the officer provides only the vaguest of long-term assurances, it's time to start shopping around for a new bank that is willing to be less demanding on the issue of personal guarantees for companies that have moved beyond the start-up phase.

Consider a Nonbank Credit Line

During the past few years, nonbank-financing opportunities have greatly increased for small business owners whose cash flow is strong enough to cover their costs. This marketplace is somewhat fragmented, and it may take some searching to track down the right loan package for your company. Potential sources of money may include credit card issuers (who sometimes provide credit line arrangements for their customers), nonbank SBA lenders, and a range of other financial institutions, including commercial lenders that focus on growth-oriented businesses and their often heavily leveraged owners. The downside is simple: They usually charge significantly

> *I own my own house without any debt. That's part of a retirement plan. I own my company and it too has no debt. That's a significant part of my retirement plan. Do I have a huge pension or retirement savings account? No.*
>
> —BARBARA B. GROGAN

higher interest rates than a bank would. But in return for those higher charges, their demands for collateral and personal guarantees will be far less stringent.

I wish that I could be more specific about the type of nonbank arrangement you should search for, but this is an evolving market, and many good options are locally based or industry specific. The good news is that this universe is much bigger than the list of all those banks that keep turning you down. The bad news is it's hard to define a comprehensive list of financing sources that don't place excessive demands and restrictions on owners, and even the Internet can't help much.

The most effective strategy here is to rely on your business networks. Talk to your accountant, attorney, the financing expert at your nearby chamber of commerce, industry trade groups, and other plugged-in corporate contacts who may be able to point you in fruitful directions. In some cases, bank loan officers themselves can offer useful leads, even if they're too skittish to make a bet themselves on your entrepreneurial venture without your personal backing.

Stage 2

To Move or Not to Move Out of a Home Office

Here's how to evaluate the consequences for your family as well as your company.

I SOMETIMES THINK I'VE HEARD every possible variation of the "in-the-home, out-of-the-home" theme during my years of covering the small business market. I've spoken to entrepreneurs who started their businesses at home, moved out, and then moved back (whether because they hated the commute, couldn't cope with the added expenses, or found child care hassles insurmountable). At the other extreme, there have been many business owners—far too many of them—who have confessed to me that they waited so long to leave home that they probably delayed their company's growth, while creating all kinds of problems on the home front.

One high-tech company grew to the point that there

were nearly a dozen full and part-time staffers crammed into the owner's dining room, living room, basement, and any other spare spot they could find. Conditions were so cramped and makeshift that employees started leaving, even though sales were booming, and the founder's family was miserable. Yet he still put off relocation because he wanted to channel all the funds he could into growth-related expenditures rather than "wasting money," as he put it, on office space.

"I was completely fixated on the costs and risks that would be involved with a move to an outside office," he recalled. "The thought of committing myself and the company to a lease—plus the added expenses that would come from extra utility costs, commuting costs, and on and on— became completely insurmountable obstacles." It took a heart-to-heart conversation with a prospective investor to change his mind. The backer decided to forgo an investment, he told the entrepreneur, because he couldn't take the company seriously so long as it was operating from the dining room table.

If you're still running your Stage Two company out of your home, you need to consider a range of financial and other matters in order to resolve whether this truly is the best of all business decisions. But be prepared: For some entrepreneurs, corporate and personal interests don't always agree to provide a neat, easy answer. At some point, you may need to make a judgment call.

Analyzing the Financial Implications

Basically, there are two sets of numbers you need to compare when deciding whether it makes dollar-sense to make the move.

❏ **Corporate effects.** Begin by estimating the financial benefit you expect to receive. In most cases, this will take the form of greater revenues than you could hope to earn if you stayed within the home office that your company is presumably outgrowing. Try to assess the trickle-down effect from these increased revenues, including whether this will help sustain improvements in your self-compensation and benefit package or simply support other growth-related expenditures. Then, calculate the corporate-cost increases that will result from your move (office rent, additional utility costs, new furniture and other supplies, office insurance, and so on). Finally, project the additional corporate tax savings you can expect to receive from deductions tied to these higher operating expenses.

❑ **Personal effects.** To balance out these business-related numbers, you must also evaluate the move's financial consequences for your household. Assess any likely *increases* in your personal costs. These might include commuting expenses, dry-cleaning bills, child care expenses, or other items. Then list *decreases* in personal expenses, including likely reductions in the household's utility bills, home insurance premiums, waste management fees, and so on.

Calculate the effect of your lost home-office deductions. Whether this will prove to be painful for your family will depend, in large part, upon how aggressive you've been on the tax front, as well as how costly a home-office operation you've been running. You may ask yourself, What do I do with all of these numbers? You may need your accountant's help to walk through all this, but that slight expense will be worthwhile if it helps you to make a better, informed decision.

What you're trying to get a sense of is whether your anticipated boost in corporate revenues (and the trickle-down effect for your household if self-compensation and benefits can be improved) will more than justify your additional corporate expenses and lost personal tax deductions.

Analyzing the Hassle Factor

These issues are tough to quantify, but they're worth considering by any home-based entrepreneur who may or

Why Move?

IF YOU DECIDE AGAINST MAKING a move at this time, remember: You're not making a lifetime commitment to keeping your business at home. Work your way through these same exercises each year, at about the same time that you're working on your business-plan projections and family financial planning assessments. If at any time a home-based office stops making sense for you, the actual relocation probably won't be half as difficult as the decision-making process was.

There are two external factors that might prompt a move at some point as your company develops. *Benefits considerations* could tip the balance. You'll discover once you start shopping around that these are tougher to qualify for if your company is a home-based business. *Financing issues* are the other biggie. Private equity investors aren't the only ones who tend to balk at the notion of providing capital to a company operating out of a home. Banks are also leery, perhaps because they view this as a sign of instability. Once you're aggressively in the market for growth capital, relocation will make a lot of sense.

may not decide to make a move. For simplicity's sake, let's boil them down to the hassle factor. There are two kinds of hassles worth contemplating: your own and your family's.

This is the time to write down (and take seriously) all the personal consequences of living with your business, quite literally, twenty-four hours a day. Does your family complain constantly, or do you yourself fantasize about having the ability to walk away from your company at least occasionally? Is your business growing so fast that it's crowding your kids or spouse out of what should be the household's living space? Do neighbors constantly gripe about all those bags of office-related garbage or delivery trucks that line up outside your home?

Or maybe none of those problems relate to your household and business, and the only reason you've been thinking about a move is because you figure you *really should* move out if you're serious about building a company. If that's the case, think again. So long as your company's growth prospects aren't constrained by its home operations, staying put is probably the smartest financial move you can make, for both your company's cash flow and your household's after-tax bottom line.

Stage 2

Planning Proactively for Erratic Cash Flow

It's now possible for you to take steps to protect your personal finances against significant problems.

IT'S DANGEROUS TO ASSUME that your company won't ever experience an unexpected cash flow disruption once it moves beyond the volatile start-up period. Problems can happen at any stage of development. When interest rates rise, for example, your corporate collections will almost inevitably slow down, compounding the financial crunch caused by the higher prices that you are paying. If your growing company relies heavily on one or two customers or suppliers, and its steady cash flow is dependent upon *their* continued success as well as your own, that can be a risky proposition. Ironically enough, cash flow crunches can sometimes result from too much of a good thing, as when expensive but irresistible growth opportunities present themselves.

In any of these instances, business owners can find themselves forced to liquidate their family's fledgling investment accounts, to raise funds by selling part of their equity stake at fire-sale prices, or to assume unwise levels of personal debt all over again—if they have failed to set up a line of defense when the company's cash flow is healthy.

The secret is just that: Your strategy needs to be set in place when the company's financial position is *healthy* rather than desperate, precarious, or even mildly shaky. Remember that old adage: Nobody wants to give you money when you need it, only when you don't. That's especially true for business owners, at least until they've achieved the longer-term growth history, maturity of corporate operations, and predictability of profits that signals Stage Three entrepreneurism.

Defensive Measures

Choose whichever of these defensive measures best suits your company's (and your family's) current situation:

❶ **Set up a corporate cash-management account** if your Stage Two business is consistently operating under positive cash flow conditions. Banks, as well as investment houses, offer some attractive options for small businesses; you may be able to link your corporate checking account to a savings account that invests excess funds in money market instruments or other safe, liquid investments.

Shopping tip: At one time, good accounts were limited to a handful of major players, such as Merrill Lynch, Citibank, and Chase. But these types of accounts are now widely available from regional as well as national firms, and there's so much competition for small business customers that it's worth shopping around to figure out who's currently offering the best deal. The easiest way to do that is through the Internet; search under keywords *cash management account* to compare fees and service options.

You'll get two advantages from setting up one of these accounts: First, your company will be able to earn some investment income and thus supplement its supply of working and growth capital. Second, by creating the corporate equivalent of your family's emergency nest egg, you'll reduce the likelihood that the company will ever need to rely on a personal bailout. In some cases, you'll be able to create new borrowing opportunities for your company as well, simply by setting up a cash-management account with a financial institution that now will have more reason to value your relationship and thus be more willing to increase your debt options.

❷ **Set in place a credit line that you currently don't need.** This piece of advice may seem perverse to you, since you probably still have only limited borrowing opportunities—and you may be convinced that you need to aggressively make use of all the funds you can get your hands on, whether those come to you from lenders or investors. But it's risky on both the personal and corporate fronts to leave yourself without *some* form of untapped credit that's readily available but won't get spent except as a last resort. Here are some suggestions.

As soon as a bank will authorize a corporate credit line that's not tied to your personal collateral or guarantee, apply for more than you need. Or, if your corporate borrowing limit is low, discipline yourself to use no more than 80 percent of whatever is available. The fees involved in securing excess credit in this way won't be significant. Some banks *do* impose some type of "use-it-or-lose-it" requirement on their business borrowers (and that *will* increase your costs, because of financing charges). If you find yourself in this circumstance, borrow the funds and bank them in an interest-bearing corporate savings account elsewhere, with the intention of paying back your credit line as quickly as possible.

If you've got credit cards in your company's name, investigate whether a credit line could be hooked up to one of them as well. American Express is particularly aggressive in offering this option to its small business customers. Although more expensive than a bank line, this still would be useful in the event of an emergency.

❸ **Consider this last-ditch alternative, if necessary:** For owners who currently have exhausted their corporate borrowing options, it might make sense to apply for a home equity line of credit. There are fees involved here as well, but they're minimal and shouldn't discourage you if you've tapped out your other borrowing and credit alternatives.

Shopping tip: Here again, it makes sense to do an up-to-date comparison of fees and interest charges through the World Wide Web; conduct a keyword search under *home equity loans.*

If you go this route, do so with the hope that you'll never have to rely on it for business purposes. Do recognize, however, that if you must do so, you'll be better off having gone through the time-consuming application process well in advance of a cash flow crunch.

Stage 2

Divorce-Proof Your Company

Unnecessary as these personal precautions may seem to you now, they can be essential to any business's long-term survival if an owner's marriage dissolves.

IT MAY LOOM AS RIDICULOUS—as well as excessively time-consuming—to plan for your divorce when that prospect seems remote and you very likely feel overwhelmed just with the challenges of starting and running a fast-growing company. Yet this risk is too serious to ignore. Without well-considered safeguards set firmly in place, a marital break-up can jeopardize a business's ownership structure and stability and may even force its sale if a divorce settlement proves financially overwhelming.

Don't brush off this advice because such a disaster seems so unlikely. Your failure to take adequate precautions can only make a bad situation much worse if you and your spouse succumb to the statistical odds of a marital breakup. One entrepreneur's story tells it all: He called me to report the unfortunate end of his company, a once-thriving automobile service firm. While the business had boomed, his marriage had suffered. He quickly came to rue his failure to follow an attorney's advice to include a divorce-contingency plan among his other early-stage business planning activities. Without a divorce plan that specified anything different, the couple's assets needed to be split fifty-fifty, because they lived in a community property state. (More on that later.)

Like those of many entrepreneurial families, this household's assets were mainly tied up in the fast-growing company—and its value was so large that the owner had no other choice but to sell it in order to pay the divorce settlement. He had tried to raise money from outside investors, but they weren't exactly thrilled by the notion that their infusion of capital would go toward a divorce settlement rather than growth-related activities.

How bad did things get? This owner actually found himself forced by a divorce court judge to accept the *lower* of two different bids, because it was a cash-only offer and his soon-to-be-ex-spouse wasn't willing to accept the financial uncertainties that might have resulted from an extended payment arrangement.

Are you convinced yet? Let me make one final point. The very fact that a divorce seems highly unlikely to you is the best proof of all that this is the ideal time to carry out this protective step. That's because neither you nor your spouse should feel threatened by what is, after all, merely a theoretical exercise in order to safeguard the long-term interests of your company as well as that of the family. Your conversations should be calm, rational, and—relatively speaking—pretty simple.

Divorce planning can and should take different forms, depending on the stage of development (as well as financial success) a company has achieved at the point its owner tackles the task. Fortunately, during Stage Two, the planning process for this is relatively straightforward. Meanwhile, the company's structure and realistic prospects for growth and profitability should by now be increasingly apparent, permitting both spouses to make informed judgments on these important matters. (The last thing you want to have happen within a heated set of divorce proceedings is to have your spouse argue that the divorce plan should be discarded because he or she never really grasped what kind of prospects your company had.)

At this time, there are basically four key issues that you two need to decide as a couple (perhaps with some input from the company's attorney or accountant):

❶ **Who owns the company's stock?** In community property states, statutes govern the division of assets, since the value of everything owned jointly *or* individually by a married couple will be split between them equally in the event of a divorce. (These states are Arizona, California, Idaho, Louisiana, Nevada, New Mexico, Texas, Washington, and Wisconsin.) Assets owned individually before a marriage generally are treated as separate property, but in some states, any appreciation in the value of those assets that occurred during the years of marriage falls into the community property category. But elsewhere, in states that are known as "equitable distribution" locations, a founder may be able to hold onto a larger portion of the company's net worth after a breakup by deciding early on to retain stock ownership in his or her name.

❷ **Who is actively involved in the company's operations?** When arriving at the value of a fair settlement, divorce court judges usually will take into account not only who holds the stock but also who has been responsible for the company's growth and development. A divorce-planning document should accurately reflect this information so that neither party can quibble over it in retrospect. There's no formal name for this kind of document: It's really just a contemporaneous description of the business and each spouse's activities relating to the company's activities.

Be as specific as possible when preparing this list. I think it's perfectly reasonable to include detailed work schedules that describe each spouse's company-related activities, both at the office and at home; comprehensive job descriptions; business travel schedules; and any other relevant information that sketches out the nature of both parties' commitment to your fast-growing company.

❸ How much is the company worth? No one would ever expect this type of document to provide an accurate bottom-line number—after all, the value of a growing company changes rapidly, and it can go down as well as up! But that's not the issue here. A founder and spouse should reach agreement ahead of time, in writing, about the valuation *method* that they would feel comfortable relying on in the event of a divorce.

This might sound esoteric, but it's not. Some valuation rules of thumb rely almost entirely on recent business-sale patterns within related industries; others concentrate on net earnings and calculate a company's value according to whatever multiples of earnings are traditionally tied to the company's industry. Valuation methods can actually vary so widely that even the accounting definition relied upon for earnings can differ. In some cases, a valuation method will take into account the worth of various assets (such as real estate, inventory, equipment, and the like) as well as its earnings or even sales history. In others, it won't.

In other words, valuing a privately held business is an art, not a science. Unlike a public company, where the value of a stock stake is simple to calculate (even though it might change daily), there's no single valuation method that offers the best-and-only answer about how much a private company's stock shares are worth. That's why the possibility exists for endless legal disputes over this issue if it's not prepared for in advance.

A safe strategy: With your accountant's assistance, choose the valuation method that works best for your industry and company size. Then agree in writing to hire three independent appraisers during the divorce. One might be hired by each spouse, with the remaining one chosen by the presiding judge. Plan to rely on the average of their assessments—or perhaps on the assessment of the closest two, if one seems wildly off base—if and when a court needs to calculate the value of a fair asset split.

A Timing Tip

IT MAKES SENSE TO INVOLVE a lawyer in drafting the initial version of your hopefully never-to-be-used divorce plan (which may include a variety of different documents, including the valuation plan and contemporaneous company description outlined above, as well as a prenuptial agreement, if any exists). Keep two copies, one in the company's files and one in your household's.

But don't forget about the plan. Since your company may well be changing rapidly during this period, it makes sense to review and perhaps revise this document annually. This needn't be a painful chore. One couple, a lawyer and a real-estate developer who both earned big salaries while running their own successful business ventures, confided to me that they incorporated this activity into their yearly anniversary celebrations to make certain they didn't forget. I'd also advise you to reevaluate your divorce plans whenever major household or business changes occur, such as the birth of a child, receipt of a family inheritance, or refinancing of the company.

❹ **How will payments relating to the company's value be made?** If the timing is left to the courts to decide, a divorce settlement may come due so quickly that an owner has no recourse except to sell the company in order to raise the necessary funds. (Remember that unfortunate automobile-service entrepreneur!) If a couple can agree in advance—when times are calm and rationality can prevail—that all corporate-stock-related payments will be staggered over time, the company's well-being will likely be preserved.

Stage 2

Diversifying Your Investments

Look for ways to increase the diversity of your personal assets as soon as possible.

ENTREPRENEURS ARE FINANCIALLY vulnerable so long as their personal holdings are concentrated in one single, precarious investment that cannot be sold or borrowed against until it reaches a level of successful growth. Some ventures never develop to the point of consistent profitability, or they may take many years before they can provide their owners with a lucrative payoff. People who diversify early into alternative investments can create valuable safety cushions and inch their way closer to achieving their family's long-term financial goals.

> *Real estate was the right kind of investment for us. I was looking for what you could call the anti-health-club investment—something that would work against the cycles of my business and help me to build credibility with the banks.*
>
> —LUCILLE ROBERTS

I've seen the value of this strategy again and again. At one financial-consulting company that I've tracked for years, the owner was able to pay his children's college tuition bills—at one point, while funding a costly diversification effort in response to a business downturn—thanks to some profitable real estate purchases and mutual fund investments that he'd made whenever cash flow was strong enough to pay him a decent salary. As soon as the company rebounded and the kids were out of college, he began aggressively investing again in a range of asset categories, first by recreating the bond- and stock-oriented mutual fund investments that he and his wife had cashed in to pay those tuition bills and eventually moving into angel investments in fast-growing companies that he came across through his consulting activities.

When should you start thinking about asset diversification? The answer is simple: As soon as possible. The tougher issue to sort your way through is how best to get started. That's because Stage Two entrepreneurs can afford to take only baby steps in this regard, mainly because it's unlikely that their young companies can manage to pay them very much in the way of a salary or bonus. Meanwhile, if growth is capital intensive and lenders and investors remain elusive, owners may well be faced by the necessity to get more heavily invested themselves or risk stalling corporate progress—despite the obvious advantages of moving in the other direction, toward alternative, noncompany-related assets.

It's sad but true: During this stage of ownership, most people would find themselves much farther along the path to safe but profitable asset diversification if they had remained in the corporate workplace, bolstered by predictable paychecks, end-of-the-year bonuses, and 401(k) accounts with matching contributions from their employers. All an entrepreneur can do, at least for now, is to set some modest objectives, while accepting the fact that business developments will sometimes make it impossible to stick to this investment plan.

Here's how to get started: If your company's cash flow is fairly even, it probably makes the best sense for you to try to save a small portion of your salary each pay period. If results are more cyclical, you may want to wait for predictable upturns in order to pay yourself a bonus that will go directly into the family's investments.

This may sound reminiscent of the strategy suggested earlier with regard to building the family emergency nest egg (see "How Much Do You Need in Emergency Reserves?" page 31). I'm repeating it here because this slow-but-steady approach works and, equally important, won't place an undue strain upon the finances of your household or your corporation.

Figure out which type of investment strategy will be best suited for you. You've basically got two choices at this stage: either lump all your noncompany investments in a single portfolio or set aside small accounts for specific goals such as college or retirement savings.

Entrepreneurship is all-consuming. You need the right kind of experts. You need great legal help. You also need great accounting assistance. Entrepreneurs who try to handle their own accounting matters don't understand their priorities.

—AARON COHEN

Each approach offers advantages. By keeping your investments together, you'll minimize fees and may be able to build up enough savings clout to qualify for special client perks or better investment terms. Personal record keeping also will be simple. But segmenting your savings into individual accounts makes it likelier that you will stay as focused on the family's specific goals as you are on your company's. You'll also be able to fine-tune your investment plans as accounts gradually accumulate value, to insure the best balance of short-term safety and longer-term growth over whatever time horizon fits each set of goals.

It really does make sense to discuss these alternatives with your spouse and any personal financial adviser you might have. I could see you making either decision without regrets. But there's one thing I should note before concluding this section: Based on my conversations with entrepreneurs, I've gotten the sense that many more of them opt for the second approach—perhaps because they *are* so goal-driven, and this approach does makes it easier to monitor the family's progress in priority personal financial matters.

Stage 2

The Pros and Cons of Investment Advisers

Once you begin diversifying personal assets outside the company, you'll need to decide whether to pay for an expert's advice or to self-direct your own investment activities.

DURING THE START-UP PHASE, your household's assets were probably so closely bound up with the company's that there was no need for an extra level of guidance beyond what your corporate accountant and attorney could provide.

But during Stage Two, once you can start moving past the safe but stodgy strategy of building the family's emergency nest egg, this issue becomes much more pressing. In part, that's because business owners often get inundated with cold calls from brokers, financial planners, and other types of investment professionals. But what also changes during this period is the potential for profit. As the household's outside-the-company savings portfolio gradually expands—whether that's in Stage Two or later, in Stage

Three—you'll find yourself with more opportunity to diversify into investments with greater possibility for reward.

Does it make sense, at this stage, to rely on an expert's guidance when exploring these unfolding investment options? Here's a self-test that should help you decide:

Do I know enough about investments to handle a beginner's activities?

Don't set your intellectual standards *too* high. During Stage Two, when entrepreneurs are still mainly invested in their company's equity, you can manage just fine by concentrating on low-to-moderate-risk mutual funds, which are simple to keep track of via major newspapers, free Web sites, and personal finance magazines.

But you do need to be capable of understanding—or learning about—essential matters such as "loads" (i.e., sales charges), the risks and rewards attached to different fund categories, and the somewhat unusual set of tax issues that relate to mutual fund investments. If you're not, then you probably do need some help from an adviser.

Cost-saving tip: At this stage, since your portfolio is small and your investment strategy relatively straightforward, you'll be best off relying on a fee-only financial planner, whose recommendations will not be affected by the receipt of commissions from investment houses whose products he or she recommends.

@ Internet Guide: One way to come up with good leads to fee-only planners is to visit the Web site of their industry group, at www.napfa.org. Once there, you'll be able to click on useful listings for fee-only planners in your area, as well as consumer tips to help you make your selection.

When interviewing possible hires, pay special attention to the planner's experience in working with entrepreneurs like yourself. Ask pointed questions, such as "How are my family's investment needs different from those of other, nonentrepreneurial families?" and "What type of asset diversification strategy makes sense for someone like me, with an equity stake in my company that's valued at _____?" (It's up to you to fill in the blank.) Also ask for references from small business clients that the planner has worked with for an extended period of time.

Can I set aside a small amount of time each month (or, at the minimum, every business quarter) to monitor my fledgling investments?

Stage Two owners should be able to manage their investments with the help of a very simple system. You can do this by setting up what's known as a cash-management account with a formal mechanism to "sweep" excess cash from checking into investments at the end of each business day. But the extra fees involved might not be worth it, since it's so simple, these days, just to arrange with your bank for a no-cost, prescheduled monthly debit and transfer of funds to your investment account.

I dropped a couple of hundred thousand dollars into a new plant for my company. What I did was right out of the textbooks: invest in real estate and lease it back to your company. But it all turned out wrong because it was in a location where the real estate market eventually collapsed.

—HOLLY HITZEMANN

Do some investigating here. Your fees for a formal sweep mechanism might run anywhere from $10 to $20 per month to more if your bank or investment house ties its fees to a percentage of your assets in both accounts. Or you might be able to eliminate the fees entirely if you keep your personal funds in the same bank with which your company does business.

But whether you choose one of these methods or prefer to send off a check to your investment account whenever you can afford to, you'll need to pay attention to the performance record of your fund portfolio. That's because the values of mutual funds fluctuate according to trends in the stock and bond markets. Funds that have been strong performers in the past may lag under changing sets of circumstances (such as shifts in management or investment strategy), and they may no longer be worthwhile investments.

I'm not suggesting that you'll want to sell an investment anytime a fund's daily price (known as its *NAV* or *net asset value*) moves an iota in the wrong direction. But if you're going to accept "ownership" of your mutual fund investments—and manage them on your own—then you need to be willing to monitor their performance regularly and to make investment changes when necessary. If you're not, then, again, you need help from an investment adviser who has the time that you lack.

One more point worth mentioning: You're still at the early stages of building a portfolio. But if you stay on track, you'll eventually get to the point where you've achieved a desirable "balance" of investments, which you should be able to define with target percentages for each asset category within your holdings. At that point, you'll want to evaluate your progress, perhaps semiannually or annually, and readjust that balance by selling or buying holdings within each of your investment categories, depending on whether they've become more or less profitable. (This is a great discipline, since it forces you to sell investments when they're high and buy them when they're not.) If you don't have the time to do this either, hire someone who does.

Could my company benefit from a relationship with an investment adviser?

This is a real possibility, especially if your business is growing rapidly and shows promise of one day either attracting private equity investors or going public. In this case, you might want to hire an adviser from a large investment house—even when your portfolio is too small to otherwise warrant the move—in an effort to build ties that could ease your way to future financing.

Tip: This move will cost you far more than either the do-it-yourself approach or reliance on a fee-only financial planner. So be certain it has the potential for payoff. Investigate the investment house's interest in *your company* as a long-term client by really forcing it to compete for your business. Ask your prospective hire to lay out a long- and a short-term plan for ways that it can help you achieve your personal and corporate financial objectives. Then double-check its credentials with business as well as personal clients who can attest to the firm's skill in raising capital in addition to paving the way toward profitable investment opportunities.

Stage 2

Creating an Investment Portfolio

The simplest way to diversify personal assets is to concentrate on a single portfolio that can counterbalance the family's high-risk investment in your company.

FOR ALL THOSE STAGE TWO entrepreneurs with little in the way of free time and limited financial resources outside the business, it can make a great deal of sense to start out with one family-oriented investment account. This can even be a stepping-stone that leads to the eventual establishment of multiple, goal-oriented accounts, once the growth of your company and investment portfolio savings can support that move.

If you decide to follow this strategy, your single portfolio can—and should—be constructed so that each new investment complements your equity stake in your company. Like any other investor, you'll want to monitor the short- and long-term risks of each investment you add to the mix. But your overall goal must be to create a group of holdings that is increasingly diversified and, therefore, less risky, less volatile, more liquid, and more predictable than is your investment in your still-developing entrepreneurial venture.

The blueprint for building a single portfolio is fairly straightforward.

Start by identifying the investment characteristics of your company

I've alluded to some of these issues before. The investment characteristics for you to consider include the following:

❑ **Financial risk.** How big is your downside? Could your entire equity stake become worthless, or is there a "bust-up value" underlying your company's asset base that would guarantee you a financial cushion? Is your potential for financial loss even greater than the current value of your stock holdings or capital investment because of personal indebtedness tied to the company? How likely is it that you would experience any of these losses?

❑ **Volatility.** Are you in a high-risk/high-reward industry, which tends to experience extreme marketplace conditions? Is the competitive arena so fierce that it's tough for you to make business predictions for anything resembling a mid- to-long-term horizon?

❑ **Liquidity.** If you absolutely, positively had to, how possible would it be for you to sell part or all of your equity stake in a timely fashion? If your company is still too young and untested to successfully carry off a stock sale, does it possess valuable assets that could be unloaded quickly if necessary? Is there anything at all that's sellable at this stage?

❏ **Cyclicity.** Is your company vulnerable to rises in interest rates, declines in consumer spending, lending crunches, foreign currency swings, or other shifts in economic conditions? Do your fortunes depend on certain broad market trends, such as the availability of consumer credit or the aging of the population? Can the timing of these shifts be predicted or in some other way be factored in to your analysis of your equity stake as a pure investment?

❏ **Investment prospects.** What's your realistic upside potential with this company? Is it a good—or even great— salary, a modestly profitable sale to a strategic corporate partner, or a break-the-bank cash-out through an initial public offering? Does whatever outcome seems likely translate into a 10 percent annual return on your investment in the business, a 1,000 percent overall return, or something in between? How does it compare to the return on a good mutual fund investment?

❏ **Correlation to other asset categories.** If your company's ability to one day earn you the investment return that you expect depends upon its ability to raise capital from private equity or other venture capital investors and, sometime soon, to go public, then your fate is even more closely tied to the rise and fall of the stock market than is that of other entrepreneurs. But stock market correlation isn't the only issue you need to consider here. Your company's investment performance may be closely related to that of other categories, such as bonds, real estate, or so-called emerging stock markets.

Working your way through this checklist will require dispassionate analysis. But until you can view your business the same way you assess any other investment, you'll be stymied in efforts to create a successful diversified portfolio.

Tip: Private companies in Stage One or Stage Two of development should be considered *growth-oriented equity investments.* Since your fledgling venture most closely resembles a so-called small-cap equity rather than a company with a large or midsized capitalization base, for now the message is simple: Stay away from *all* growth-oriented equity

> *I don't electronically trade stocks—what a waste of time that would be for someone who's as preoccupied as I am with running a growth-oriented company!*
>
> —AARON COHEN

investments (which includes stocks, mutual funds, and investments in other private companies) until you have adequately diversified your family's holdings elsewhere.

Evaluate the investment dynamics of your industry or sector

Work your way through the same checklist of characteristics that you explored in the first step. This may seem redundant, but it's not. That's because your overall industry may be vulnerable to a larger set of marketplace issues than seem to relate directly to your company from the perspective of its small but growing business niche. As an investor, you'll want to take these issues into account from the broadest possible vantage point so as to diversify most effectively away from the risks tied to your equity stake. For example: If your industry thrives mainly when new-housing starts are strong and your family's only noncorporate asset is your house, you wouldn't want to invest spare cash in commercial real estate.

Appraise the adequacy of your emergency nest egg

If it seems large enough to provide your family with all the short-term safeguards it may require, then you're ready to

get involved with moderate-term, moderate-risk investments. Since you'll want to stay away from the equity markets at this point (remember the tip in step #1!), a good
alternative is the bond market. Few Stage Two entrepreneurs have enough spare cash to support the purchase of a
portfolio of individual bonds, so it makes best sense to consider a bond-based mutual fund.

Investigate a number of choices. Funds that invest in
short-to-moderate U.S. treasury instruments, U.S. government agency debt, or high-quality corporate bonds all
could offer a balanced (and acceptable) mix of risk and
reward. But since your investment in your company is not
very liquid (meaning marketable) at this stage, avoid long-
term investments, such as zero coupon bonds or U.S. savings bonds. You also cannot afford to tackle the kind of
interest rate exposure tied to bond funds that specialize in
long-term treasuries. In addition, you'll want to avoid the
risks tied to volatility and possible defaults that are associated with junk bond holdings.

Branch out cautiously

Although entrepreneurial work occurs at an accelerated
pace, your activities on this front must proceed gradually.
While it's true that the quicker you can invest, the quicker
you can start spreading your investment risks around, you
probably won't be able to proceed quickly at all. Your biggest
handicap will be your inability to pay yourself enough of a
salary or bonus to support a full-scale investment campaign.

But once you find that you've been able to invest a
small sum each month (and haven't needed to reach into
your nest egg for emergency relief from corporate cash
flow crises), the time will come relatively soon when you'll
be itching to get involved in other types of investments.

At this stage of diversification, it still makes sense to
stick with mutual funds, since many are designed to accept
minimal investments and they offer investors the advantage

When Can I Buy Stocks?

For most stage two entrepreneurs, the risks attached to stocks and stock-based mutual funds are simply too high and the size of their portfolio too skimpy to warrant such an investment as a diversification play. There's no safe way around this rule (such as, for example, deluding yourself into believing that an index-based mutual fund is somehow less risky than other equity investments simply because it aims to track, rather than outperform, the markets). You cannot afford to add to your equity exposure in any way at all at this stage, until you reduce your risks with other types of investments.

If you're in doubt about the wisdom of "just saying no" for now, try this simple exercise. Calculate the current value of each of your investments, then label it according to broad categories: money market funds (or equivalents), bonds, real estate, and equities. Don't forget to include an estimate of the value of your company, which will likely amount to your only equity holding at this point.

If your equity in your company doesn't dwarf your entire household's other investments, you're an unusual entrepreneur! In that case, you—and you alone—may be ready to start shopping for some blue-chip stocks. Otherwise, you need to wait until you enter Stage Three, with consistent profitability and operational stability.

of well-diversified portfolios. Here are two good alternatives to consider:

❑ **Convertible bond funds** provide the safety of bonds as well as some upside earnings potential, since they invest only in bonds that can be converted into stock shares when the equity market is strong.

❑ **REITs** (real estate investment trusts) hold multiple commercial properties, which are usually hotels, office buildings, or retail malls. Although they've got their own risks, they can offer a good investment hedge against the volatility of the equity markets if they don't put you in conflict with step #2.

Stage 2

Saving for Your Children's College

If family circumstances convince you that it's time to plan for college tuition costs, here's how to get started without disrupting your company's growth.

PERSONAL FINANCE EXPERTS always advise parents to start saving for college as early as possible—ideally from the moment their children are born. But it's tough (and often impossible) for entrepreneurs to stick to that kind of steady savings discipline while they're also trying to build a fast-growing company.

If you're motivated to try to do both, however, Stage Two can be a good time to begin. So long as your company can pay you a regular salary that more than covers the household's monthly living expenses, you should be able to set aside a small sum each month as part of a college savings plan. Just keep in mind three important points:

RUSH!

NEW SUBSCRIBER SAVINGS!

Visit us at: www.gunsandammomag.com

❶ College savings plans work best when they're based on long-term investment strategies. Unfortunately, that makes them similar to your investment in your company—not as risky, perhaps, but fairly illiquid. (Many of the best savings options are designed to mature as tuition bills come due and can't easily be cashed in or sold sooner if you need to do so.) That means that this type of savings account is of only limited value when it comes to a Stage Two owner's important goal of asset diversification. So no matter how worried you are about college costs, you've got to accumulate other kinds of investments too.

❷ Entrepreneurs may be able to save less and still cover tuition costs if they make creative use of their ownership options. Here's some good news. So long as your company's cash flow is stable, there are ways that you can use it to help shoulder some of the costs of educating your kids. One possibility is to put your teenager on the company's payroll. If you can justify the salary for tasks that might include mail-room work, copying, filing, or making deliveries, the paycheck will be tax deductible like any other business operating expense. There's also a personal tax benefit if your child is over fourteen, since that income will be taxed at his or her (lower) tax rate rather than your own.

Here's another option: Consider setting up an educational assistance program for all employees and their family members, including your own. But be careful here. In order for the company's tuition reimbursements to be tax deductible, they need to be provided on a nondiscriminatory basis to all full-timers. Under current regulations, employer-provided tuition assistance plans can pay up to $5,250 per year of college costs, without imposing a personal income tax liability on the employee.

One caveat: You'll have to meet the 5 percent test in order for company expenditures to be tax deductible. This means that owner-employees (and their families) can receive no more than 5 percent of the benefit from the plan. Check with your accountant if you're uncertain whether you'll fit the requirements.

❸ **If you want to achieve your college savings goals, you *must* protect these funds from the demands of your growing company.** One of the saddest stories I've heard is from an entrepreneur related to a tuition savings account that went completely awry. This owner had made the foolish (if understandable) mistake of using the family's college savings as collateral against a business-based loan. Some of the investments within this were publicly traded technology stocks. (*That* was a mistake too, but it's not the point of my story.) As stock prices slid throughout the second half of 2000, the value of this collateral base sank below the level deemed acceptable by the bank, so the loan was called in for repayment even though there wasn't any other problem with it or the company. Difficulties escalated quickly. Since the company was in a fast-growth mode, it didn't have sufficient available funds to meet the bank's demand, so the owner needed to cash in the entire college savings account to make up the difference. The moral of this story: No matter how big this investment account gets, keep your company's paws off it.

> *Once the company gets to the point where it's making a profit and cash flow is strong, set up an automatic debit arrangement for your business as well. Have the funds go into some kind of safe, cash-management arrangement.*
>
> —HOLLY HITZEMANN

Some Investment Options to Consider

For people who aren't business owners, the best bet is to invest their college savings accounts in stocks or stock-based mutual funds with long-term growth potential. But since entrepreneurs are already so heavily invested in growth equities through their own companies, it makes sense to rely on other savings vehicles here. Some good choices include the following:

❑ **State college savings plans** (known formally as Section 529 plans or qualified state tuition programs) are available almost everywhere; they vary in their design, but all offer parents some type of tax-advantaged opportunity to save funds for college. Some state plans allow families to prepay their tuition bills entirely, at significantly discounted rates. These are definitely worth investigating, although options vary a good bit. Every plan permits its savings to be used at institutions of higher education anywhere across the United States, but some plans offer significantly better advantages for savers who use their funds at in-state colleges and universities, which can be limiting.

One great advantage to these plans is that they're open to all state residents, regardless of income levels. So if you find your salary increasing as your company grows, you won't have to worry about being disqualified from further participation.

One more tip: If you don't like your own state's 529 plan, you might want to consider one offered by any of these states, all of which permit participation by out-of-state residents: Colorado, Connecticut, Delaware, Indiana, Iowa, Montana, New Hampshire, New York, Rhode Island, and Utah.

Thanks to tax relief from Washington, D.C., 529s now look better than ever. New rules provide that no tax will be owed by anyone (either parents or children) when funds are withdrawn after January 1, 2002, to pay for college expenses. The regulations also make Education IRAs (the so-called E-IRAs) worth more serious consideration: Parents with combined household incomes of up to $220,000 can save up to $2,000 per year, starting in 2002, on a tax-free basis, with funds permitted to be used for college or private elementary and secondary schools.

❏ **Zero coupon bonds** are bonds that are sold at a significant discount to their face value. (The trade-off is that their investors don't receive any interest payments, unlike regular bondholders.) They've got two big advantages for college savers: certainty (because investors know exactly how much each bond will be worth at its maturity date, which is usually timed for when a child turns eighteen or so) and flexibility (since the funds can be used, once the bonds mature, to pay for college costs anywhere). There's also not much risk attached to these bonds, since they're usually issued by U.S. government agencies. But they too have a downside that could scare some business owners away: They're very illiquid, because it's difficult to resell a zero coupon bond during the long period before it matures.

Series EE Savings Bonds may also be worth considering, since their investment income receives tax-free status if the proceeds of the bonds are applied to college tuition costs (but not toward the expenses of room and board or books and other supplies). Their interest is compounded semiannually, calculated at 90 percent of the average yield of 5-year Treasuries for the preceding six months.

Since this means that their interest rates basically are tied to inflation, they offer little prospect for making significant investment gains, especially during low interest rate periods like the one that prevailed during the late 1990s. That can be discouraging for college savers who need all the help they can get. They're also not as liquid as you might imagine: If you need to cash in an EE before it's at least five years old, you'll face a penalty—sacrificing the most recent three months' interest.

It's also worth pointing out that the rules governing the education tax exclusion on EEs are fairly restrictive. The bonds must be purchased by someone who is at least twenty-four years old and can only qualify for a tax break if that person has an income under certain limits at the time that the bonds are redeemed. The exclusion limit currently phases out for joint filers on adjusted gross incomes between $83,650 and $113,650 and for single taxpayers between $55,700 and $70,750. If your company winds up being as successful as you expect it will be, you could find yourself with a low-return investment and no tax benefits at all by the time you redeem the bonds and send your child off to college.

For up-to-date information on EEs, visit www.savings bonds.gov.

Stage 2

Retirement Planning: Make Moves Now

As you begin to diversify assets away from your company, it's time to take some baby steps in the direction of retirement saving.

MANY ENTREPRENEURS' RETIREMENT plans are fairly simple: Build their companies up to become very large and very successful, then sell them (or carry out a glitzy initial public offering) and live out a cushy existence afterwards. Some people modify this strategy, with the intention of starting and selling multiple companies before settling down into their easy chairs. But their visions are usually founded on the optimistic assumption that their company's long-term development will more than compensate for any lack of short-term planning and saving on the retirement front.

The risks inherent in this strategy (or lack of strategy, as it might better be described) should be all too obvious. Many entrepreneurial companies fail—or they limp along in a slightly better than break-even mode that will *never* attract future buyers or open the door for a lucrative IPO. If their owners omit the important act of setting aside personal funds for retirement (and developing an appropriate investment strategy for these funds), they will pay the consequences during financially strapped retirement years.

That said, during Stage Two, most companies' growth demands and cash flow constraints are such that owners can—and should—take only modest steps in this direction. There are three retirement savings options worth considering:

Individual Retirement Accounts (IRAs)

For many early-stage entrepreneurs, IRAs are probably the best way to go since they combine the advantages of a personal tax deduction, so long as you meet the income guidelines, with a lack of corporate baggage (meaning you don't have to worry about providing this benefit to your staffers as well). For tax year 2002, contributions of up to $3,000 per year are permitted for each working spouse; a married couple with one nonworking spouse can set aside up to $6,000, so long as no more than $3,000 goes into either the husband's or the wife's account. The ceiling on tax-deductible individual contributions will rise to $5,000 by 2008, thanks to tax relief. Then, any investment income earned on retirement savings qualifies for tax-deferred status until it is withdrawn after age 59½. (Before then, there's a 10 percent penalty, as well as income tax assessment, on early withdrawals, so entrepreneurs need to consider this savings account *off-limits,* even when they're hunting for funds to invest in their companies.) Also worth noting: Business owners who are older than fifty (and have the cash to spare) can take advantage of a new "catch-up" clause, which permits every individual to set aside an extra $500 per year starting in 2002, and $1,000 per year as of 2006.

One caveat: The income guidelines that govern deductibility are fairly limited, so you won't be able to continue this strategy (at least in a tax-advantaged manner) once your company grows sufficiently to start paying you the kind of salary you well deserve. A married couple filing jointly can contribute $3,000 apiece and receive a full tax deduction, so long as their adjusted gross income adds up to no more than $49,999. Between $50,000 and $59,999, the deduction is gradually reduced—and by $60,000 and over, it disappears.

> *If I've got one regret, it's this: I really didn't have a personal financial adviser at the beginning, when I started my company thirteen years ago.*
>
> —BRIAN SULLIVAN

Roth IRAs

These attracted some attention when they first were unveiled back in 1998 since they offer savers one big advantage: Investment income from a Roth IRA can be withdrawn on an entirely tax-free basis, so long as it's been held in an account for at least five years and the policyholder is over 59½ years old.

But their downside is significant for early-stage entrepreneurs, who need their financial benefits in the short-term as well as the long-term: Contributions are not tax deductible in the year in which they are made. Given the other constraints on the family's pocketbook, this disadvantage may push the Roth beyond your realm of possibilities.

If your family is fortunate enough *not* to depend on a tax benefit to ease the pain of retirement savings, I'd urge you to consider a Roth IRA, at least for now. But do be aware that you'll likely outgrow this vehicle if your company becomes increasingly successful. Contribution limits are currently phased out between $95,000 and $110,000 in adjusted gross income for single taxpayers and between $150,000 and $160,000 for married couples filing jointly.

SIMPLE IRAs

For business owners who are afraid to make a commitment as potentially costly and administratively time-consuming as setting up a 401(k), yet they want to offer their employees some type of retirement benefit, this can be an attractive compromise. The name stands for Savings Incentive Match Plan for Employees. (You get the idea, which is that the company is required to do some matching of employee contributions. But these rules aren't too burdensome, especially for Stage Two owners who don't yet have many employees.)

The good news is, you and your staffers can contribute *more* of your earnings into a SIMPLE IRA than its traditional counterpart with that $3,000 limit. Here, the cap is as high as $6,500, which gets subtracted from people's paychecks on a pretax basis.

Your company also gets to qualify for a tax deduction for matching contributions (which can be a 100 percent match of the first 3 percent of salary deferrals or as little as a match of 1 percent of pay for two out of five years). These options may seem complicated, but your corporate accountant should be able to help you figure out which one makes the best sense, given your company's current financial picture and near-term cash flow prospects.

Corporate Retirement Plan?

I CAN'T DENY THAT I'VE HAD many heated conversations with business owners over the years on the issue of whether they should *ever* consider setting up a corporate retirement plan. These plans have a bad rap among entrepreneurs who worry about bogging down their businesses with unnecessary costs, over-the-top paperwork hassles, and inflexible government regulations.

I try very hard to change their minds—especially if they're facing stiff competition for skilled employees in technical and financial fields, or if they're trying to build a good management team. I'm convinced that retirement plans (even something as simple as a SIMPLE IRA) give out clear signals that you're serious about building a big business and treating your employees right. I'm also convinced that you'll stand a better chance of taking care of yourself and your family in this regard once you set a corporate plan in place.

Trust me: By Stage Two you and your company are ready to take on these relatively minor administrative and financial responsibilities, and the rewards will be well worth it.

There's also another benefit worth considering on the corporate front. The employer contribution is not subject to payroll taxes, which can amount to significant savings. Expect your administrative costs to be minimal—generally between $10 and $50 per year per participant; don't worry about costly IRS filings or discrimination tests, since none are required for companies that set up SIMPLE plans.

A Simple Tax-Reduction Strategy

The least costly and less complicated way to carry out estate planning is to get started before your company becomes significantly profitable.

HOW MANY ENTREPRENEURS are ready to contemplate their own mortality, let alone devote the time and money that are usually necessary to set in place a full-scale estate plan, complete with trusts, trustees, and state-of-the-art tax-reduction enhancements? So here's some good news. For business owners who are willing to face this issue during the earlier stages of their company's development, the process can be relatively painless.

The secret: You can take advantage of the gift-tax exclusion rule, which permits every person to give away up to $10,000 in cash or assets *tax-free*; best of all, this exclusion can be applied to a limitless number of recipients each year.

Some quick background: The tax that's relevant here isn't income tax but rather the federal gift and estate tax. This is levied against the value of each person's total property transfers—whether made during his or her lifetime or at death—above an exemption level that is currently set at $1 million for 2002 and scheduled to rise to $3.5 million by the year 2009, while top estate and gift tax rates are due to decline during this period according to a graduated schedule. Thanks to recent tax relief, estate taxes are now set to disappear entirely in 2010 (although the gift tax is scheduled to remain in force). But there's too much room for congressional maneuvering between now and then for me (and most estate-planning experts) to be willing to bet the bank that large estates will ever reach tax-free status. So it's hard to avoid the issue: After all, for quite a few years to come, this tax rate will still hover around 50 percent. Meanwhile, for many people, there are also state "death" taxes to worry about. So it's important to take steps to avoid estate taxes, especially in entrepreneurial situations in which fast growth is likely.

That brings me back to this $10,000 exclusion. What makes this annual tax loophole especially effective for early-stage business owners is the fact that their stock won't be worth very much—if anything at all—during the days before the company achieves profitability. Meanwhile, so long as they transfer only a minority stake to family members or others, the IRS permits the *taxable* value of a private company's shares to be discounted even further, making it extremely unlikely that any of these early gifts will wind up crossing that $10,000 threshold.

There's an interesting trend that I've noticed during the years I've spent covering the small business marketplace. Owners of early-stage companies are often so preoccupied with the challenges of running their businesses (or so poorly advised, because cash flow constraints prevent them from hiring top-notch advisers) that they fail to take advantage of this estate tax break during the days when it's easiest and most profitable for them to do so.

But whenever entrepreneurs repeat the start-up experience, by launching new businesses after that first one, this is one mistake they don't make twice. One "repeat entrepreneur," whose new venture was in the direct-marketing business, told me that she had gifted nearly half of her stock holdings into trust funds for her children during the company's first year of operation, without incurring any tax liability at all. "That way, no matter how big it grows or how valuable it gets, I never have to worry about that stock again," she noted. Good point.

Don't feel bad, however, if you—and your company—have made it past the start-up phase without setting this type of basic estate plan in place. You're scarcely alone. And I'm convinced that during Stage Two, your company still should be able to achieve major benefits from the $10,000 exclusion rule, mainly because its lack of consistent profitability and long-term cash flow stability should justify your claim that its stock is still worth relatively little. (That's especially easy to argue when you plan to give away only minority stakes in the company.) If your company has already built up enough value to make this difficult, here's the solution: Stagger your stock-gifting activities over a number of years to make certain that you don't trigger unnecessary tax consequences by giving away too much.

There's one more issue worth mentioning here. This strategy can get a little more complicated once you reach the point where you've got outside investors, especially the kind of large-scale angel investors who may represent your first step toward venture capitalists or other professional private equity investors (see "Moving Away from Friends-and-Family Financing," page 177, and "Where Can You Find Angel Investors?" page 184). They may not want you to muddy the waters of your company's ownership mix by adding new owners whose priorities might be different from your own.

So it makes sense to act early, before bringing these kinds of investors on board. Another alternative is to get around these objections by gifting shares that don't possess voting rights. This should be simple to carry out if you've adopted a C corporate structure, which permits multiple categories of stock (see "Incorporation Issues," page 34).

Making lifetime gifts of your stock to family members or others during Stage Two (or even earlier) isn't difficult. If your children or other intended recipients are adults, you'll probably want to transfer ownership to them directly. But otherwise it makes sense to consider setting up some kind of trust. Various options will be discussed elsewhere in this book (see "When Estate-Planning Trusts Can Help," page 259).

While the actual transfer of stock will not be difficult or time-consuming, you should involve your corporate attorney (to handle the paperwork) and your accountant (who should report the transfer to appropriate tax authorities). Either adviser should also prepare documentation that will be kept in your company's files to justify your assessment of the stock's minimal value at the time of your gift; this is an essential safeguard to protect you (and your estate) against audit risks at some later point.

Don't be put off by the necessity of paying for their services in this regard. Your overall cost should run no more than $2,000 or so—a small price to pay for the gift and estate taxes you'll save by not postponing these stock transfers until your company becomes profitable and therefore much more valuable than it is at this stage of growth.

Stage 2

Do You Need an Independent Board of Directors?

A well-chosen board can help business owners steer a safe course between corporate and personal objectives.

MANY BUSINESS FOUNDERS delay bringing outsiders onto the board of directors, in large part because they fear unwanted interference or challenges to their authority. That's shortsighted. If a board is constructed to include people with expertise in legal issues, accounting, and tax matters—as well as some experienced entrepreneurs—this group will enhance the growing company's management sophistication and network of contacts. Odds are strong that board members also will bring with them an understanding of the owner's personal priorities and a desire to help achieve those along with the corporate goals.

Some quick background first: As soon as you incorporated your company (see "Incorporation Issues," page 34), you were probably required by your state's regulations to set up a formal board of directors. But in most states, as is the case in Delaware and New York, that requirement is about as loose as it can get. Your board can have only one director serving on it, and it's undeniable that most owners of entrepreneurial ventures just choose themselves. In such cases, the board is really more of a fiction than a reality.

I frequently try to sway owners in a different direction.

There are compelling personal, as well as corporate, reasons why it makes sense to establish a broadly based board of directors as soon as a company's operations stabilize during Stage Two, if not earlier. Since such boards, at least theoretically, possess independent authority within the corporate structure, they can be a great line of defense against personal tax audits (which become an increasing risk for owners on both the federal and state levels once their companies can support better self-compensation packages and the introduction of benefits and perquisites).

I ended up giving my key people a total of 16 percent of the company's stock. But that kept them with me through my firm's growth and sale. The truth is, the cost of giving those small stakes away was much more than offset by the benefits that the company received in return.

—BRIAN SULLIVAN

So don't postpone this decision any longer. Just follow these four steps to make certain that your upgraded board helps you achieve your personal as well as corporate objectives:

❶ **Keep your board professional.** The instinct to appoint only close friends and relatives is misguided, since their lack of experience will, if anything, hinder the company's development. In the event of an audit, meanwhile, they'll never be able to convince any tax agency that they did anything other than rubber-stamp the founder's decisions on compensation and other matters. If your directors instead possess legitimate business credentials as well as firsthand knowledge of key financial issues, they'll be able to make their own informed judgments and, hopefully, assuage the tax authority's anxieties.

❷ **Establish subcommittees with prescribed responsibilities.** One of the first to be established should be a com-

Keep Board Minutes

You can't be too careful! Comprehensive board minutes should be retained for at least seven years in order to protect companies and their owners against the possibility of tax-related challenges. But there are other reasons why it makes sense to keep a complete set of these records even longer. Investors, lenders, or possible buyers may want to investigate the board's actions at any point in the company's history. So save two copies, storing one at corporate headquarters and the other at your attorney's offices.

pensation committee, whose tasks should include setting the owner's salary and those of all the other key managers. There should be a formal set of procedures that this committee follows each year. These should be reported to the board as a whole at the same time that the committee makes its salary recommendations.

Tip: Once cash flow is strong enough to support the creation of corporate benefit or perquisite packages, a separate benefits subcommittee also should be set up to handle these issues in a similar manner.

❸ **Encourage directors to be active and inquisitive.** The best way to help build an effective board is to keep it well informed on both corporate and personal financial matters. One example: While it's perfectly appropriate for an owner/chief executive officer to tell the board's compensation subcommittee how much salary he considers desirable, these directors also should receive relevant input from the outside world, such as survey results that reveal how much CEOs at similar companies are being paid. In order to maintain some distance, you'll be best off asking your accountant to research this matter and provide the subcommittee with necessary background data.

❹ **Keep comprehensive minutes of all board meetings.**
Minutes help reinforce the board's stature as a well-informed, independent entity and will go a long way toward justi-
fying any corporate or personal financial decision that may
be challenged at some point in the future. The board's
minutes should reflect the complexity of its discussions, as
well as the outcome of all votes taken. Subcommittee
reports, including a description of procedures followed
and any research material that may be relevant to their
recommendations, should be included in board minutes.

Stage 2

Moving Away from Friends-and-Family Financing

*As your company becomes more capable of
raising funds from a variety of sources, you'll
increase your credibility in the capital marketplace
if you wind down your financial relationships with
most types of early-stage investors.*

MY, HOW QUICKLY THINGS can change in a fast-growing entrepreneurial venture! Once business operations become
established and the company has amassed a series of quan-
tifiable corporate achievements, financing prospects
should gradually broaden to include a bank credit line,
other credit prospects, and equity investments from some

type of independent investor—typically an angel or strategic corporate partner at first.

Harsh as this may sound, this is the time when dispassionate business logic *must* supersede a founder's emotional attachments to any friends-and-family investors who helped get the start-up off the ground. Odds are strong that the company's long-term growth prospects will depend on its ability to make the transition from personal to professional capital relationships. After all, few maiden aunts or ex-kindergarten buddies possess the financial wherewithal to bankroll today's increasingly necessary investments in costly areas such as technology and marketing. The problem is, despite their good intentions, F&F investors may scare off better-heeled second-stage providers of capital, because their involvement conveys the potential for complications from unsophisticated or even disruptive backers.

It may be hard to believe that your relatives or friends could actually turn into a liability for your fast-growing company, but it's true. A financial consultant who frequently advises large-scale angel advisers confided to me recently that he won't even take a serious look at entrepreneurial companies that have more than a couple of friends-and-family backers. As he put it, "It's a messy situation with too many unpredictable parties involved. If I like the company otherwise, I'll encourage its owner to clean up the problem, end those financing relationships, and then come back to me for a second look."

Some business owners don't face significant difficulties on this front. Their friends-and-family investors intend right from the get-go *not* to remain involved in the new venture any longer than absolutely necessary. This often occurs when initial investments take the form of a loan (usually conceived of as a short-term arrangement made with either the company or its founder). In such cases, the loan should be paid off as soon as corporate cash flow permits it. Included with the principal payment should be an interest payment that—at a minimum—matches the bank rate that would have been charged during the borrowing period.

Tip: If your company is doing well enough that you can afford a somewhat higher interest payment, don't hesitate to make it. Your early backers deserve that extra thanks, after all, since their loan was a high-risk proposition that bailed you out when banks were not willing to take a gamble on your new venture. Remember, so long as the original loan was documented in some way, all interest charges should be tax deductible as a legitimate business expense.

That's the best scenario for winding down an F&F investment. The most problematic is one that involves an equity-based relationship with a friend or relative who wants to have an active say in the company's growth but is ill equipped for the role. Such relationships scarcely can be hidden from prospective investors, since most will carefully investigate and even interview your early investors before making a decision about whether to get involved.

The safest strategy is to try to extricate such investors from your company before you even approach a likely new source of capital. In order to reduce possible personal complications, you may rely on your company's attorney or accountant to broach the possibility of buying out their investment. Here again, it makes sense to factor in a good return on their initial infusion of capital. Since it was probably small, paying it off profitably should be manageable now that cash flow has stabilized and you've got a bank line of credit to dip into if necessary.

Be creative: If your earliest investors are unwilling to completely liquidate their holdings, suggest a minirecapitalization scheme that might involve some type of initial payoff (along the lines of the loan repayment sketched out above) and the replacement of regular equity with some type of second-class stock that explicitly contains no voting rights and perhaps even commits to a buyout at a specified later date. To avoid future complications, fully document the transaction and include a clause in which both parties agree that your F&F investor will not be involved in the company's operations in any way.

It's worth emphasizing, however, that there's no need to elbow out an initial investor who in any significant way adds to your credibility in the capital marketplace. If you received an early investment from a former business colleague or personal contact who possesses strong business credentials, make the most of this by asking him or her to serve on your board or as an informal adviser. You may even want to involve this person in your approaches to possible new investors (see "Where Can You Find Angel Investors?" page 184).

Stage 2

How to Make the Most of Strategic Partnering

Forming alliances with other corporations is an increasingly popular growth strategy, but entrepreneurs need to plan ahead in order to best control the personal risks and rewards.

AS YOUR COMPANY DEVELOPS, you will likely find yourself with more opportunities to negotiate so-called strategic partnerships with other corporations whose interests may be aligned with your own—perhaps relating to a single business niche or segment of your customer base. When structured to benefit both partners, these relationships can help galvanize growth while potentially creating all kinds of future options for corporate fund-raising, diversification, or even, one day, the lucrative sale of an owner's equity stake.

It's been interesting to watch this strategy take on increasing importance within the small-business community, especially after the stock market started weakening in mid-2000 while credit markets tightened. Since entrepreneurs are an endlessly inventive breed—particularly when it comes to the search for capital—they've become much more aggressive about pursuing these deals with large, usually well-funded corporate players. And that makes perfect sense in an environment in which it's now tougher for many growth companies to obtain loans from traditional bankers or equity investments from professional backers looking for a quick exit strategy tied to a lucrative initial public offering.

> *If you find that your company is in trouble for three months, figure out a way to change things. Don't take it as a personal failure.*
>
> —HOLLY HITZEMANN

Yet, for all the advantages that can come from a short- or long-term strategic alliance with another corporation, entrepreneurs need to remember that these business deals carry personal financial implications. It is best to plan for these in advance, while negotiating all the other terms. Here are the key issues to focus on:

❑ **Equity.** If there always must be an exception that proves the rule, strategic partnerships offer the exception for Stage Two owners' being advised in all other cases to avoid adding new stock stakes to their personal holdings since investments in their own companies already tip the balance so heavily in this direction (see "Creating an Investment Portfolio," page 154). But there's an irresistible logic behind equity swaps here, since corporate partners band together because they both believe that they stand to benefit from an alliance, presumably through profitable revenue growth that will translate into higher stock values for each company. You'll be best off if you negotiate an equity swap with a company that is significantly different from your own. Look for partners among public corporations, businesses that are much larger than yours, or companies that operate in other industries.

❏ **Debt.** In the world of strategic partnerships, anything goes, so you may find yourself considering a wide range of debt-related proposals. Some will carry with them an unacceptable level of risk for a Stage Two entrepreneur: It never makes sense, for example, to agree to a deal that involves your signing a personal guarantee to support a loan that goes directly to your corporate partner. (It's only slightly less dangerous to provide the personal backing necessary to obtain credit for your joint business alliance.) A safer course of action: If you and your strategic partner need to borrow funds to support your joint activities, both companies should be willing and able to provide business assets as collateral.

On the other hand, if you are considering a relationship with a much larger and better-established corporation, you may be able to obtain valuable financing assistance as part of your new deal, which could help your family reduce its level of debt-related risk. Consider proposing any of these possible arrangements:

Your new partner might be able to help convince its banker to provide your company with a line of credit that does not require you to provide personal guarantees (or will require them only for a short-term transition period in which you establish a good payment history).

Your partner might decide to make an infusion of capital into your original business, with the understanding that you will use these funds to help pay down a bank loan

Key-Man Insurance

WHETHER OR NOT YOUR STRATEGIC partner raises the idea of life insurance as a precautionary measure, it's worth your brief consideration at this stage. A key-man policy makes sense only if two factors come into play. First, the success of your strategic partnership must be essential to your company's future. And second, the partnership's outcome must depend upon either your own involvement or that of your counterpart at the other company.

If an insurance policy seems to make sense under these circumstances, rely on the same kind of term-life policy that you've already set in place for your family and company (see "Life Insurance Protection for Your Family," page 66, and "Business-Oriented Life Insurance," page 69). Purchase enough of a death benefit to shelter your company (and indirectly, your household) from whatever financial blow could occur if an unexpected death terminated the strategic partnership. Comparison shop for this policy the same way you would for any other term-life policy. Two sites worth visiting are www.directquote.com and www.insweb. com.

or outstanding credit card bills and thus strengthen your Stage Two company's financial position (and thus, indirectly, your personal financial stability).

Your corporate partner might be willing to guarantee a growth-oriented business loan that will benefit either your company or your joint venture. (Just because you wouldn't agree to that deal doesn't mean you wouldn't be willing to accept another company's aid!)

Stage 2

Where Can You Find Angel Investors?

When your company reaches the stage at which it can start attracting capital from private investors, your personal finances may benefit in five important ways.

ONCE YOUR COMPANY HAS BEGUN to demonstrate the validity of its business plan projections as well as its long-term potential, you may be able to tap into what's commonly known as angel financing. Angels are private individuals, often themselves experienced entrepreneurs or other businesspeople, who possess the financial resources to make relatively large investments in young companies, up to $100,000 or even more in some cases.

Not every growth company requires an infusion of outside capital. But many do—especially now that electronic commerce and other technological developments have raised the ante on most companies' cost of entry and expansion into the marketplace. If you decide to seek out potential angels—or, better still, find yourself being pursued by them—there's more to think about than simply how much money they'll be willing to invest. While there's no single right or wrong answer here, these are some issues you'll want to consider:

❶ **Can an angel's involvement help reduce your family's financial exposure to the company?** The answer may be no: Your prospective investor may have no interest other than in providing enough new capital to galvanize your business's growth. But there *may* be opportunities worth investigating. Don't be shy here: If you're still carrying personal credit card obligations tied to corporate expenditures, and your company can't yet spare the cash from its growth funds to pay you back, your angel investor might be willing to help (since it's in no one's best interest to prolong this level of financial risk for an entrepreneur and family).

One solution might be to negotiate a loan from the angel at the same time that the equity-oriented investment gets made. The purpose of the loan, which should be explicitly stated in a formal promissory note, would be the payment of all company-related credit charges currently held in the owner's name. The loan could be structured to provide annual interest payments from the corporation, assuming that its cash flow is sufficient to handle these. Payment of outstanding principal could be either scheduled for a specified date in the future or tied to the company's next round of financing, whichever occurs first.

❷ **Might your angel's involvement improve your company's ability to raise funds from banks without putting the household's finances at risk?** If your angel has a record of backing successful entrepreneurial ventures, his or her financial involvement should make your young company appear more creditworthy for two reasons. First, the new money helps because it broadens your company's capital base, which is one factor that bankers consider when deciding whether to approve a business loan. Second, it functions as a kind of business credential, because the investment proves that you've been vetted by an independent expert. If you've never been able to qualify for a corporate credit line before, these factors should tip the balance in your favor. What if you've already got one in place? Then your angel's involvement might convince your banker to remove personal guarantees and some other restrictions.

❸ **Does the angel possess business contacts that could lead to fruitful strategic partnerships?** Such alliances, especially with larger corporations, could also carry strong weight with potential bankers and help limit your family's credit risks—even in cases when an angel's involvement cannot single-handedly convince lenders to loosen the purse strings. Another option: Since Stage Two companies should be thinking about ways to create, at the minimum, an in-house package of health care benefits, it's worth investigating whether you can reduce such costs or improve the quality of your corporate alternatives by piggybacking your plan with those offered by either a strategic partner or an angel who's also a full-time business owner.

❹ **Can this new infusion of capital provide you with the chance to start diversifying into other investments?** Obviously, your primary objective when raising funds from an angel investor is to increase your company's supply of growth capital. But you may be able to give your family's finances a boost at the same time, if your prospective investor is amenable.

Here's how this might work: The bulk of the stock transfer would involve the sale of authorized—but still unissued—shares from the company itself (see "Structuring Your Company's Stock," page 38, for background on this). But a small portion of the equity that gets sold to your angel could come from your personal holdings; therefore, the funds tied to this part of the transaction would go directly to you and be available for your personal investment outside the company.

One caveat: When negotiating the sale of stock from multiple sources, it's possible to lose sight of dilution issues and wind up transferring a higher percentage to an angel investor than you might otherwise intend. So be sure to involve your corporate attorney or accountant before finalizing the terms of any stock transfer.

Angel Leads

WHILE IT'S APPEALING TO THINK of the Internet as an up-to-date, comprehensive source of leads to the massive (and fragmented) universe of angel investors, I'm convinced that the best way to hook up with these men and women is through your personal networks. I've interviewed countless angels over the years, and most have told me that they try to confine their financing commitments to companies close enough for them to "kick the tires"—meaning to visit regularly and, usually, to be actively involved during fast-growth, high-risk periods.

So it may not be worth your time and effort to pursue potential angels electronically if they're located too far from your home base. Look for better leads through your corporate accountant and attorney, industry associations, the chamber of commerce, regional economic development organizations, and local angel groups. The one exception: If you've established a strong market niche and ties to large corporate customers or suppliers, you might be able to generate angel-investment interest among key executives at these companies, wherever they're located.

❺ Can your new angel bail out friends-and-family investors who are looking for ways to reduce their exposure to your growing business? It's a good idea to at least raise this possibility whenever your company brings in a new source of capital. If your F&F investors are looking for an exit and your angel is willing, structure a multipart equity sale as outlined above.

@ **Internet Guide:** As you'll see if you search the Web under the keywords *angel investing*, there's an ever-

growing number of sites devoted to hooking up small business owners with angels. But some websites charge unnecessarily high rates, and many are far from effective in living up to their promises. One site worth investigating is the Angel Capital Electronic Network (ACE-Net), which is sponsored by the Small Business Administration's Office of Advocacy; it's located at www.sbaonline.sba.gov/ADVO/acenet.html.

Stage 2

The Self-Test

Here's how you can tell when your company has moved into the next stage of development— Stage Three—which means it's time to upgrade your personal financial plans.

BY ONE MEASURE, IT SHOULD be fairly simple for entrepreneurs to detect the transition between Stage Two—operational stability—and Stage Three—profitability. Their companies need to be logging financial results that are consistently in the black. The financial anxieties of start-up and early growth should be behind them. Once, one might have described such a company as a "mature" business, although that term carries with it such images of age that it scarcely seems to apply to many of the fast-growing companies that now dot the United States' business horizon.

The fact is, however, the course of development for an entrepreneurial company is seldom this clear-cut these days. In many industries, competitive pressures now force founders to think in broader terms than they once might have done—which takes many companies down paths of hyperaccelerated growth, international development, and, increasingly, electronic diversification. It's not always simple to tell when your company and your personal financial plan are truly ready for Stage Three. The self-test below should help you decide:

❶ **How would you truly characterize your company's profitability?** Remember, you're not selling your business to an investor or a customer when you answer this question; you're going to be making some decisions with important financial implications for yourself and your family— and you won't gain anything from being either excessively optimistic or pessimistic. If profitability seems to you to be either sporadic (meaning a month-by-month pleasant surprise), insignificant (too small to sustain any key lifestyle improvements), or shaky (vulnerable to likely downturns in your industry or overall economic trends), you're not yet ready to leave Stage Two.

❷ **What are the bottom-line implications of your current growth strategy?** These days, many entrepreneurial companies transition quickly back and forth between profitability, break-even, and operating loss situations—not because their fundamental business plans are flawed but because their growth opportunities, costly though they may be, are simply irresistible. Although you seriously may want to upgrade your personal activities by diversifying more of your personal assets away from the business or by rewarding yourself with some of the more generous perquisites of ownership, you cannot safely embark upon Stage Three's aggressive strategies until you are fairly certain that the company can continue to grow while remaining consistently and significantly profitable.

❸ **Have you already achieved the personal financial goals you set for yourself when the company entered Stage Two?** If you haven't, then you're probably not ready to accelerate your financial plan regardless of what state of growth and development your company is in. You'll be best off establishing a prolonged transition period for yourself in which you clear up any personal problems or catch up on overlooked areas. Here's the logic behind that statement: Stage Two is the ideal time in which to balance the status quo—as well as your financial plans—for your family. During this period, you should have eliminated credit problems, otherwise reduced your household leverage, and continued to look for ways to scale back your personal exposure to your growing company. Meanwhile, your baby steps as an investor should have laid the groundwork for what will hopefully develop into a long-term commitment to asset diversification away from your business. In addition, you should have broadened your company's employee benefit blanket, while exploring some basic ownership perks (and starting to reward yourself for the time and other investments you have made in the business).

Notice how broad and well balanced this list of Stage Two achievements is? Between them, the items on this checklist position entrepreneurs for the very different approach to financial planning and goal achievement that makes sense once Stage Three arrives. At that point, corporate profitability levels allow owners to become much more aggressive in their pursuit of whatever financial goals matter most to them on the personal front. For many people, these tend to center on just a handful of priorities—those that provide a tremendous impact on their family's current lifestyle and long-term potential. During this upcoming stage, personal preferences drive an owner's financial planning activities just as surely as a lack of cash restricted them during the company's earlier development.

That's why it doesn't make sense to move up to Stage Three before you've built a solid and broad base to support your household's financial health. You'll never regret delaying the transition. After all, there should be plenty of time later on to enjoy the rewards of owning a successful and profitable business.

Entrepreneurial Insights

EARLIER IN THIS BOOK (see pages 89–101), I quoted some personal finance strategies that a number of well-known and successful entrepreneurs had relied on during their companies' start-up and fledgling growth stages. Although their advice didn't always exactly match my own recommendations, these real-life anecdotes provide what I believe are valuable insights into the challenges and motivations that can affect an entrepreneur's activities, especially on the personal front. You may even want to try out some of their ideas yourself!

In the pages that follow, you'll again hear from a diverse group of men and women who are running fast-growing, successful ventures in a wide range of industries. Some are better known than others, some are farther along the growth spectrum, but all of these company founders have devoted a good bit of their energy and brainpower to the personal financial issues explored throughout this book. The stories and strategies they share with us here are best suited for the owners of established companies, those that I term Stage Two and Stage Three businesses. I hope that you'll find them as fascinating as I do.

SELF-COMPENSATION AS
THE COMPANY GROWS

❑ Aaron Cohen

"As your company grows and you start dealing with the question of whether to pay yourself a raise—and if so, how much—there are other factors that you need to keep in mind. It's not appropriate for the CEO to take advantage of the company's capital base. On the one hand, it shouldn't be a problem if you pay yourself the highest salary within your company. But there may be plenty of reasons why you might decide not to.

"For example, at my own company, I didn't take home the biggest paycheck. What you want, above all, is for your salary to convey to potential investors and other outsiders a sense of professionalism and your commitment to your business's growth."

❑ Lillian Vernon

"I managed my company according to the philosophy that entrepreneurs should never overpay themselves, and I have held true to this belief. My salary today is modest compared to the salaries of other chief executive officers who have companies of comparable size. I also have not compensated myself with a bonus since 1995. My advice to entrepreneurs who are just starting out is to pay yourself modestly, buy only what you absolutely need for the growth of your company, and don't spend your profits on personal luxuries."

❑ Robert F. Young

"Red Hat is the third company I've started in my career. But I relied upon consistent personal strategies across those three start-ups.

"I started paying myself a salary eighteen months after

establishing the company, once my personal savings ran out. In Red Hat's case, that first salary was the smallest possible amount that I could survive on in Westport, Connecticut, with my wife, three daughters, and a mortgage.

"As the company has grown, my raises have been in line with the best guess at the 'industry average for my position and responsibilities' that I, and the people I relied on for advice, could estimate. Once the business was established with outside investors and a board of directors, we always adopted compensation that included incentives in the form of bonuses for achieving annual goals adopted by the board.

"My advice for entrepreneurs is that they should be careful to ensure that they don't overpay themselves. It conveys the wrong message to investors—namely, that you are not in it for the long haul but prefer short-term rewards. On the other hand, don't underpay yourself—if you can afford to pay yourself. Underpaying yourself results in your personal life being more difficult, and those difficulties can reduce the effort you put into building your company."

BENEFIT STRATEGIES

❏ Tom Stemberg

"When we founded our company in 1985, all the founding partners took at least a one-third pay cut. The pay cut was in exchange for large equity stakes in what was at the time considered a fairly risky venture. But because from that point forward we always raised more money than we needed, before we needed it, we never faced a financial crisis starting out.

"As the company has expanded, we have continued to believe that part of an entrepreneurial culture is to have a relatively spartan, egalitarian benefit/perk plan that remains egalitarian even as benefits grow. To this day, our most senior *executives travel via coach, have no reserved parking spaces, and share the same medical benefits as other employees."*

❑ Aaron Cohen

"When the company got a little older and stronger, we kept improving our benefit plan. We offered gym membership, a whole wellness package. I felt as though benefits like that, which impacted everyone at the company, were more important than spending money on something that would only affect me, like having a company car and a driver. That would have been nice but just wasn't worth the money at a time when we were concentrating on growth."

❑ Ruth M. Owades

"As your company reaches the break-even point and reaches profitability, certain things are possible, and benefits can be implemented gradually, when you can afford them. It's important to bring in as many benefits as soon as you can—health, 401(k), vacations, holidays—and to create a pleasant work environment. This tends to come at a time of profitability and success. By the time I founded Calyx & Corolla, I had visibility and credibility and the company was seen as a good place to work. I was able to hire a number of experienced executives."

❑ Barbara B. Grogan

"Most entrepreneurs think that their retirement plans are their companies. And in the end, I'm not really all that different.

"I own my own house without any debt. That's part of a retirement plan. I own my company, and it too has no debt. That's a significant part of my retirement plan. Do I have a huge pension or retirement savings account? No.

"Now, I do have a 401(k) plan through my company. But between all the rules and regulations, I can put very little into it. It's a very small number in the larger scheme of things, compared to my other assets. So it's not surprising that I don't

think of it as a major part of my retirement plan. My company is my retirement."

❏ Brian Sullivan

"The question of whether or not to share equity with your key employees is a really complicated one. We've all got a very strong psychological desire to hold onto the equity. But at a certain point in my company's development, it became clear to me that in order to retain my top producers, I had to give away some.

"Eventually, I ended up giving my key people a total of 16 percent of the company's stock. But that kept them with me through my firm's growth and sale. The truth is, the cost of giving those small stakes away was much more than offset by the benefits that the company received in return. After all, your key people probably have that same passionate desire that you have to say, 'Yeah, I'm an owner. I'm a partner in all this.' It motivates them in very important ways.

"When I felt that it was the right time to sell the company to a major international player in our industry, my employees who were minority owners all supported the sale. And, in fact, they were essential ingredients in making it all happen. Giving them equity was one of the smartest decisions I ever made."

AN ADVISER'S ASSISTANCE

❏ Aaron Cohen

"From my perspective, entrepreneurship is all-consuming. As a result, you need to build an infrastructure that includes all the right kind of experts. You need great legal help. I relied on the same firm for corporate and personal advice. You also need great accounting assistance. My accountant is a value-added

financial adviser when it comes to both business and personal matters. I believe that entrepreneurs who try to handle their own accounting matters don't understand their priorities.

"Whether my stock in Concrete had ended up being worth $100 or $100 million, I certainly intended to carry out some very traditional personal planning. I don't want to become an expert on this. I've got more than enough to keep me occupied, concentrating on what I do best, which is building businesses. I plan to rely upon a very good professional, whether it comes to setting up a college savings account for my young child or diversifying my assets outside of my businesses."

❑ **Brian Sullivan**

"If I've got one regret, it's this: I really didn't have a personal financial adviser at the beginning, when I started my company thirteen years ago, and I should have. It's funny. I had all the financial discipline and business management skills I needed when it came to knowing where the receivables were and keeping the business on a fast-growth track, but I didn't have those skills.

"If I had sought out this kind of advice early on, when the company was still very small and not really profitable, I would have had tremendous opportunities to set up trusts and other plans. Those kinds of things would have been especially beneficial to have in place before I sold my company in 1999.

"But instead, I waited until after the sale to consult someone with estate-planning and investment management expertise. And you know what he told me? The first thing he said was, 'I wish you'd come to me two years ago. There are still things that you can do—but we could have accomplished so much more if you'd started this process earlier in your company's development.'"

LATER-STAGE INVESTMENT STRATEGIES

❏ Aaron Cohen

"Thanks to my entrepreneurial activities, I've been the share-holder of three companies that were privately held. There's tremendous risk in my private-equity portfolio.

"As a result, I'm a very low-risk guy when it comes to my other investments. I have a 401(k) plan. I have a very diversi-fied portfolio, in which I include my investment in my home. I don't electronically trade stocks—what a waste of time that would be for someone who's as preoccupied as I have been with running a growth-oriented company! Entrepreneurs who decide to spend their time and energy on their investments are actually distracting themselves from the more important task they've got at hand. I feel very strongly about that. I do know some fellow CEOs who invest in the markets as a hobby. This makes sense, but not for me. I try to play golf or watch the Knicks during my downtime.

"You know what stocks I follow? I follow the stocks of my competitors, because the knowledge that I get from doing that helps me run a business better. But I don't actively follow the stock market in search of prospective investments."

❏ Holly Hitzemann

"Nobody ever warns you in advance how tough these person-al issues can be for you when you're an entrepreneur. Once my company moved out of the start-up phase and began gener-ating sufficient cash flow, I took steps to diversify my assets. I dropped a couple of hundred thousand dollars into a new plant for my company.

"What I did was right out of the textbooks. It makes sense to invest in real estate and lease it back to your com-pany. And I made my purchase at what seemed to be the right time. The market was growing; projections for future

growth were strong. What can I say? I did the right thing, but it all turned out wrong, because the plant was in a location where the real estate market eventually collapsed. Meanwhile, my industry changed out from under us in ways that no one could have ever expected. The fact that everyone now has a personal computer and printer on their desks means that we didn't need to have a production facility. In fact, my company transformed itself from a production company to a licensing company to what we are today—an intellectual property company.

"But I was trapped in a hard asset whose value had collapsed, and this investment meant that I couldn't pivot as quickly as I should have in making those transitions. Ironically enough, even though you would have thought that the real estate would—at the very least—have been useful as collateral when I needed to borrow money for the business, it was worthless in that regard. The banks weren't interested in it.

"Looking ahead, I can certainly hope that the market rebounds to a point at which this will turn out to have been a profitable investment over the long term. But my advice for business owners, based upon my own experience, is to stay liquid. Be free. Because the fact of the matter is, industry after industry has gone through massive changes on the technological front. And I believe that the odds are very strong that unfolding technologies and geopolitical changes will continue to produce exponential changes that many entrepreneurs will need to be able to respond to, if their companies are going to grow and thrive. The best way to position yourself to accomplish this is to keep yourself—and as much of your company's assets as possible—liquid."

❏ **Lucille Roberts**

"As soon as the money started coming in and I could pay myself regularly, my husband and I began to buy real estate, mainly by concentrating on locations where I had health clubs.

"Real estate was the right kind of investment for us. I was

looking for what you could call the anti-health-club investment—something that would work against the cycles of my
business and help me to build credibility with the banks. Real
estate was so real. Nobody had to worry about whether or not
it was a fad.

"Those investments worked just the way we hoped they
would and did a great job of balancing out our risks. That's not
to say that real estate is the right investment for everyone. We
got into it in part because that was my husband's business
line. But I'd advise any company owner to look for an alternative investment that fits two requirements: It should be something they know about, and it should be very different from
their company."

❏ Barbara B. Grogan

"Business is an increasingly dynamic process. I don't know if
there really is a Stage Three—or if there is one, if an owner
can hope that things remain stable and secure for more than
a nanosecond. And that's true for big companies as well as
small ones. I sit on the boards of three large companies.
They're all in a position where cash flow is great, but they're
Old Economy businesses. So they're in the process of reinvent-
ing themselves. And that's a constant need for all of us.

"Having said that, there's certainly a difference between
the very early start-up phase—when most people go into
hock and have little net worth, or no net worth, or negative
worth—and those later stages when you've built up a sizable asset base in your business. It's easier to take huge risks
when you don't really have anything to lose. When you've
built up your personal assets, it's important for an
entrepreneur to think about diversification so that you can
spread those risks around.

"I decided very early on that one of the ways that I could
diversify fairly safely was by buying the commercial property
that Western needed for its headquarters. That was a way of
investing without being speculative. After all, I knew the tenant,

and I knew that she was a pretty reliable character. I knew she wouldn't run out on me without paying the rent.

"I have a stock portfolio and a bond portfolio. As an investor, I think in long-term, conservative strategies. I've worked too hard with my company to ever risk losing what I've achieved so far.

"Recently, I made an angel investment. It's a little technology company that was started by the son of a friend of mine. Bless his heart—two-and-a-half years later, the company is still in business! They've got revenues! So things are going well.

"I actually hope to make more angel investments, especially as I get closer to retirement. I like the idea of helping other entrepreneurial businesses get off the ground. So, these days, I'm trying to educate myself about all this. I attend a lot of angel-investment events because they're a great way of getting up to speed on this and learning about the kinds of opportunities that exist. It's an exciting prospect."

BANKING ISSUES

❏ Ruth M. Owades
"Until a company is profitable, any bank line of credit requires the founder's signature, and if you default it's your house, your car, your savings. You have to make that decision and understand the risks and work to build a viable business and get your personal signature off the line of credit as soon as possible!"

❏ Holly Hitzemann
"Once the company gets to the point where it's making a profit and cash flow is strong, set up an automatic debit arrangement for your business as well. Have the funds go into

some kind of safe cash-management arrangement. The trick is, don't touch this money unless your business gets into trouble and you absolutely must tap into these savings.

"Finally, you've got to be realistic. If you find that your company is in trouble for three months, figure out a way to change things. Don't take it as a personal failure—in my case, the industry changed all around me. It wasn't my fault. I needed to change the company to keep up. But sometimes entrepreneurs get into a position where they can't or won't make those kinds of big changes. Then they wind up draining their personal funds and putting themselves at all kinds of risk, because they can't face reality."

❑ Lucille Roberts

"When you own your own company, you can't ever keep all your eggs in one basket. You believe in your company, but you can't ever predict what's going to happen. When I first started out, people would say to me, 'All this exercise stuff is a fad.' You do the best job you can, but you never know. That's why you need investment balance.

"No matter how much my company has grown, I've always followed the same saving and investment strategy. I have a certain amount of money taken out of my paycheck each week. Forced saving really works. When I started doing this, and the company was small, it would just be $25 or $50. Now it's much more. But it's amazing how much can accumulate. Now what I do is look at that account four or five times a year and make some investment decisions at that time."

CRISIS MANAGEMENT

❏ Holly Hitzemann

"I started my company with a personal loan—even back then, there was no capital around for start-ups. I got off the hook for that loan after a few years and managed to keep my personal exposure to the company at a minimum for quite a while.

"But then three or four years ago, my whole company needed to make a major transition, in order to keep up with changes in the marketplace. I had to make a very big investment in new technology. And that transition took place at the wrong time for the banking world. Capital was tight once again, and banks weren't interested in making loans to companies like mine. The rest of the capital markets didn't hold out any opportunities for non-high-tech businesses. So I again had to borrow for my company, using my personal credit cards and lines of credit against my house.

"Now that I've made that investment and successfully repositioned the company, my husband and I are once again trying to pay some attention to our personal financial priorities. We've set ourselves the goal that in a year or less we want to reduce our outstanding personal debt (nonmortgage) by 50 percent. In another year after that, we want to eliminate it entirely. To accomplish that goal, we're making huge payments and going through a lot of pain and agony in the short term. Meanwhile, I'm making a bet that for twelve or fifteen months, I can say no to some if not all growth-oriented investments in my company and putting personal matters first.

"Is that hard to do? Absolutely. When you're an entrepreneur, it's as though you're always caught between two lovers, your business and your family. There's no easy way to figure out how to balance their two interests or when to put one set of interests ahead of the other."

PREPARING FOR YOUR COMPANY'S SALE

❑ **Brian Sullivan**

"The real reason I decided to sell my company was that I could see the way my industry was changing. I realized it wouldn't be possible—no matter how successful we were—for me to achieve what others had done ten years earlier. We needed to be part of a larger corporation.

"That said, the smartest thing I ever did as an entrepreneur was to get heavily involved in my industry association. I'm a big believer in this. It had a huge impact on the way I ran my business at all stages of its growth. It also raised my visibility within the industry, which certainly helped when it came to creating possible sale opportunities for the company.

"I cannot stress how strongly I believe that getting to know your competitors, especially the senior executives and company leaders, is important for any entrepreneur. Lots of people shun this, but that's not a sophisticated approach to running any business. You can learn a lot from them. And you can benefit from them knowing you.

"Heidrick & Struggles first wanted to buy us in 1993, but I wasn't ready back then. We ended up doing the deal in '99.

"If you're getting to the point where you're negotiating for the sale of your company to a strategic buyer and you plan to stay on—as I did—here are some things I'd recommend: Make sure that you agree upon a floor compensation for yourself, no matter how much of your future pay will also be tied to growth-related contingencies. Also negotiate for a mandated title and guaranteed responsibilities. Finally, I think it also makes sense to aggressively negotiate a time, in the not-so-far-off future, when you can leave the company. You might not want to set up a competitive operation one day—but you might just feel as if you're ready for early retirement. Try not to lock yourself into a very long-term commitment."

❏ Aaron Cohen

"If you're in the position we were in, and are selling or liqui-dating your company, my advice is to have great in-house and outside counsel; to stand by your creditors and fight for them; and not to run your company to the edge so that you cannot provide a transition severance. Every employee at Concrete recieved severance."

P

ersonal finance possibilities gain a different profile as your company becomes consistently profitable, cash flow is positive, and your business operations are mature. You've reached …

STAGE 3

Planning for the Next Level

Once your company achieves target levels of growth and profitability, you should be able to pursue more of your personal, as well as business, objectives. Here's how to fine-tune your agenda.

FOR THOSE ENTREPRENEURS fortunate enough to get to it, Stage Three is close to nirvana. Their companies have survived the rocky periods of start-up and early growth; they've found their market niche, achieved a consistent level of profitability, and—by this point—have very likely either successfully won financing from bankers or outside investors or generated sufficient cash flow to fund their corporate growth. In either case, the businesses are finally robust enough to reward their owners for all the hard work and sacrifices that went into getting them off the ground.

One might think that financial planning at this stage of corporate maturity would be as simple as saying, "Let the good times roll." But that's not quite the case. Your personal plans and activities at this stage must be coordinated with your realistic longer-term plans and objectives for your business. That's because you cannot safely design a structure for rewarding yourself unless you take into account your company's future development, whether that will include your own likely continued involvement or some type of exit. To get a feeling for which type of financial plan makes the best sense for you at this time, consider the follow scenarios:

❶ My company is still fairly young, and so (relatively speaking) am I. I'm having the time of my life and hope to grow, along with my business, for many years to come. If this sounds familiar, you're a traditional entrepreneur. Once you achieve success with a business venture, you plan to stay with it for quite a while (and probably don't intend to start and run multiple companies during the course of your career). The good news is, you're perfectly positioned to start reaping the full rewards of ownership during Stage Three, in large part because there's no need to worry about someone coming in and second-guessing you the way they might if you later tried to sell the company or take it public. Your options are numerous, and I'll explore them all here. You can pay yourself as generous a compensation as cash flow constraints—and the IRS—will permit. This is also the time to expand your benefit plan in ways that will reward either all your employees or at least yourself and key players.

It's worth pointing out that Stage Three can last a very long and profitable time. During it, you should be able to achieve most or all of your investment priorities, including saving for retirement and other goals such as college for your children.

❷ I've got no plans to sell my little gold mine. But I do hope to pass it along to my family members. Follow the same approach to financial planning that's outlined above. But given your own stage of development, as well as your business's, it's essential that you pay special attention during Stage Three to estate planning and management succession issues (see "When Estate-Planning Trusts Can Help," page 259, and "Exiting through a Long-Term Succession Plan," page 267). Fine-tune the strategies you select in Stage Three to best match your mature company's value.

❸ I know that I'll be buying or starting other businesses as I pursue my entrepreneurial vision. Does it really affect today's financial planning decisions whether I end up selling this company first or not? The "repeat" entrepreneur has become increasingly common during the past decade, with some people preferring to start and sell one business at a time and others diversifying into multiple business holdings. Depending on which type of strategy you decide to follow, you'll need to structure your personal plans and activities differently in Stage Three.

> *Once the business was established with outside investors and a board of directors, we always adopted compensation that included incentives in the form of bonus for achieving annual goals adopted by the board.*
>
> —ROBERT F. YOUNG

Let's consider first the owner who does not plan to sell company number one before starting company number two. He might still be able to reward himself fairly lavishly—his intended long-term ownership gives him this prerogative. However, he'd be best off confining his rewards to salary and bonuses. Extra funds should be invested in fairly conservative and liquid investment vehicles so that they will be readily accessible when it comes time to fund a new venture.

The owner who plans to sell one company before starting another is in a different position. On the one hand, there is less need for easy-to-cash-in savings since the business's sale will likely raise more than enough funds to support a new start-up. But it makes sense to moderate self-rewards during this stage and channel excess cash flow into the kind of growth activities that will make the mature company more attractive to buyers.

(That's because if growth seems to have stalled, it will be tougher to carry out a sale and then move on.) For entrepreneurs who fall into this category, a safe course would be to steer clear of the more costly strategies outlined in Stage Three and instead pursue no more than two or three expanded personal options.

❹ I'm running this company with a clear exit in mind—most likely a strategic sale to a larger corporation or an initial public offering. What's the impact on my personal choices during Stage Three? It's a big one. Entrepreneurs who pursue this vision—and still believe, by this stage of development, that they're likely to achieve it— have no choice but to continue to delay their personal gratification in the interests of best preparing their businesses for sale. All decisions relating to compensation (their own as well as the rest of the staff's), perks and benefits, corporate and personal tax strategies, and the like need to be weighed against one basic measure: Will it make my company more or less marketable?

I can't emphasize this point strongly enough. Any choices that can be viewed as excessively rewarding the owner—at the possible cost of corporate growth—can come back to haunt you. The typical criticism I've heard is that this gives the impression that the owner didn't believe in the company's long-term future, so wasn't willing to invest in it. A better approach is to think about personal rewards like a Stage Two owner. Only opt for upgrades in your financial planning activities that won't cost your company much money. Yup, that means concentrating on matters like estate planning and low-cost benefit strategies.

Stage 3

The Wisdom of Deferring Your Compensation

***Your compensation potential may now be so high
that it makes sense to defer part of your paycheck
or annual bonus in order to reduce your personal
tax bill and enhance your long-term security.***

DECIDING HOW MUCH TO PAY yourself when you're an owner
is seldom a simple matter. But here's a big surprise: As your
company grows and becomes more successful, the issue of
owner's self-compensation becomes *more* complicated, not
less so. That's because many alternatives become possible
once your company is securely anchored in Stage Three of
consistent profitability. But it's not always clear which personal financial priorities loom largest, which can make it
difficult to figure out which option works best for you and
your family.

Let's say you find yourself in the following (very attractive) situation. Your company's growth has supported
steady and significant increases in your total compensation
package, and you've used that money wisely, meaning
you've spent it in ways that have enhanced your family's
lifestyle while also accomplishing the household's important savings and investment goals. Your company's cash
flow and external financing resources are sufficient to support its future growth activities. And you now find yourself
in the enviable position of not needing all the money that
your company could afford to pay you.

I'd argue that it's time to think about setting up some

type of deferred-compensation arrangement. (In fact, if you're in a situation as sweet as the one I've just described, you probably could have set up one of these even earlier, but there's no point in worrying about wasted opportunities!) The logic? They're another way of boosting your retirement savings—always an important goal. And depending on the type of deferred-comp plan you set up for yourself, you also may be able to reduce your current tax liability.

Recent tax relief from Washington makes deferred-comp arrangements even more appealing, since the top bracket is scheduled to drop from 38.6 percent (in 2002 and 2003) to 37.6 percent (2004 and 2005) to 35 percent (2006 through 2010). Although there is no guarantee what will happen after that point (the top bracket is scheduled to rise back to 39.6 percent as of 2011), this declining schedule now makes short-term deferral plans worth contemplating—as well as longer-term arrangements that defer compensation until after retirement.

Before getting into the different design possibilities, it's important to understand the major distinction between a deferred-compensation arrangement and whatever other retirement benefit you already may have set up or be thinking about launching at your company. Plans that cover all employees (not just owners or key executives), such as 401(k)s, are commonly known as "qualified" retirement plans, which means that they meet a variety of requirements imposed by the Internal Revenue Service and Department of Labor. Those plans don't discriminate among employees; all can participate. (In fact, these plans must be able to document the participation of many employees at a wide range of salary levels.) Because these plans are deemed "qualified," they provide valuable tax deductions for your company as well as for you and your employees (see "The Case for Setting Up a 401(k) Plan," page 221).

Those tax breaks are great. But for a business owner in

your current situation, there are plenty of advantages to thinking outside the box, which in this case means opening your eyes to the wide world of "nonqualified" benefits. A deferred-compensation plan is one of them. It doesn't qualify for special tax benefits for the company, because it's a discriminatory benefit (more on taxes later). If you set one up, you—like many business owners—may decide to reserve this goody for yourself. Or you may offer it as an option to one or more of your key executives. The choice is entirely up to you.

As I emphasize when I talk to business owners about these plans, flexibility is really what they're all about. You can set up your own deferred-compensation plan—if you want one—to delay your receipt of a percentage of your salary, or you can take home your full paycheck and decide instead to defer your annual or quarterly bonus. You can do this one year, when your family's current expenses are low, and never delay another year's compensation until all twelve of your children graduate from college. It's your call.

If you're intrigued, however, I do need to warn you that the rules governing these types of arrangements can get complicated. There's one essential decision you'll need to make when designing your company's plan: Do you intend for your company to actually set aside the deferred compensation during the year in which it is *earned* although not paid? (When this happens, the money is usually placed in some type of trust, of which you will be the ultimate beneficiary.) Or will your company leave the plan unfunded until the deferred compensation payment becomes due?

Here are the consequences of each decision:

❏ **If your company funds your plan in advance,** it will qualify for a tax deduction during the year in which the money is set aside (even though you won't actually receive it until a later, specified date). There are two advantages to going this prefunding route: It's a guarantee that you'll

Guidelines for a Deferred Compensation Plan

WHICHEVER TYPE OF PLAN you decide to set up, keep these caveats in mind:

❏ **There's no relief on the employment-tax front.** Your company needs to pay employment taxes on any deferred compensation during the year in which it is earned, not paid. That's true whether your plan is funded or unfunded.

❏ **You'll need a written document that describes your plan.** Don't try this without an attorney's assistance. Your plan document must spell out key details such as when you'll receive the deferred compensation, how it will be paid (whether in a lump sum or specified regular payments), and escape clauses, if any (which might allow you to take an immediate payout, minus a financial penalty, under certain circumstances such as the sale of your company). Expect to pay $1,000 to $3,000 in adviser's fees at setup, depending on your plan's complexity, but afterwards, your legal and paperwork expenses should be minimal. Don't forget to have your board formally vote to approve the plan; keep a record of this vote in your board minutes.

❏ **Your company may be able to use an annuity or insurance policy** to help guarantee the eventual payment. This can help you avoid some of the problems associated with prefunding a deferred-comp plan. But these multipart deals can get complicated, especially when it comes to possible tax consequences. Again, consult your attorney.

receive the money eventually, which you can't be absolutely sure of if your company simply intends to pay you out of cash flow at some point in the future. Also, the assets in a funded deferred-compensation plan will be protected from your company's creditors. But there's one significant disadvantage, which does discourage many owners from going this route: At the time that your plan is funded, you'll owe personal income taxes on it, just the same as if you had actually taken home that paycheck. If your current salary isn't large enough to cover that tax bite, you may need to cash in savings or investments (which will erode your asset-diversification accomplishments, at least for now).

❏ **If your company doesn't fund the plan in advance,** all those pros and cons get flipped. There won't be any corporate tax deduction until the compensation gets paid to you, presumably after your retirement. But you won't owe any personal taxes until that point either (and by then, you'll probably be in a lower tax bracket). But— and it's a big but—your eventual payment is hostage to your company's long-term fortunes: If it experiences a cash crisis or gets socked by lawsuits from disgruntled customers, investors, or employees, you may watch your money go out the door in another direction from your household.

Stage 3

The Medical Savings Account Alternative

Here's a cost-effective way to give yourself and your employees sound health care coverage, a valuable personal tax break, and a chance to boost retirement savings.

BY THE TIME ENTREPRENEURIAL companies reach this level of growth and success, most owners have been in business long enough to develop some real frustrations with their health insurance options. (Usually they've set up some type of medical coverage plan by some time during Stage Two; see "Bringing Medical Benefits In-House," page 114.)

For small businesses—even those with a cash flow strong enough to support setting up a comprehensive employee-wide plan—problems abound. As one furniture importer complained to me, "Companies need to believe in the value of my product before they'll buy it—why doesn't the world of health insurance work that way? Where's the value in a policy whose prices keep going up, up, up, even though you need to have five different arguments with the insurance carrier every time you file a claim?"

When established entrepreneurs contact me with complaints like these, I usually recommend that they explore medical savings accounts (MSAs, also known now as Archer MSAs)—although that task sometimes isn't a simple one since many insurance brokers and carriers don't offer them. Still, I believe MSAs are worth the extra digging, because these relatively new health care products offer some important advantages for companies in that hard-to-satisfy category of fewer than fifty employees (which also includes sole proprietors, freelancers, and independent contractors). Among their benefits: low corporate cost, personal tax breaks, potential retirement benefits from an IRA-like savings vehicle, and participants' ability to choose their own medical professionals. It's impossible to overstate how much of a selling point it can be with prospective hires when they learn that your company won't force them to accept HMO coverage!

Medical Savings Accounts were first launched by the federal government in 1997 as an experimental pilot plan that was due to expire at the end of the year 2000 or whenever 750,000 policies were sold, whichever came first. But thanks to strong bipartisan support, the plan was extended for at least another two years, along with the guarantee that any company that sets up a plan can continue to operate one, no matter what happens to the program in general. While there would, obviously, be more certainty to these plans if the federal government just would come right out and give them permanent status, most of the insurance brokers and health care industry experts that I've spoken to seem fairly confident that these will be part of the horizon for many years to come.

Here's how MSAs work. They consist of two components:

❶ **A very high deductible insurance policy.** This is purchased directly from an insurance carrier (or through a broker or agent). Owners typically choose a deductible of $2,000 for individual coverage and $4,000 for families; the reason they do this is simple—the higher the deductible, the lower a company's policy fees.

Tip: Since you still want to be able to direct corporate cash flow toward growth-related activities and, whenever possible, owner-related rewards, it makes sense to keep health care outlays as low as possible, even if your company can actually afford to pay more for a lower-deductible alternative.

❷ **A savings account.** This is what separates MSAs from any other high-deductible insurance plan you may have considered (and probably rejected) in the past. It's also the feature that makes medical savings accounts so attractive for employees and owners alike, even while they need to put up with those onerous high deductibles. Every participant in your company is allowed to set aside personal funds—up to 75 percent of the deductible for family coverage or 65 percent of the deductible for individuals—in a special savings account that offers them the same tax advantages that an IRA would. This means that annual contributions to an MSA are tax deductible and can earn tax-deferred interest until they're withdrawn.

Here's the special kicker: It's up to each of your employees (and to your own family as well) to decide whether to use the money in your medical savings account to pay uncovered health care bills each year or to keep the funds invested until you reach retirement age. For people who choose the latter option, MSAs become a supplemental retirement benefit (and we all can use as many of those as we can find!).

There are only a couple of difficulties that I warn business owners about. MSAs can't solve every single insurance problem you're likely to face. If your company is very small (or has only a single employee—you), you probably won't be able to include extras like prescription drug or dental benefits in your coverage. In that case, you and your employees can choose either to use personal MSA funds to cover these costs or just bite the bullet and pay them out of pocket.

There are also a fair number of regulations you'll need to get used to if you decide to give the plans a try. These include one dictate that doesn't make a whole lot of sense to me but remains completely inflexible: You must set up your plan so that either the participant or the company, but not a combination of both, makes those annual savings contributions. So you can't have the company pay $1,000 into each MSA account as an extra benefit and leave each staffer to contribute the rest. As a result, most small companies leave it up to their employees to make whatever savings contributions they can afford.

Here's my advice (at least for those companies whose cash flow is strong and employee base is relatively small): If you, like many Stage Three owners, are motivated by the desire to take spare cash out of your company in any legitimate way that won't raise your audit risks or already high income tax bill, consider having your business make the full savings contribution permitted under the law during any year in which corporate results are strong.

I know that could add up. But your company may be perfectly capable of handling this additional cost, at which point it makes sense to use this vehicle to help boost your business-funded personal retirement savings. Best of all: Since MSA rules are flexible, you can discontinue this practice whenever cash flow seems shakier, or the company needs more growth capital, or your staff starts growing.

@ **Internet Guide:** It's rules like these that really require you to spend a little time up front comparing design options, as well as the MSA's overall pros and cons for your company. A good broker can help. To find one who works with this type of plan, contact www.room100.com/msa, a site managed by the National Association of Alternative Benefit Consultants. Another valuable site is the Health Insurance Association of America (www.hiaa.org), which offers a guide to insurers and MSAs.

Stage 3

The Case for Setting Up a 401(k) Plan

Many entrepreneurs shun 401(k)s because they're worried about excessive cost and administrative complexities. But the benefits of these plans can outweigh their disadvantages, thanks especially to new options that are available on the Internet.

AN AGGRESSIVE APPROACH to retirement planning makes sense for Stage Three owners for a variety of compelling reasons. One is very basic: Entrepreneurs, like everyone else, need a safety net to insure their long-term financial well-being at a time when the Social Security system remains precarious (and none of us, after all, would really be too happy ending up relying on its payments as our sole source of retirement income). Another reason is conservative (although a better term might be *realistic*): No matter how successful your company is now, there's just no guarantee that it will either exist profitably for as long as you might want it to or that you'll be able to sell it, whether to a strategic corporate partner, an individual buyer, or the investing public, and retire with a pot of gold.

As I stress to Stage Three owners all the time, there's also a very concrete reason why retirement planning is a savvy step, especially now that your company's cash flow and profitability levels are strong: taxes. Other personal financial strategies might help you achieve asset diversification, but retirement planning can carry with it some significant tax benefits, especially for business owners. Fortunately, you and your company are ready to profit from Uncle Sam's largess.

Although 401(k) plans have a bad rap among some small business owners, they are well worth considering—if only as one part of the multitiered retirement-saving strategy you develop during this period. You already may have been exposed to these plans if you're a veteran of the corporate world. Many large businesses permit every employee to set aside a portion of salary each month that can be contributed, on a pretax basis, to a self-directed investment account. Retirement-saving limits are regulated by Congress. The annual cap on personal contributions is currently set at $10,500. This limit will increase to $15,000 by 2006. As with IRAs, recent legislative changes now permit extra "catch-up" contributions by workers older than fifty, starting at $1,000 per year in 2002 and increasing to $5,000 in 2006.

Let's quickly run through the upside and downside of 401(k)s. When it comes to taxes, setting up one of these plans is a win/win strategy for both you and your business. After all, your personal contributions reduce your taxable income, which cuts your tax bill. And given your company's growth and development, you've probably reached a compensation level at which income tax deductions are more valuable to you than whatever disposable monthly income you'll find yourself sacrificing in the interests of long-term retirement savings.

Meanwhile, your—and every other employee's—contributions cut your company's tax bill too. That's because any pretax dollars deposited in an employee's 401(k) account reduce his or her taxable income, which likewise reduces the company's payroll tax obligations. One more point: Recent tax relief measures now include a financial incentive in the form of a tax credit to help encourage business owners with fewer than 100 employees to set up their first qualified retirement plan.

Should you provide some type of employer match of employees' contributions? The rules that govern 401(k)s are flexible on this point, so it's up to you to decide whether the company's cash flow can handle this extra expense. If it can, then your 401(k) plan will carry with it two other benefits worth considering. When you institute a matching plan (perhaps contributing 50¢ for every $1 set aside by each staffer), you've managed to find another legitimate way to channel funds from your company to your own long-term savings. Your company will also receive a tax deduction based on its total matching contributions, which are considered a business operating expense.

Now for the downside. When you set up a 401(k) plan, with or without a matching enhancement, your company is obligated to offer it to every employee. (There's just slight room for maneuver on this end: When designing your plan, you can insist that participants work for the company for a specified period before becoming eligible; you can also include vesting rules, which provide that employees who leave the company before working for, say, three to five years will forfeit all matching contributions.) In order to make certain that your plan isn't discriminatory—meaning that it doesn't favor either you, as the owner, or only high-income employees—your company will have to pass compliance tests each year.

That's undeniably a hassle. Companies are required to document the salary levels of participants to prove that participation occurs on all rungs of the corporate ladder rather than basically being reserved for the people at the top. This usually requires employers to spend some time on employee education seminars as well as some money on promotional materials, since younger or lower-income staffers may need to be convinced about the long-term benefits of setting aside a portion of their current salaries in order to help secure their retirement futures.

But these hassles may be worth tackling if your com-

Two Alternatives

IF THE COSTS AND COMPLEXITIES connected with 401(k) plans still seem off-putting to you, there are two other kinds of retirement plans you might want to investigate with the help of a benefits consultant or your corporate accountant:

❑ **Simplified employee pensions (SEPs).** With these plans, it's only the company—not you or any of your employees—that contributes money into a retirement account, which is actually just a variation on an IRA. That limits the benefit, since there's no tax relief at the individual income-tax level, but still offers you and your employees the chance to build your retirement savings.

Two pluses: There's no need to set up a huge administrative apparatus in order to administer a SEP, and your company is under no requirement to make contributions during any particular year. But if it chooses to do so, it must follow formal nondiscriminatory guidelines that limit contributions to a fixed

pany is relatively small or its cash flow is strong enough to cover the additional short-term costs. Besides the personal and corporate benefits that accrue from 401(k)s, there's another incentive: In industries in which competition for skilled and experienced employees is fierce, these plans can be an appealing recruitment and retention tool.

@ **Internet Guide:** Comparison shopping among plan administrators is essential if you're thinking about setting up a 401(k) plan. There are three major costs you'll need to investigate: start-up expenses (which include the cost of preparing plan documentation for government regulators), annual administrative fees, and yearly investment management fees. Some firms also tack on various supplemental formula of no more than 25 percent of employees' salaries (or $40,000, whichever is less) and—here's the rub—a specified lower contribution level for you and any other owner.

❑ **SIMPLE plans.** The name stands for Savings Incentive Match Plan for Employees, and the design is fine-tuned for smaller companies; in fact, you can't set up one of these if you have more than 100 employees. Basically, you can structure one of these plans as either an IRA or a 401(k) plan (for more details, see "Retirement Planning: Make Moves Now," page 165).

These plans aren't very flexible. For example, they can't be coupled with any other corporate retirement plan or modified to reward older employees or owners. But their advantage really is simplicity. Companies can qualify for that tax deduction without subjecting themselves to any of the onerous federal tests that otherwise apply to qualified plans.

charges as well. A good source of comparative data is www.401ksource.com. You'll need to pay a fee, but its data on more than 100 providers is valuable.

Another issue worth investigating: Some providers have started offering online delivery of their 401(k) administrative and customer services, often at reduced rates. Since this trend is developing, you'll be best off conducting a keyword search under *401(k)* to see what's new. Two sites that are currently worth visiting are www.401keasy.com and www.401k.com.

Stage 3

Broadening the Benefit Blanket

From a personal perspective, it makes sense to add the benefits you need yourself to your company's mix. These cost-effective strategies can help reduce the hit to your business's bottom line.

THERE'S NO EXCUSE, ONCE YOU'VE achieved cash flow stability and consistent profitability, for failing to create exactly the benefit plan that you and your family need. At some point during Stage Three of your business's development, it will become possible for you to achieve many of your goals. This point may not occur today or tomorrow. But whenever it does, you'll be able to shift your mind-set from the defensive benefit strategies that characterize entrepreneurial companies during Stage One and Stage Two to a very different, proactive approach.

You've got opportunities now. Start taking advantage of them. Figure out your own personal priorities and design a tax-advantaged benefit package that includes as many of them as your company can afford.

Keep one complication in mind, though, before proceeding further. The same tax rules apply here as with other benefits you may have already set in place. If your business is structured as an S corp, a partnership, or a sole proprietorship, you cannot receive health care coverage on a tax-free basis if it's paid by your company. That problem doesn't exist for owners of C corps.

There is a way around this problem if you find yourself

in the wrong corporate category, at least when it comes to this issue. If you own the stock in your company in your own name and you're interested in employing your spouse, he or she can receive such coverage without incurring a personal tax liability—like any other staffer—and then you'd qualify as well, through a family plan.

Setting—and Achieving—Your Priorities

Now for the fun part. Drawing up your household's benefit wish list should be simple. Does everyone in your family wear eyeglasses? Then you'll probably want to opt for a vision-care benefit (which could be as bare-bones as joining an HMO-type network of vision-care professionals or subsidizing the cost of prescription glasses, or could get as elaborate as a plan that reimburses the cost of laser eye surgery). Are your kids approaching the age when they'll need braces? Or are you the potential problem, as you're getting closer to a number of costly periodontal procedures? Then you might want to add a souped-up version of dental coverage to your benefit mix, which would include orthodontic or periodontal care.

Don't be frugal when drawing up your wish list. You might want to consider adding fitness club memberships to your benefit package. (Remember when calculating the cost that this is not tax deductible for the company if the gym is off-site; in that case, you and your employees will also owe taxes on this benefit.) If you're in your forties or fifties, it's also a good idea to think about long-term-care insurance. (While the odds of your needing this coverage in the short run may seem low, studies suggest that as many as two out of every five people may need some type of nursing-home care during the course of their lifetimes.) Given the enormous personal costs that this insurance can shield you against, it's likely to be an important element in protecting your family's, as well as your company's, long-term security. After all, the last thing you'd want is to see your business sold off in order to pay a nursing home's bills.

Once you've developed your family's wish list, take a frank look at your employees and their own likely requirements. If your workforce is small or your staffers tend to be young and single, they may not need many of these benefits or actually use them, even if your company signs up. (That's an ideal scenario for any business owner, although, obviously, it's not one that you can control.) On the other hand, if you've got a large number of older staffers, that reality alone could push the cost of certain benefits out of your company's reach. In this case, for example, it undoubtedly would be more cost effective simply to decide to pay for a long-term care policy by yourself. If the cost of an individual plan seems excessively high, you may be able to boost your bonus to help cover the premium fees.

*W*hen the company got a little older and stronger, we kept improving our benefit plan. I felt benefits that impacted everyone at the company were more important than spending money on something that would only affect me, like having a company car and a driver.

—AARON COHEN

One tip: Do some comparison shopping, perhaps by consulting an insurance agent or your trade association, to see which of these extras your company really can or cannot afford for next year's plan. Think of this as an incremental process. Now and throughout Stage Three, your goal should be to continuously look for manageable ways to enhance your corporate package with as many additional benefits as are desirable for you and your family.

Some Attractive Compromise Solutions

If your company is not yet at the point where it can afford to meet all your personal benefit goals, I'd recommend that you consider some tax-advantaged cost-control strategies:

❏ **Cafeteria plans.** Although these are more commonly used by large corporations, I'm convinced that they are a natural for mature entrepreneurial companies. With a cafeteria plan, what you'll basically do is design a package—and put it in writing—that allows your employees to choose between receiving a cash payment of a certain amount or any of a number of benefits, which between them will cost the company that much in premium fees.

As an owner, it's up to you to set this financial cap at a sum that your company can afford, while also guaranteeing you the benefit choices that you personally value. As long as your cafeteria benefit menu is offered on a nondiscriminatory basis to everyone in your workforce, its corporate costs will qualify for tax-deductible treatment. Best of all, these plans really can help to keep your company's premiums relative low, because people tend to prefer a full or partial cash payment over a full-service benefit package. That's especially the case if they're younger and don't think they need the coverage or are married and can qualify for a spouse's plan instead.

❏ **Flexible spending accounts (FSAs).** So what if your company can't yet afford to foot the bill for 100 percent of the cost of all those benefits that you and your employees might want? The truth is, no matter how big or profitable your business gets, you may never choose to enhance its benefit package to that extent, given how pricey health care benefits can get. That's why FSAs are worth your attention.

Flexible is a good word for these plans. You can set up a corporate FSA to permit you and your staffers to use pre-tax salary dollars to help pay any number of different costs associated with medical care. This might include any insurance-premium expenses that aren't paid for by your company, which can be a big help if you decide, as many small and large corporations do, that you can't afford to pay the entire cost of family coverage if an employee wants it. Flexible spending accounts can also be used to make out-of-pocket medical expenses more affordable (if your company plan has a high deductible or can't yet cover pricey items such as periodontal visits or prescription drugs).

There are two reasons why an FSA would help many Stage Three owners. First, if you participate yourself, you can reduce your own taxable income by the amount of money that you expect to spend on health care through contributions to your flexible spending account. Tax reduction is an important priority for most owners of mature companies.

Second, these plans save taxes for your company too. That's because every dollar that you and your employees contribute to an FSA account is free of FICA taxes (which can save your company as much as 7.65 percent in payroll taxes). Unless your Stage Three company is still in a super-fast growth mode, requiring extraordinary expenditures of capital, tax minimization is undoubtedly an important corporate priority as well.

One caveat: Although the personal tax break you'll receive here is attractive, it has limits. Thanks to government regulations, FSA contributions fall into the category of "use it or lose it," so participants have a strong incentive to be cautious when they decide how many health care dollars to deduct from their paychecks. That's different from the situation with Medical Savings Accounts, where owners and other participants are able to boost their retirement savings by any extra funds that they set aside and don't spend for health care services (see "The Medical Savings Account Alternative," page 217).

Stage 3

Ways to Enhance Your Company's Retirement Plan

If you feel caught between your desire to prepare for a comfortable retirement and your company's need for a tax break, consider some owner-advantaged options that meet with IRS approval.

I'M ALWAYS DISAPPOINTED when I see an entrepreneur's eyes glaze over when the conversation turns to qualified retirement benefits. (That may sound like an opening line to a joke, but I'm quite serious about this issue.) Some people worry excessively about costs and paperwork complications, and as a result, they deny themselves, as well as their employees, the opportunity to start planning for a secure retirement (see "The Case for Setting Up a 401(k) Plan," page 221). But others make an even more foolish mistake: They won't consider qualified plans at all because they're convinced that any workforce-wide benefit can't really offer significant value to a business owner.

For Stage Three owners whose companies have the cash flow to support comprehensive benefit packages, that can be a costly oversight. Profitable ways exist, in fact, to tweak the design of your qualified plan to provide yourself and your family members with exceptional rewards while still holding on to those valuable business deductions relating to the costs of administration and corporate contributions. Here are some of my favorites:

❑ **Age-based profit sharing plans.** These make sense if your payroll is relatively small and you, as the owner, are significantly older than the rest of the people you employ. Here's why: With this type of plan, corporate contributions are tied to two factors—the age of each employee and his or her compensation level. Granted, the rules that govern these calculations are very technical. When designing the plan, you have to specify an age for retirement and then figure out what the present value is of a single life annuity for someone starting at that age and then ... enough already, you get the idea. You'll need an expert's help if you want to get one of these plans up and running, but the personal financial advantages may be worth it.

I'm the first to admit that these plans aren't for everyone. One financial consultant confessed to me recently that the only reason he regrets his hiring strategy (all back-office personnel are mature older women—meaning, really mature) is his inability to take advantage of this type of plan, which he well knows and recommends to many of his clients. These plans also, of course, don't work with Stage Three owners who still pay themselves an unnaturally low salary compared to the rest of their management teams (usually because they're delaying their payoff until a company sale or IPO). That said, however, I'm convinced that for many owners of mature companies, this simply can be a great way to carve out a bigger share of a plan's contributions than the rest of the staff receives.

❑ **Unit benefit plans.** This is a type of defined (meaning guaranteed) pension plan whose benefit is tied to job tenure. If you're in a situation in which you have put in significantly more years at your company than any of your other employees have—or if it's the nature of your industry to experience frequent job turnover—you'll again find yourself receiving a benefit that outweighs anything other staffers receive.

But, but, but. There's one caution that is certainly worth pointing out here. Many large corporations have

Go See Your Accountant

IF YOU'RE STILL LOOKING FOR WAYS to get the most bang from your buck out of your company's retirement-benefit-related expenditures, you'll be well advised to invest $1,000 or so in a long session with your accountant (don't forget to go armed with a bottle of aspirin).

You may learn that your company is eligible for other so-called top-heavy ways to design your retirement or pension plan. (This term refers to plans that mainly benefit owners and other high-level executives, if any exist.) Or you might be able to reduce the cost of your company-wide program through a loophole called "permitted disparity," which allows owners to take into account the benefits that their employees will one day receive from Social Security at the time that the company makes its annual corporate contribution calculations. You also might be able to provide yourself with some additional retirement security by setting up a plan tied to your compensation as a board director rather than as an employee of your company.

But all of these strategies are enormously complicated, and there are plenty of tax risks if you fail to comply with strict government regulations. You'll also need an expert's help in figuring out which of these souped-up models, if any, will add significant value, given the particulars of your business and personal situation.

taken a variety of steps to pull out of defined benefit plans because they can represent such a huge, inflexible expense and even a drag on growth. You probably wouldn't want to set up one of these plans if you weren't completely certain that your company's cash flow was lush and secure (and also that you won't be bringing aboard a large number of employees).

❑ **Pensions for relatives.** This strategy has plenty to recommend it for an owner with a comprehensive set of long-term financial goals for his or her entire household. Let's say that your teenager, adult child, or spouse works for your company on a part-time basis. (I'm not talking about the odd Saturday-morning appearance. The IRS's rules here require a minimum of 1,000 hours annually, which boils down to a twenty-hour-a-week commitment with two weeks off each year for good behavior, or an extremely intensive work schedule during summers, occasional weekends, and college-vacation breaks.)

The good news is this: Your company is allowed to make a $10,000 minimum pension contribution to his or her account, regardless of how much your family member was actually paid during the year. Here again, the rules are a little complicated, but they're worth investigating. That $10,000 must get discounted by 10 percent for each year under a decade that your relative has worked for you. So it pays to start setting up this strategy sooner rather than later!

Depending on your particular situation, there are other ways that you also may be able to use company funds to help finance a relative's retirement savings. One strategy worth checking out is appointing a spouse or other family member to your company's board of directors. Different tax-planning and retirement-planning options then exist, depending on whether the relative is also on the company's payroll. (Do exert some self-control here, though, or you'll create more problems than you solve; see "Do You Need an Independent Board of Directors?" page 174.)

Stage 3

Should You Add Real Estate Investments to Your Portfolio?

If you haven't yet diversified into this potentially lucrative market, this may well be the time to make a major move.

I'M ASSUMING THAT YOUR household's investments by now are broadly diversified, even if they still lack the depth that you hope they will one day possess. Your portfolio should include a safe and liquid emergency reserve fund; one or more retirement savings vehicles; and a mixture of different classes of stocks and bonds, whether through direct holdings or mutual funds. So it's time to consider adding a significant investment within an asset category that can benefit almost every Stage Three entrepreneur: real estate.

The advantages for an owner of a mature, or maturing, privately held company are numerous, starting off with the fact that real estate tends to have little correlation in its cycles or risk factors with either the public or private equity markets. This makes it an excellent investment diversification vehicle for later-stage entrepreneurs whose personal assets are heavily concentrated in a successful, if currently illiquid, business.

It makes sense to think about this investment market in a different way than you may have done earlier. When your company was younger and more fragile, the best real estate holding for you was undoubtedly your home, which provided you with two very important kinds of shelter: a living space for your family and an asset to be borrowed against for your business. As you slowly began to take baby steps into the world of alternative investments, you may have dabbled with REITs (real estate investment trusts), which allowed you to invest in commercial-property portfolios that were professionally managed and as simple to buy and sell as mutual funds.

Now that your company has reached a stage at which its profits are consistent and cash flow is both positive and predictable, you're ready to make a different and larger bet on this market. For Stage Three entrepreneurs, it's a natural step to invest in an office building, warehouse, or other commercial property that can be used (if only partially) by

Make It Manageable

ALTHOUGH BUSINESS OWNERS often prefer to invest in commercial properties that are tied in some way to their companies, you may want to investigate other types of real estate investments. Your ties to a key customer or supplier may alert you to potentially lucrative opportunities elsewhere. Be careful, though. The farther afield you get, the tougher your properties will likely be to manage, which could be a problem, given the fact that this is an investment sideline rather than your chosen calling.

If your child is attending college, you might want to consider investing in a small-scale apartment complex that he could live in—thus saving room and board—and also manage for you. Plan to sell the property after he graduates; if the market is hot, you may earn enough profit to cover all those tuition bills.

their businesses. Such a deal can be structured in a variety of ways, depending on personal priorities.

If your goal is to diversify personal holdings while finding additional ways to take cash out of your company, then your family should purchase the property and your company should lease it from you, thus providing your household with an additional monthly source of income. Structure this arrangement the same way you would with any third-party landlord, which means documenting the transaction with a lease and assigning a monthly rent that will be defensible, given current norms, if the IRS or one of your investors challenges the arrangement.

I'd advise any company owner to look for an alternative investment that fits two requirements: It should be something they know about, and it should be very different from their company.

—LUCILLE ROBERTS

What if you can't afford to make the purchase or don't want to tie up family funds for the down payment? With your corporate attorney's assistance, you should be able to safely borrow money from the company's coffers. Just make certain that you've got a promissory note that spells out your family's interest- and principal-payment obligations to the company. You'll also want to confirm that the anticipated rent your family will receive from your business (as well as from any other commercial tenants) will more than compensate you for your financing costs.

If your goal is to sell your company at some point in the near-to-moderate-term future, then it may make better sense to structure this as a corporate transaction instead. On the one hand, choosing this course deprives you of the potential to supplement your paycheck and bonuses with another nice monthly check. But by adding a significant tangible asset to your company's holdings, you should increase both its value and sales prospects. That's a longer-term payoff that may be worth waiting for.

There's another possibility: Benefit your children or heirs by making them, or a trust fund that covers them, the real estate's owners. This type of strategy can help later-stage entrepreneurs who are focused on college planning (by providing older kids with future tuition funds in the form of monthly income that gets taxed at a lower rate than your own) or estate planning (by transferring to them an asset that has value in and of itself, as well as to the family's business). But to do it right, you'll probably need some help from your attorney or accountant, since you'll want to carry this out in a way that won't trigger unwanted income- or estate-tax consequences.

Stage 3

Investing in a Second Home

Vacation properties offer another appealing way to diversify personal investments, but proceed cautiously.

IT OFTEN MAKES SOUND FINANCIAL SENSE to invest in your corporate headquarters, but that decision doesn't add much in the way of fun to your family's lifestyle. That's why plenty of business owners who have reached the point where they've got cash to spare opt instead to purchase a second home.

Is that a financially savvy decision? Here's the advice

that I give to business owners when they write or e-mail me with questions about this strategy:

❑ **First, examine your family's personal asset base.** Despite the allure of owning your own getaway, entrepreneurs should only consider this type of luxury investment *after* they've adequately diversified away from the risks and illiquidity embodied in their companies. That means the purchase of a second home should occur only after owners have accumulated the broad-based asset mix that I described earlier (see "Should You Add Real Estate Investments to Your Portfolio?" page 235).

❑ **Next, consider your household's current income and expenditure pattern.** Unless you're contemplating renting out your vacation home for most or all of the year, making this purchase won't generate the kind of additional monthly income for your family that buying the company's headquarters would. Should that be a deal-breaker? Not if your compensation is already so large and secure that you don't need any extra boost. If that's not your situation—and if you don't want to be tied to a commercial property instead—then it makes sense to delay this decision until a later date.

❑ **Try to predict how much time you'll actually be able to spend at your second home.** If you're running a demanding and fast-growing company, you might find yourself free to escape from the office for only a week or two each year, plus a few long weekends. If that's the case, why add the hassles (and expenses) of vacation home ownership to your already overloaded life as an entrepreneur? Probably you'll be better off splurging on a luxury vacation and investing some of your spare cash in a real estate investment trust (REIT) or commercial property transaction.

❑ **Finally, consider this purchase from an investment-only perspective.** Since most of your personal assets are already tied up in one illiquid property—your company—

you want to make certain that any real estate you buy doesn't compound your family's potential problems. The way to do that is by realistically assessing how marketable your proposed vacation property would be if you needed to bail out quickly. Although there are no guarantees, you also should try to predict what kind of investment return you might expect to earn over a moderate- to longer-term period (maybe a three-to-seven-year horizon). Depending on current real estate conditions in your region, you might decide that a commercial property would be more marketable—or that you'll earn a more lucrative return by investing in a hot nearby vacation spot instead.

How important is it to consider issues like these before plunking down a deposit for that beach house or ski chalet you've always dreamed about? For an entrepreneur whose top priority is still the growth of the company, this process is downright essential. A small custom manufacturer I know bought a second home *before* his company's finances were truly stable enough to guarantee his monthly paycheck. "After all those years of sacrificing the family's interests to the company's, I *wanted* to believe we were ready. But I got fooled by a couple of unusually strong quarters when I was able to pay myself some extra bonuses that made everything seem affordable," he recalled.

By the time this owner decided that it made sense to rent out the vacation home—to supplement the family's realistic income levels—the summer rental season was behind him, and he learned, to his dismay, that there weren't any attractions for a year-round tenant. Eventually, as he reported to me, he managed to sell the property at a loss. But before that happened, he was forced to boost his monthly paycheck in order to cover all those additional personal costs, at the expense of the company's growth activities. These problems should have been completely avoidable.

Yet there's no reason to nix a vacation home purchase

Tax Tip for a Second Home

WHEN CALCULATING WHETHER this is the right kind of investment for you to make, it pays to check in with your accountant to make sure that you don't wind up with unanticipated tax headaches. The biggest one is the potential that second-home ownership might trigger an Alternative Minimum Tax liability. (That's because one of the itemized deductions that get added back in this calculation is real estate tax.) Don't let this factor alone discourage you. But it does make sense to know going into the investment what its overall cost, including taxes, will be for your family.

if your personal, corporate, and local real estate prospects are all strong enough to support the decision. I'd recommend, however, that you take these four steps to keep your family's finances on track.

❶ **Supplement your emergency nest egg** (or set up a separate vacation home reserve fund) to cover unanticipated—but all too predictable—costs for repairs, refurbishment, weather-related damage, and more.

❷ **Help cover your costs** by taking advantage of a great tax loophole that allows people to rent out their vacation homes for up to fourteen days without incurring any tax liabilities on the extra income.

❸ **Look for ways to minimize your big expenses,** typically the home mortgage and insurance fees. Bankers and insurance carriers often charge higher rates for second homes; you may be able to find discounts by approaching the companies that currently cover your primary residence.

❹ **Hire a local caretaker who can handle minor repairs** and help keep your hassles to a minimum. This is good advice for anyone who lives more than an hour or so away from a vacation home, but it's especially important for entrepreneurs who simply don't have the time or flexibility to leave town every time some shingles blow off the roof.

Stage 3

Making Your Own Angel Investments

Once your company's cash flow and profits are strong, you may be tempted to invest in other people's entrepreneurial ventures. Here is a risk/reward strategy that will maximize your potential for personal financial success.

ODDS ARE VERY STRONG THAT at some point during Stage One or Stage Two, you were approached by would-be entrepreneurs who viewed you as a sympathetic soul and potential source of capital. During your company's earlier, more vulnerable stages of growth, you—hopefully—turned down those pitches, recognizing that your first priority was investing in your own entrepreneurial venture, while your second priority, as soon as you had the time and energy to focus on it, should have been to protect and improve your household finances.

But now that your company's results are strong and you've presumably taken a series of steps to diversify your family's savings and investments, it's time to evaluate the prospect of an angel investment differently. Don't act precipitously, however: Unlike investing in a stock, bond, or mutual fund (which you can easily unload if you find that you really can't afford to hold it as a long-term investment), angel deals are tough to extricate yourself from if you find that you've overestimated your readiness for this type of market play.

One early-stage owner wrote to me after having made the mistake of investing in a friend's entrepreneurial venture; he had decided to give angel investing a whirl because he felt that one strong operating quarter was a sign that his own young company had surmounted its early hurdles. What had really happened instead was that his company had managed finally to collect some large overdue payments from one-time customers. Its cash flow was scarcely abundant. "If I had really analyzed the patterns in our orders and receivables, I would have recognized that conditions were still precarious, or at least unsettled," he told me, "but I was just so optimistic that I leapt at the first sign of good news. And I thought that I could multiply my prospects for success by investing in other good entrepreneurial ventures as well as my own."

When his company's conditions returned to their more normal (and precarious) state, it was strapped for funds—and forced to rely on the owner's personal credit cards and emergency savings, since he had put all of his other spare funds into the angel deal. Worst of all, this misguided investment in his friend's start-up was completely illiquid, which meant that there was no way of recovering his personal funds in the foreseeable future. (And conditions stayed at this impasse for years. The last time I talked to him, he was still cursing that investment decision.)

So there certainly are risks connected with these deals. But if you and your company are ready, the following are all good reasons to seriously consider getting involved:

❏ **Your company's operations are spinning off so much cash** that your current compensation can easily cover your household living expenses plus current investment goals—with a healthy surplus.

❑ **You've identified business niches** whose profit potential matches your own entrepreneurial guidelines, but you don't have the time or inclination to start up another company to tap into them yourself, at least for now.

❑ **Your network of business contacts** has brought you an exciting opportunity in an industry you know and understand, and you can get a piece of the action for a price that won't negatively affect either your company's growth strategy or your family's lifestyle.

Business owners sometimes cite a fourth motivation as well. When the public equity markets become weaker or more volatile, as happened in the early days of the new millennium, investing in a good privately held entrepreneurial venture can seem to offer far greater prospects for a favorable return. But this motivation needs to be examined very closely. Regardless of whether current returns are up or down for stocks, bonds, mutual funds, real estate investment trusts, or other publicly traded investment vehicles, these will always be less risky, more liquid, and far less volatile than any type of private investment, whether it's your own company or someone else's. That means that an angel deal can scarcely be viewed as a safer alternative or a hedge against market risks.

The bottom line: Choosing an angel investment for no reason other than the weakness of the public markets is shortsighted. After all, if that weakness continues, you may never be able to cash out of your investment—and thus never achieve your payoff goals—because the company

> *Recently I made an angel investment. It's a little technology company that was started by the son of a friend of mine. Bless his heart—two-and-a-half years later, the company is still in business! They've got revenues! So things are going well.*
>
> —BARBARA B. GROGAN

you bet on will probably fail to go public or attract a large strategic buyer.

That caveat aside, for many Stage Three entrepreneurs, it may well make great sense to explore the angel market-place. Below, I've suggested some guidelines that should help you protect your personal interests while maximizing the potential for profits.

❶ **Start by searching for deals through your personal network of contacts.** Your corporate attorney and accountant can be great sources of leads worth exploring; local trade groups and your chamber of commerce may also yield prospects. But don't stop there. You may come across an interesting and potentially investment-worthy young company in your larger community of suppliers, outsourcing providers, or even customers.

❷ **Stick to what you know best.** Think of this as financial self-defense. When you're buying shares in a mutual fund, there's little danger in reaching far afield, since you can rely on the expertise of a (hopefully) skilled professional who will give the fund's investments full-time attention. But whatever your intentions may be, you can't turn your full energy toward any investment as long as you're an active entrepreneur. You don't have the time to teach yourself everything that a savvy investor truly needs to know about an industry that is completely unrelated to your own and *then* to stay on top of that industry's changes, fast and furious as they may come. So give yourself a break here. If you invest in a noncompetitive company whose business niche you understand and track regularly, it will be far easier to evaluate your investment's business activities and progress.

❸ **Consider joining an angel network.** There's a lot to be said about the advantages of pooling your own investment capital with those of other well-heeled entrepreneurs. For one thing, it frees you from the necessity of putting all your eggs in one basket; networks typically aim to invest in a handful or more business ventures at a time. If you and the other members of your network come from a range of industries, you can put together a diversified group of holdings, thereby spreading your risks and probably improving your prospects for return.

Tip: Angel networks exist in many metropolitan regions, but if you can't find one that fits your location or interests, don't hesitate to start your own. Just make certain that you limit membership to fellow entrepreneurs who share similar goals and attitudes about the act of building a successful business.

❹ Be wary of Internet "opportunities." A number of websites exist—and more keep cropping up—with the intention of hooking up would-be angels with business ventures in search of capital. But there are a number of reasons to approach these with caution. For one thing, most sites offer little in the way of due diligence or quality controls. They may list any capital-hungry business willing to pay their registration fees and, thus, be chock-full of mediocre prospects looking for naive investors with more cash than common sense. Also, it's at least questionable whether, simply by publicizing their business plans on the Internet, listed companies have given up a competitive advantage and thereby weakened their future prospects. If you've got other ways to develop angel-investment prospects, you're probably best off relying on them.

@ Internet Guide: If you're looking for ways to educate yourself about the ins and outs of angel investing (which really is, whether you want to believe this or not, different from the act of starting and building a company yourself), these free websites do a good job of providing the need-to-know basics: www.ace-net.sr.unh.edu, www.earlybirdcapital.com, and www.seedstage.com.

Stage 3

Repeat Entrepreneuring: Is It for You?

Be certain to minimize any risks to your existing business, as well as your family's finances, by following the strategies outlined below.

IN THE ENTREPRENEURIAL CLIMATE that has flourished in the United States since the 1990s began, it has become increasingly common to see business owners start multiple companies. Sometimes they plan to run the businesses simultaneously, and other times they wait to sell the original business, perhaps to a strategic corporate purchaser or to public investors through an IPO, before launching the next. The advantages to either course are obvious: Thanks to the intense learning curve involved in starting and running a company, most people get better and better the more times they do it.

For Stage Three owners with a good new idea and the energy to give it a try, there's often no reason to delay the repeat experience. But it's essential to make certain that they launch their new companies in ways that will not put their business and personal financial achievements at risk. Below are some guidelines that should help you steer a safe but profitable course.

❑ **Don't try to start a new business until your existing company is ready.** Here's what that means: All vital operations should be stable. This includes sales and marketing, bill collecting, purchasing, and inventory management, if applicable. Profitability should be consistent, and your company's budgeting and financial reporting processes should be reliable. Above all else, you should have a management team in place that is qualified to cover for you during those inevitable moments when all hell breaks loose and your start-up needs you twenty-five hours a day.

❏ **Don't repeat your past mistakes—especially on the financing front!** It's one thing to put all your personal assets at risk when you don't have any other choices and you don't have much in the way of assets to lose. But that was then and this is now. You can't afford to jeopardize your successful company and with it the comfortable lifestyle and diversified investment portfolio that it supports.

So rely on safe ways to capitalize your new venture: Outside investors are particularly desirable and may be easily accessible now that you've got a proven track record. Or tap into spare savings, meaning family funds that are not tied to essential goals such as emergency reserves, col-

Turbo-Level Tax Advantages

ONCE YOU START OWNING MULTIPLE companies, your estate planning challenges—as well as opportunities—multiply as well. As with any business venture, you'll be able to save the most in taxes if you begin carrying out stock gifting and other strategies sooner rather than later—ideally, before your new venture develops any value in the eyes of Uncle Sam (see "A Simple Tax-Reduction Strategy," page 170).

Don't try this without the help of a good trusts-and-estates attorney. You may be able to compensate this time around for tax-minimization opportunities that you overlooked in the frenzy of building your first company. It will all depend on the care you take in creating a comprehensive estate-planning package.

lege tuition, or retirement planning. Try to avoid tying any bank loans to your personal guarantee or your original company's assets. As a better last resort, there's always your home equity.

❑ **Protect your household and your existing company by keeping all business ventures separate and legally sound.** Remember how important it was to set up the right corporate structure and personal financial defense mechanisms the first go-around (see "Incorporation Issues," page 34, "Structuring Your Company's Stock," page 38, and "Record-Keeping Rules: Save Everything!" page 42). Back then, sound preparation involved sorting your way through a wide range of issues that could affect your business's growth potential as well as your household's long-term financial picture.

All this is just as important, maybe more so, with each new business venture that you launch. You can keep these tasks fairly simple

> *I've been the shareholder of three companies that are still privately held. There's tremendous risk in my private-equity portfolio. As a result, I'm a very low-risk guy when it comes to my other investments.*
>
> —AARON COHEN

if you choose to diversify within the corporate umbrella of your existing company rather than to set up a new and separate operation. But there's a downside to this approach since it may limit your future ability to spin off discrete business entities and realize different payoffs at different times.

To give yourself the most flexibility, bite the bullet and tackle legal and other complexities up front, before launching your new venture. Establish a separate corporate structure, with its own insurance blanket, financial reporting system, tax-filing operation, and record-keeping arrangements. Make sure that your existing investors and lenders understand the nature of this new business (and that they are not connected with it in any way, either in terms of increased financial exposure or added profit potential, unless they make new infusions of capital into this start-up). Although you'll face some added adviser fees, it pays to involve your corporate accountant and attorney in figuring out how to best set in place new systems that will keep up with your current, somewhat more complicated, situation.

Stage 3

The Financial Benefits of Charitable Giving

Now that contributions have become affordable for your family, you'll want to weigh the pros and cons of several gifting strategies.

WHENEVER I THINK ABOUT entrepreneurs and charitable donations, I can't help recalling one huge blunder that a business owner confessed to me some time ago. "You'd never think so many problems could result from what was basically just my desire to share some of my success with other people" is the way she put it.

This CEO ran a small but profitable niche publishing company and had wanted, years earlier, to share her good fortune with a local nonprofit organization whose social priorities matched her own. She had contemplated, she told me, an outright donation of cash but felt that her opportunities were limited in this regard, since most of her personal assets were tied up in the company. So, rather than making what seemed to be a too-small cash contribution, she decided to gift a minority equity stake from her own holdings of the business's stock.

It was yet another one of those classic seemed-like-a-good-idea-at-the-time entrepreneurial errors. From a personal financial perspective, there was little to recommend the gift, since it qualified for only a tiny tax deduction. That's because the IRS discounts the value of any private company's stock—since it's so illiquid and perhaps even impossible to sell—and then further discounts the value of minority stock holdings like this one. From a corporate-management perspective, meanwhile, the gift was a downright disaster, since the nonprofit organization turned into a vocal and usually dissident shareholder. A crisis developed when the nonprofit planned to sell its small stake to an unwanted suitor of the publishing company. The entrepreneur found herself forced to buy back her own stock (at an inflated cost!) in order to avoid future complications.

Get the message? As appealing as it might seem to look for ways to blend your entrepreneurial activities with your charitable commitments, it's far safer to keep them as distinct as possible. I'd recommend one of these donation strategies instead:

❑ **Gifts of outright cash.** This is a simple way to go, and it's the one I prefer, especially if you are just starting to get involved in significant gifting. In order to claim a tax deduction for the full value of your gift, retain any documentation that the nonprofit provides.

Here's a tip: If your company's cash flow is thriving, you might want to consider adding an employee benefit that's offered by many large employers: a charitable-gift match. So long as your business matches donations made (whether by you or your staffers) only to accredited nonprofit groups, this expense will be tax deductible as a legitimate business expense and may well earn some brownie points with employees and your community.

❑ **Gifts of appreciated stock.** The advantage to this strategy is purely a financial one. If you donate, for example, stock shares that you purchased for $1,000 that are now worth $10,000, you'll get a personal tax deduction for that full $10,000, regardless of your initial expense. Meanwhile, you won't owe any capital gains tax on the $9,000 of appreciated value, and neither will the nonprofit—which is why charitable groups are just as happy to receive stock donations as they are to get cash.

But there's an important reason why I believe business owners should think twice before making any gifts of publicly traded stock: It can undermine your hard-won accomplishments in asset diversification. Unless you've reached the point at which your portfolio is so large and diverse that it counterbalances your huge investment in your company, I'd argue that you're just not ready to start giving stock away. Stick to cash or postpone your household's large-scale donations for now.

❑ **Charitable trusts.** Let's say you're not quite in the Donald Trump category but your company seems profitable and secure, your investment portfolio is at least fairly diversified, and you've accomplished the family's key goals (such as saving for college for the kids or your own retirement). If you're charitably inclined, you might want to investigate these kinds of trusts, which allow people to make larger contributions than they might otherwise feel ready to handle.

Here's how they work. You donate an appreciated asset (which is usually stock in a publicly traded company but might just as easily be a piece of real estate or a work of art) to a trust in the name of your charity of choice. In return, the charity promises to pay you a fixed rate of interest (at least 5 percent per year) for whatever length of time you choose. That's what helps make these gifts affordable for those who are well-heeled but usually not yet wealthy. When making the gift, some people request a payment from the charity's trust throughout the remainder of their lifetime. Others specify a number of years, which might be tied to their planned retirement or the sale of their companies.

If you're intrigued, there are two caveats to keep in mind. First, these don't qualify for the same kind of tax deduction you'd receive if you just bit the bullet and made an outright gift of either cash or stock. The IRS will discount the value of your gift based on a number of factors, including your age and the amount of income you plan to draw from the trust during the course of your lifetime. Second, these are irrevocable gifts, which means you shouldn't contemplate making one—any more than you should think about giving away stock or cash—until you're certain that your family and your company are financially secure enough to support it.

❑ **Charitable gift annuities.** These are similar to charitable trusts, with one important exception: They only work with gifts of cash. Basically, what happens with these annuities is that you donate a sum of money, which might be as low as $5,000, and in return a nonprofit promises to pay you a return (which might be as high as 10 percent per year) for the rest of your lifetime. It's a fairly simple arrangement, since you don't have to set up the trust yourself or worry about a lot of paperwork or legal issues. But here again, the gift is irreversible, and the tax deduction is limited, based on your age and other factors.

Stage 3

Protecting Your Downside in Lawsuits, Hard Times

Entrepreneurs perpetuate unnecessary risks when they don't take steps to shelter their personal assets from negative marketplace trends.

HOPEFULLY, WE'VE ALL LEARNED some lessons from watching what happened to many of the dot-com millionaires. So long as your wealth is basically tied up in the value of a single private (or even public) company, the family's finances are exposed to some powerful marketplace risks. If the company's revenue stream or its sources of financing suddenly dry up—or any of a number of other business-threatening events occur—the value of an owner's equity stake can shrink precipitously. Other difficulties may follow, tied to personal liabilities, declines in self-compensation, tax problems, and more.

Given the personal financial stakes involved, it may be no surprise that partners at some of the nation's most elite corporate law firms have confided to me that they're spending more and more time working with even their most successful clients on asset-protection plans. As one explained to me recently, "Entrepreneurs who started their companies within the past ten years just don't realize how much more aggressive people will be about turning to lawsuits when business problems arise and times are tough. When the economy is as strong as it was during the 1990s, there's more of a willingness to move on, because there's always another potential deal worth pursuing." At the most aggressive end of the downside protection spectrum, some advisers are forcefully recommending the establishment of offshore trusts and foreign corporations as ways to keep an owner's personal assets as safe as possible from legal challenges.

For most business owners, however, I'm convinced that there's little justification for resorting to such costly and complicated sheltering devices. If you follow these six steps instead, you should be able to significantly reduce your downside risks.

❶ Keep yourself and your company as separate as possible. I can't overstate the importance of this, nor can I possibly detail all of the ways that I've heard business owners go wrong here—running the gamut from comingling their personal and corporate funds or credit cards to failing to keep adequate records of which assets belong to the family or the business to blurring the distinction between themselves as individuals and as corporate officers when they sign business documents.

When owners fail to observe proper procedures—more often because of carelessness or attention overload than bad intentions—they "pierce the corporate veil" in legal jargon. That leaves the way open for a judge in a bankruptcy court or lawsuit to poke even bigger holes in the legal safeguards that are otherwise provided to entrepreneurs through their company's formal status as a C or S corporation, partnership, or limited liability company.

Believe it or not, you could risk losing your corporation's personal-liability safeguards if you fail to schedule annual meetings of your board of directors and then keep records of what's been discussed, even if these meetings take place by telephone. Your corporate advisers should be able to instruct you about the procedures to follow, regardless of whether you have any outside board members or other shareholders besides yourself. Don't overlook anything: You've also got to keep all corporate annual filings up-to-date, along with your business tax returns, if you want to be certain to maintain your corporate status.

When owners ask me how to clear up problems in any of these areas, I advise them to consult their corporate law firms—right away. That's because it's essential that all legal ambiguities (or errors) be fully corrected if their personal assets are not to be fully exposed in bankruptcy proceedings, corporate lawsuits, business loan foreclosures, or other crises.

❷ Document any personal infusions of cash that you're forced to make in order to keep the company afloat. It's remarkable how many owners were forced to reach into their own pocketbooks after capital sources started drying up during the spring of 2000. If that happens to you, don't try to second-guess how long it will take for the company to make a repayment. For some owners it never happens, especially when prolonged downturns within the debt and equity markets keep cash flow pressures strong.

In cases like these, it makes sense to follow the same simple strategy that I recommended to start-up owners in Stage One: Keep careful records that describe the date and amount of each loan (see "Should You Rely on Personal Funds in Corporate Crises?" page 53). Assuming that you've got other employees, it's a good idea to ask another corporate officer to sign these promissory notes. Then retain copies in your corporate and personal files. Don't skip this safeguard. If your company ends up in bankruptcy court or undergoes some other type of financial restructuring, this is the only way to guarantee your stature as a creditor who may also deserve some measure of restitution.

❸ Don't rely on risky personal leverage techniques that may prop up your ailing company while creating dangerous exposure for your family. My list of no-no's here includes borrowing in any way against the value of your entrepreneurial stake or business-related assets.

All you need is a down market in order to see just how

dangerous this strategy can be. This past year I was contacted by a number of tech entrepreneurs who lost big chunks of their equity when what were basically business-oriented loans (backed by personal guarantees tied to the owner's stock holdings) were called after corporate problems developed while the economy worsened. These owners got hit by a domino effect. When downturns within their companies forced them to disrupt the banking covenants that were tied to their business borrowings, the banks called in their loans. The companies didn't have sufficient cash flow to pay. So the banks did what banks will always do: They turned to the loan collateral, at which point it became clear that the owner's stock holdings were severely depressed in value (not too surprising in a bear market!). In each of these cases, the banks ended up seizing much larger portions of the owner's stake than anyone might have imagined possible in order to pay off the outstanding loans.

This isn't the only way an owner can get into trouble. It's also risky to leverage your family's other investments in order to raise cash for the company. That's because these loans compound your business-related risks by also exposing you to stock or bond market volatility. Downward market trends could cause your personal loans to be called in for repayment—which could devastate your family's safety net or the stability of a college savings or retirement savings plan.

❹ **Keep your personal tax reports timely and accurate.** Business owners are always popular targets when it comes to audits. That's especially true when corporate problems raise red flags for the tax man. Don't adopt aggressive tax-reduction techniques that may come back to haunt you.

❺ **Take advantage of whatever legitimate creditor-protection loopholes are permitted under your state's regulations.** All states offer "homestead" exemptions, which will shield some or all of your family's equity investment in your home in the event of a bankruptcy or creditor lawsuit. These limits are currently set locally, with Florida at the top of the class, thanks to its unlimited exemption. But that situation might change, thanks to a federal proposal to limit homestead exemptions in bankruptcy cases to just $125,000 in total. Some states, such as New York, also permit people to shelter those funds they've invested in insurance policies from all types of creditors. If that option is open to you—and if it seems to make sense, given the condition of your personal finances as well as your company—you might want to consider bolstering your retirement savings by socking away funds in an annuity or other investment-oriented insurance product.

❻ Explore ways that trusts can give you added asset protection. Here's why this precaution may make sense. If a serious problem affects your company, it's not impossible to imagine a scenario in which lawsuits could follow, whether from customers, suppliers, investors, or other interested parties. They'll look for ways to sue you personally, as well as your corporation, in an effort to tap into as deep a pocket as possible.

Investigate your options with an attorney. There are some fairly simple ways that business owners can shield personal assets from all creditors, including funding their 401(k) plans to the maximum levels permitted under federal laws and setting up irrevocable trusts for their children (which is a strategy that also makes good sense from an estate-planning vantage point). Depending on your tolerance for complexity, you may also want to consider establishing something that's known as a family limited partnership, which can provide some levels of protection by containing within it your equity stake as well as other investments.

Occasionally I hear about an entrepreneur who combines the use of a family limited partnership with various trusts, both domestic and foreign. That strikes me as being completely over-the-top, unless you want to be perceived as walking on the wild side. As one attorney commented to me recently, if an owner goes this route and then, later on, experiences a significant downturn in the company's operations, he can expect to be "tarred and feathered" in the eyes of investors, business associates, and creditors, whether or not he is actually guilty of any wrongdoing.

Stage 3

When Estate-Planning Trusts Can Help

Once an entrepreneur's company—as well as personal assets—accumulate significant value, it can make sound financial sense to investigate setting up one or more trusts for heirs.

ONE OF THE MOST HOTLY debated tax issues in the new millennium is the so-called death tax, which currently can consume as much as 50 percent of a business owner's estate, once state and federal taxes get factored in. With the estate tax scheduled to gradually shrink and finally disappear by the year 2010, it might seem tempting for entrepreneurs to sit back and hope for the best (especially if they've built their companies to Stage Three of growth without taking precautionary tax-reduction steps at some earlier point of development).

But I'm convinced that the risks of this strategy are enormous, given two very significant "unpredictables." First, although I certainly hope this won't be the case, you may unexpectedly die during the eight-year window before the tax vanishes. Second (and perhaps more likely), if and when the political climate changes in Washington, D.C., the estate tax may be reinstituted. Either way, your family, as well as your company, could suffer. So if you're running a successful and profitable privately held company and have yet to develop a full-scale estate plan, it's time to get started right now.

One caveat: As the estate tax laws now stand, each person possesses a total lifetime gift-and-estate tax exclusion, currently pegged at $1 million per individual and due to rise to $3.5 million by the year 2009. Some variant on this level of lifetime exclusion does seem likely to survive long term, which might mean that a married couple could safely count on bequeathing to heirs a business and other assets worth something in the range of $3 million to $4 million without triggering a significant tax liability, if any at all. Since that's the case, entrepreneurs whose companies will likely grow only to this level of value might be able to avoid the whole trust issue and other complicated estate-planning strategies. But if you imagine that your company could grow to be worth much more (and certainly if you expect that an initial public offering or $5-million-plus sale to a strategic buyer is likely), read on.

The reason it makes sense to think about trusts at this stage of corporate growth is quite simple. The value of your company and other assets is now simply so high that you won't accomplish much in the way of tax reduction if you confine your activities to the $10,000 a year gift giving that was outlined earlier (see "A Simple Tax-Reduction Strategy," page 170). Now you need to find ways to transfer more value more quickly. These trusts can help:

❑ **Grantor Retained Annuity Trusts (GRATs)** work like this: You transfer some of your company's stock shares to a trust established in the name of your children (or other heirs), but the transfer isn't an outright gift. That's because you will receive a significant interest payment (or annuity) tied to the stock, perhaps in the form of a large dividend payment to be paid to you annually for some time to come; at the end of this term the ownership rights pass to your heirs. Pay special attention to the length of time you select as the trust term for these retained rights. If you die before the term ends, the contents of the trust will pass back into your estate, and the estate will be liable for all taxes on it.

The bottom line: Because you retain a financial stake in the assets within the trust through this annuity payment, the IRS greatly discounts the value of the stock that you've transferred into it. The greater the discount, the smaller the gift tax liability. Best of all, there's an additional tax discount you'll be entitled to so long as your gift is of a minority stake. As a result you should owe very little, if anything at all, in taxes for such stock transfers made during your lifetime.

❑ **Life insurance trusts** should be a no-brainer for any entrepreneur who can envision passing a sizable estate on to his or her heirs, whether in the form of company stock or other household assets. That's because these trusts, if set up correctly, manage to exclude a life insurance policy's death benefit from the taxable portion of a couple's estate. This benefit is especially important in cases in which heirs will need extra cash to help cover estate-tax liabilities, which can hit them from any number of different directions, including tax bills for angel investments in other companies that you may have made during your lifetime.

An insurance tip: Ask your broker and accountant about the possible benefits of using a second-to-die insurance policy with one of these trusts. These basically will insure both your own life and that of your spouse but only pay death benefits after both of you die. There are two major advantages: The cost is generally lower than for two individual policies, since the payoff is delayed, and the payoff comes when it's most necessary, which is after your com-

An Outright Gift?

IF THE VALUE OF YOUR COMPANY and other personal assets has gotten so sizable that it seems impossible to avoid a hefty tax bite even through the use of one or more trusts, you may want to consider making a large outright gift and paying the tax now rather than later. That's because of a subtle difference in the way the government levies estate taxes and gift taxes. Put simply, if you give a gift of $2 million worth of company stock or other assets to a child during the course of your lifetime, you would owe roughly $1 million in taxes, adding up to a total expenditure of $3 million. If you died leaving that same $3 million worth of assets in your estate, you would owe about $1.5 million in taxes, leaving your heirs with only $1.5 million (as opposed to the $2 million they would have received from a lifetime gift). Discuss the pros and cons of making a large lifetime gift with a trusts-and-estates specialist. Tax relief regulations have made this decision even more complicated, since the estate tax is scheduled to disappear in 2010 but the gift tax is, so far, scheduled to remain in force. Can you count on either of these two eventualities? Get an expert's advice about how the possibilities relate to your own situation.

pany and other assets get transferred to the second generation—the transfer that triggers the estate tax.

If you decide to set up a life insurance trust, remember that it's essential to rely on an estate planner's assistance, to make sure your decisions don't jeopardize this vehicle's tax-free status. You'll need to appoint a trustee, who must be the person to actually handle the application process and paperwork for the life insurance policy. You should be able to transfer an existing policy to any life insurance trust you now set up, but this too is complicated, so don't try it on your own.

It also makes sense to involve your accountant as well as an attorney when it comes to figuring out how much insurance to purchase and how to structure your payments for it. To get the most tax benefits, you'll want to carefully plan and time your insurance fees so that payments will qualify for the annual $10,000 gift tax exclusion and thus not trigger any unwanted tax liabilities.

Stage 3

Starting to Think about Your Exit

Whichever end-run strategy you now choose will shape the outcome of your personal financial plan.

THERE'S NO DOUBT THAT THE LATE 1990s were a wild and crazy time for American entrepreneurs. It seemed as though anyone with the right business scheme and enough energy to work 24/7 could count on—or at least hope for—the prospect of an initial public offering that would, sooner rather than later, produce riches beyond logic or fantasy.

That was a great dream, but as I regularly tried to remind start-up and early-stage owners, it was one that bore little relevance to most people's business or personal lives, let alone their financial futures. Now that the stock market and U.S. economy have returned to Earth, that's a message more entrepreneurs are open to hearing. Regardless of what's going on in the current IPO market and whether your company is actually a likely candidate for a public stock offering or not, there are a wide range of so-called exit strategies that you can and should explore.

> *I waited until after the sale to consult someone with estate-planning and investment management expertise. And you know what he told me? The first thing he said was, 'I wish you'd come to me two years ago.'*
>
> —BRIAN SULLIVAN

I'd urge you to start thinking about this issue in a systematic way as soon as your company stabilizes within Stage Three of growth. You might not be ready to take action yet. In fact, you might need to spend some time researching the various options, in order to get a true sense of what could be possible for you and your company at some point down the road.

But I cannot emphasize to you strongly enough that every profitable exit strategy takes planning, on both the corporate and personal fronts. There's no guaranteed happy ending here: Statistics suggest that the majority of entrepreneurs find themselves unable to cash in on their companies when they're ready to sell or retire. Those are often the same people who find themselves unable to achieve many or most of their long-term personal financial objectives, despite years of hard work and business ownership.

Throughout the remainder of this book, I'll walk you through specific action blueprints tied to popular entrepreneurial exit strategies. But to get you started thinking in practical terms, I offer this checklist:

❑ **How long-lasting is your commitment to the company?** It's amazing how many times I ask an owner this question only to be told, "You know, I've never thought about it in those terms." Stage Three is the perfect time to wrestle this issue to the ground. If you're the kind of business founder who thrives on creativity (or chaos), or if you find yourself looking back longingly on the days when you were your only employee, or if you know in your heart of hearts that you're just not suited to run a large and well-oiled corporate machine, you may not want to stick around forever, no matter how much you love this baby of yours.

On the other hand, you may feel as though you couldn't imagine life without this company—not, at least, now that it's finally capable of rewarding you for all your hard work and personal sacrifices. Depending on your age and the nature of your family obligations, you might want to concentrate on succession planning and estate planning issues instead (see "Exiting through a Long-Term Succession Plan," page 267). Remember, this is one decision that isn't cast in stone. After a few years of successful Stage Three operations—or even longer—you can always decide to re-explore the company sale option.

❑ **What kind of entrepreneurial payoff are you looking for?** Here again, there's no right answer, only the one that feels right to you. Fantasies of dot-com billionaires aside, there are countless owners, I'm convinced, who don't need or want a huge one-time payment for their companies. And then, of course, there are plenty who do.

When I ask owners this question, I urge them to be as specific as possible. There are many people who have told me that the pot of gold they're seeking is a lucrative, predictable paycheck, supplemented by bonuses and other ownership perks, the right kind of jobs for their spouses and children, and the ability to be their own bosses forevermore. For them as well, succession planning would be more appropriate than exit planning. If you, on the other hand, are looking for a big pile of cash, either to support your early retirement or to finance your next entrepreneurial venture, a sale or IPO makes sense. But don't waste your time pursuing a bid from a larger corporation, since it would probably expect you to accept its stock as full or partial payment (and might also demand that you delay your departure for one to three years).

❑ **Don't overlook your company's glitches and glitz factors.** If your business niche is tiny, obscure, or just plain unsexy, you're going to have to come to terms with its limited cash potential. That's not to say that your company is not salable, although some companies simply end up this way. But if you've got a business that only a founder could love, you're going to have to be energetic and creative if you aim to do anything other than pass it along to your kids. I'd suggest that you focus your efforts on two promising exit strategies: a sale to employees if you're looking for an immediate cash payment, or a sale to another corporation if you've got a supplier or customer who understands the business's potential and you're willing to accept its stock in return for your own. Plan to start early, whichever strategy you choose. If you find yourself in this category, a profitable departure is probably going to take some time.

Then again, if you're fortunate enough to be in an industry niche that the capital markets have deemed "hot," your prospects for quick cash are good. You've probably already taken steps to pave your way to a lucrative IPO or corporate sale by forming alliances with professional or strategic investors (see "Moving Away from Friends-and-Family Financing," page 177, "Where Can You Find Angel Investors?" page 184, and "How to Make the Most of Strategic Partnering," page 180). If that's the case, they—and you—will probably aim to carry out your company's exit strategy as soon after you've entered Stage Three as market conditions permit it.

Stage 3

Exiting through a Long-Term Succession Plan

You may have no desire (or financial need) to think about selling your company now or anytime down the road. But you still can't afford to overlook the exit issues raised by your decision to retain long-term ownership of a successful family business.

THERE ARE MANY STAGE THREE owners for whom the prospect of selling their businesses is only slightly less unimaginable than the thought of selling their children.

That's not too surprising, given the intensity of many founders' emotional attachments to their entrepreneurial ventures. They've devoted an enormous amount of time to helping the companies grow over the years. Their work can finally begin to pay off once cash flow stabilizes and profitability reigns.

What is surprising to me, however, is the way that such owners often mistakenly convince themselves that they're making a "no-exit" choice, which translates into a "no-planning" choice. In fact, as I warn entrepreneurs all the time, there's no such thing as a "no-exit" option. Even if you don't have any intention of selling your company now or later, you're simply opting for a delayed exit, with your eventual departure probably coinciding with either your retirement or your death.

Once you face this reality, it should become clear that your decision to retain long-term ownership of your company requires the same type of corporate and personal preparation that any other exit strategy does:

Business Planning

Unlike all those owners who are focused on the prospect of a sale to an individual or a corporate buyer or an initial public offering, *you* don't need to be worried about the outside world. (In fact, if you're serious about never selling your company, it's very likely that you don't even have any investors to answer to—because they'd probably be pressuring you either to sell the company or to buy them out before you get too comfortably settled in Stage Three!) So long as you're up to date with the IRS and your financial reports work just fine for you, your managers, and your bankers, there's no reason to consider spiffing up your accounting team or to worry about the difference between business brokers and investment bankers. (After all, you don't need help selling the company from either one of them.)

Your focus should be strictly on your family and your key employees. That's because you need one thing and one thing alone: a succession plan. In any family-owned business (which is really the category that you've chosen to place yourself in, whether or not any other members of your family currently are involved with your company), a comprehensive succession plan covers two essential points: management and ownership.

The bottom line: Right now, while you are healthy, alert, and actively engaged in running your company, its management and ownership are probably centered on one person—you. But if your long-term goal is to keep your company strong and your family financially sound, you must plan ahead for a different set of contingencies, which might include your eventual retirement, your physical or mental incapacity, or your death.

Unfortunately, succession planning isn't a simple, fill-in-the-blanks process. Business owners rely on a wide range of strategies here. At the simplest end of the spectrum, those entrepreneurs who feel confident in the management capabilities of either their spouses or their adult children may designate (and then should begin to train) a single successor. In those cases, in order to solidify this heir's control over the company, it makes sense to bequeath to him or her a majority of its stock. If your company is structured as a C corp, you can even create multiple categories of stock, so that nonmanagement heirs possess fewer or no voting rights.

In other more difficult cases, owners may not be able to identify a family member who is qualified and motivated to take over the management of the company. Although they may choose to pass on the majority of its stock to family heirs (whether directly or indirectly, through trust arrangements), they also may decide to leave a small stake to a key employee, in the hope that this person will take over the helm in the absence of a family leader.

You'll need to figure out the plan that works best for your company. I urge you to consult your accountant, attorney, and other financial advisers, in addition to fully discussing these matters with your spouse, adult children, and other heirs. Put your plan in writing. Then, revisit it every two or three years, or sooner if business or family changes warrant this.

Personal Planning

I'm sorry to report that in certain ways, a delayed-exit strategy raises more personal financial complications than any other exit. That's not a reason to avoid this choice. But it certainly does mean that you'll need to plan carefully for problems that may occur now or later on:

❏ **Less liquidity.** Although no one may ever come right out and say this to you, the decision to retain long-term ownership of your company means, basically, that the only way you'll ever be able to take money out of it is through your salary, bonuses, and other perks. That means you'll probably never buy that custom-designed yacht or villa in Tuscany that you've always fantasized about. After all, it's highly unlikely that you'll ever be able to raise a block of cash by selling a minority portion of your equity stake to somebody else. (As I mentioned earlier, outside investors generally have their sights fixed on the prospect of an exit, whether you do or not.)

One solution: You'll need to rely more heavily on those savings and investment disciplines that you practiced during Stage One and Stage Two if you're going to achieve high-end financial goals.

❑ **Limited growth options.** Let's say you want to propel your company into a faster growth mode (maybe because its current levels of revenue, cash flow, and profitability aren't sufficient to pay you the financial rewards that you believe you deserve). Here's the problem. The capital markets, as we know them, are simply not designed to provide growth funds to owners who aren't interested in selling equity and then eventually cashing out through a corporate sale or an IPO. So unless your business fits a banker's description of creditworthy, either because it's asset rich or you're willing to put up significant personal holdings as collateral, you'll be stymied when it comes to raising expansion funds.

One solution: If your company possesses nonessential assets or business lines that might prove salable on their own, this might be one way to raise personal or corporate funds while protecting your ownership stake.

❑ **Long-term financial risks.** As long as your personal assets remain heavily tied up in your company, you and your family face a range of future problems. Unless estate taxes disappear completely and forever, or your company remains so small that its value won't trigger a liability after your death, you'll need to provide your family with a financial cushion so that it won't be forced to sell the company to pay the taxes. One solution: insurance, and plenty of it.

Since you haven't opted for a liquidity event like a sale or an IPO, your next best option is to invest heavily in a life insurance policy (see "Life Insurance Protection for Your Family," page 66, and "When Estate-Planning Trusts Can Help," page 259). If you haven't been able to set aside significant retirement savings, you may also want to investigate the purchase of some type of annuity, which would guarantee you a predictable monthly income for your later years. Meanwhile, I'd also advise you to consider a long-term-care policy as well, since you may not have the deep pockets to shelter your company from a forced sale if you or your spouse eventually require nursing home care.

Stage 3

Exiting through a Sale to Another Individual

Here's how to prepare and plan for the personal financial consequences.

THE RECENT AND PROLONGED U.S. business boom produced many benefits. But one of the biggest often gets overlooked by entrepreneurs—at least until they start thinking about parting with their companies. It's the unparalleled abundance of possible buyers, thanks to a number of different trends that have left plenty of people well capitalized, unemployed, and far too young and energetic to retire. Some are the recipients of hefty severance or early-retirement packages tied to company downsizings. Others are successful investors who used their stock market profits to finance flights from the large-corporation world. And quite a few are former entrepreneurs themselves.

For most business owners, I'm convinced, this large pool of potential buyers offers their best prospects for a timely and fairly priced sale. Although this type of transaction doesn't carry with it the same super-high payoff potential of an initial public offering or deal with a large corporation, it's got some very big advantages, which are especially valuable in tougher economic climates. First, because these kinds of buyers tend to personally finance most or all of the cost of their purchases, they don't tend to be dependent on the availability of bank credit. That makes these deals far less vulnerable to economic downturns than, say, IPOs or those sales to corporations that are paid for with cash rather than stock.

> *I cannot stress how strongly I believe that getting to know your competitors, especially the senior executives and company leaders, is important for any entrepreneur. Lots of people shun this, but that's not a sophisticated approach to running any business.*
>
> —BRIAN SULLIVAN

As I frequently emphasize to all those business owners who come to me for advice about how to sell, there are other benefits: Individual buyers typically are much more open to a wide range of industries and market niches than corporate or professional investors might be. They're also far likelier to shop among small-scale companies, meaning those whose growth potential won't ever push them into an eight- or nine-figure revenue category.

Business Planning

If you're convinced that this type of sale might be the best exit strategy to pursue, start preparing your company sooner rather than later. Hopefully your objective isn't an imminent sale. In an ideal situation, you'll have at least a year or so to make certain that your financial records and other corporate documentation are in order. I'd advise you to take three steps at this initial stage:

❶ Make certain that your annual financial reports are audited by a certified public accountant. Savvier buyers will probably insist on more than one year's worth of audited returns. If time pressures don't permit you to build this kind of paper trail for, say, this year and next, hire a CPA firm to assess or supplement prior years' financial reports.

❷ Look for extra ways to document your company's strengths and growth potential. Any or all of the following details can be helpful in building your case to a potential buyer: a comprehensive analysis of revenue and profit streams by major product or service line; specific breakdowns of your company's operating costs, cash-flow patterns, and short- and long-term financing needs; and full details about your historic and current customer and supplier bases.

If your ultimate objective had been an IPO or a deal with a large corporate player, you would have hired an investment banking firm to coordinate the various tasks associated with step #2, along with many others. But in this lower-end segment of the for-sale marketplace, you'll need to carry out most of this preparation by yourself (or with the help of your attorney or accountant).

❸ Search out and eliminate red flags that could scare off possible buyers. At many entrepreneurial companies, these take the form of comingled personal and corporate assets or overlapping financial transactions that could make it tough for an outsider to evaluate the boundaries between your company's coffers and your family's pocketbook.

If your company is carrying what might be seen as an excessive amount of debt—whether to credit card companies, banks, friend-and-family lenders, or your own household—you'll be best off establishing a payment plan that will gradually reduce or eliminate these obligations before you hang up your for-sale sign. Make certain, though, that the repayment schedule won't significantly disrupt cash flow or growth-related activities.

Once you've carried out these three steps or at least gotten started in the right direction, you're ready to reach out to potential buyers. There is a range of alternatives here. You can try to handle the transaction yourself, which carries with it the advantage of saving yourself a sales commission. The traditional method for handling a sale this way involves personal networking, perhaps with friends or relatives, and advertising the company, usually through local newspapers, trade publications, or regional business magazines. Thanks to the rise of the Internet, do-it-yourself sellers now have a second, although more costly, option, which is to list their companies at one of a variety of electronic websites.

Having tracked the business-sale market closely for nearly five years now, I wouldn't recommend either of those two alternatives. If you're running a growth-oriented company, I just don't believe you have the time or the resources to carry out an aggressive sales effort all by yourself. (As one owner who tried recently and unsuccessfully to sell his financial services firm told me, it's also very difficult to be an effective and objective negotiator when you're so closely and emotionally tied up with the company you're trying to sell. "I found myself getting prickly," was the way he put it, "when people asked questions that made it seem as though they didn't appreciate my business. That scared them off, because it seemed as if I had something to hide.")

As for the Internet option, my objections here are quite similar to the ones I've raised earlier in my discussion of websites that aim to attract angel investors (see "Where Can You Find Angel Investors?" page 184). Although these sites are proliferating and clearly do attract their share of window-shoppers, I just don't see signs of enough deals getting concluded this way to justify the cost of these listings.

Instead, what I'd recommend is that you track down a good local business broker whose qualifications include familiarity with your industry and experience selling companies that are fairly similar to your own. These days, most successful brokers will use the Internet as well as traditional marketing techniques in order to maximize your prospects for attracting buyer interest.

The best way to generate good leads to business brokers is by networking with your accountant, attorney, banker, chamber of commerce, and local trade associations. Check credentials carefully and be certain to interview entrepreneurs whose companies were successfully sold by the broker and not just by his or her firm.

One final tip: Stay away from business brokers who try to charge you an up-front fee as well as a sales-based commission. It's usually unnecessary and, on occasion, can be a warning sign of a fraudulent professional.

Personal Planning

I apologize in advance if anything that I'm about to say destroys your illusions. But if you're thinking about selling your company through this method, there are a few points you need to focus some attention on.

First and foremost, don't lose sight of the fact that in return for whatever sale price you negotiate, you're going to be giving up your salary, bonuses, and any other ownership perks you've set in place by Stage Three. Under current marketplace conditions, transactions like these tend to command a sale price that ranges somewhere between three and six times EBITDA (an accounting term that means earnings before interest, taxes, depreciation, and amortization).

If you're even thinking about the sale of your company

Unusual Niches

AT SOME PRIVATELY HELD COMPANIES—especially those that operate within small or unusual business niches—it can be tough to attract the interest of outsiders, no matter how profitable the business may be. Their advantages are simply too much of a secret. In those cases, I advise owners to look inside their organizations, since their best chances for completing a successful sale may come from a management or employee buyout.

Here are three of these strategies worth exploring:

❑ **A gradual or complete sale to a key executive.** It will probably be up to you to broach the possibility to any of your top managers who might seem to be likely candidates, since the prospect may not otherwise cross their minds. If there's interest on that end, you can help the deal to happen if you offer to personally finance whatever portion of the sale cannot be covered through your employee's savings or borrowing capabilities.

❑ **The creation of an employee stock ownership plan (ESOP).** Once, but no longer, popular at large publicly traded companies, ESOPs now are mainly used by entrepreneurs who are looking for ways to finance their departures from private companies. You'll need legal and accounting help to structure

to an individual buyer, I'd urge you to calculate two sets of numbers: (1) your annual total compensation, meaning the value of all those goodies you now bring home each year plus whatever you manage to sock away in some type of retirement savings or deferred compensation account, and (2) your likely selling price range.

What if that second number is not significantly greater than the first? Then I'd speculate that it doesn't really make much sense for you to sell the company, at least this transaction properly. Once your company's stock ownership plan is in place, however, it should be able to borrow sufficient funds from a bank to purchase some or all of your stock (and then gradually begin to transfer it to your employees).

Tip: You may be able to defer your taxes on a sale to an ESOP if you fit certain criteria and you reinvest the proceeds of the sale into so-called qualified replacement property, which refers to stock or bonds issued by U.S. corporations. Again, don't try this without an expert's guidance.

❑ **The recruitment and hiring of your eventual successor.** Think of this as a last-ditch option, since it will likely take some time and delay your eventual exit. But if you don't have anyone on staff who seems interested in purchasing the company (or is qualified to do so), start thinking about expanding your management team to bring such a person on board. In this case, you'll want to be pretty frank with your potential hires about your longer-term objectives. But don't place yourself on the defensive: If your company is profitable and you're willing to help provide the financial wherewithal to support its purchase by an insider, you'll probably find that this job attracts lots of qualified and motivated applicants.

under your current set of financial realities. Maybe what you need to do instead is concentrate on some accelerated growth strategies that might increase your firm's ultimate sale price. If you can't sell your company for at least three (and ideally, more than five) times your total compensation package, you could find yourself in the worst of all worlds—forced to go to work for somebody else sometime soon, unless you've built up a very large and diversified investment portfolio to supplement your sales package.

If you're in this boat—and, at the same time, your company currently is supporting you in a comfortable lifestyle with plenty of added extras—I'd at least consider the prospect of hiring a high-level manager and scaling back your time commitment to the company rather than cashing in at a price that's ridiculously low. Then again, you might want to proceed with the sale, even at a reduced price, if you're nearing retirement age and feel physically and emotionally ready to cut back to an easier (and less expensive) lifestyle.

But there's no single right answer here. After all, you might find yourself in a situation in which your anticipated profits would be sufficient for you to be able to reinvest them in a new entrepreneurial venture that will, hopefully sometime soon, replace your current compensation package with one that's even more lucrative. In that case, you won't need to worry about raising so much money since you are planning to invest it and use the proceeds to supplement your retirement and other savings.

If you decide that you want to do this kind of deal now but need to look for ways to squeeze some additional income from it, there are some kickers you might want to consider. Instead of selling real estate or heavy equipment that your company is dependent on, segregate these assets from the rest of the business and propose leasing, rather than selling, them to your buyer. That will guarantee you a revenue stream moving forward (which will help ease the pain from that forgone paycheck) and, at least in the case of the real estate, might also allow you to reap additional profits later on if the property appreciates in value. You might also consider offering to partially finance the deal (again, think future revenue stream) in return for an attractive interest rate, a somewhat higher sales price, or a bonus arrangement tied to future growth achievements.

One last caveat: Since a sale like this one usually involves the transfer of a large block of cash to an entrepreneur, I think it's essential to have an advance plan for how you'll handle all that money, especially during the early days after the sale, when you can expect to be in a fairly emotional (and perhaps even erratic) frame of mind. I've heard some real horror stories from sellers about the ways that they frittered away or misinvested valuable funds as they coped with feelings of guilt, disorientation, or even boredom.

Here's what I'd suggest: After the closing, put all that money away someplace safe (and preferably, hard to get at) for at least three months, to give yourself some time and space to consider your options. Investing in 90-day certificates of deposit isn't a bad idea at all, although a money market fund would work just as well, so long as you don't need a lock and chain to keep you away from your booty.

Then, during this period, carefully explore your options with some help from your accountant, attorney, and perhaps a personal finance adviser. Keep in mind that you'll owe capital gains taxes on this transaction for any payments you receive during the year in which your sale closes. If the sale is structured to include installment payments, capital gains taxes will be assessed during any year in which you receive those payments. Depending on how much you've received, as well as its timing, you'll also probably need to adjust your estate-tax plan to take into account the longer-term consequences of cashing in your company. Finally, you'll also want to work out a new or adjusted savings and investment strategy that's appropriate given your age; the status of your family members, retirement savings, and projected needs; and the depth and breadth of your current investment portfolio.

Stage 3

Exiting through a Sale to Another Corporation

Although there are cons as well as pros to this strategy, you may be able to achieve greater profits and long-term personal financial security.

THE BUSINESS-SALE STRATEGY that I'm about to discuss won't work for every company, nor will it fully satisfy every owner's personal financial objectives. But its advantages are so significant that you may be tempted to give it a try anyhow.

Go right ahead. I wouldn't discourage any owner from at least investigating this option if the time and motivation to do so are there. That's because a sale to a corporate buyer offers most entrepreneurs the best chance they'll have of earning a truly lucrative payoff (since, after all, even in the best of economic times, an initial public offering is truly a long shot).

As I tell owners when they call me with questions about these transactions, their advantages all boil down to one factor: money. These types of deals tend to be priced at higher valuations than sales to individuals do, which makes sense because corporations usually have deeper pockets that they can dip into, as well as existing credit lines and other financing options. They're often willing to pay more as well, because they'll typically only contemplate an acquisition like this when it promises to deliver valuable synergies to their existing businesses, which usually take the form of enhanced revenue potential, anticipated cost efficiencies, or broadened customer bases.

There are other advantages, but they also fall into the category of dollars and cents. That's because these deals often involve terms or contingencies that can create greater upside potential for a seller (although they may increase a deal's risk factors as well). These might take the form of a long-term bonus, on top of the fixed sale price, which would be tied to the achievement of the acquirer's growth objectives; equity stock payments, if the purchaser is a publicly traded company; or some type of stock warrant or option payment, if the purchaser is another privately held company with plans to eventually carry out an IPO. For owners who are concerned about their future income streams, it's worth pointing out that many corporate suitors will agree to—or even insist upon—a moderate-length employment or consulting contract with the seller.

When I felt that it was the right time to sell the company to a major international player in our industry, my employees who were minority owners all supported the sale. And, in fact, they were essential ingredients in making it all happen. Giving them equity was one of the smartest decisions I ever made.

—BRIAN SULLIVAN

All this may sound very appealing to you. But there are downsides to this exit strategy worth keeping in mind. You'll have a hard time attracting corporate interest if your company is small; depending on your industry, that might describe a revenue base of anything less than $5 million to $10 million. You've also got to have great growth potential, or be able to build a good case that your business lines will help galvanize sales growth elsewhere when they're combined with those of a well-heeled business suitor.

Get the idea? You (or your company's sales adviser)

need to be pretty proactive to make one of these deals happen. They require much more creative planning and legwork than it takes to reach out to the individual-buyer market. And that's not all. If you manage to close one of these sales, you'll need to be prepared for a package that will seldom involve a full and outright payment of cash. All those quirky terms with great payoff potential will usually tie your fate to that of the buyer's for years to come. (That's a reality a large number of sellers have come to regret after the stock market collapse of 2000–01. "I sold my life's work for nothing," one former entrepreneur complained to me as he reported that the stock he had received in return for his own had collapsed from a value of $16 per share to below $2. And there wasn't anything he could do about it.)

Then again, every segment of the for-sale market contains stories of failures as well as successes. If you're still interested in pursuing a corporate buyer, here's a two-part action list.

Business Planning

❑ **Get your *p*s and *q*s in order fast.** You won't find yourself with any wiggle room when it comes to presenting your company's financial reports, as you might in a sale to an individual buyer. You'll likely need audited financial returns for at least the past two years. In this part of the for-sale market, your company can never be too well credentialed or documented. My advice? If your accounting firm isn't a major national or regional player, make the switch today and then wait for this year's audited results before proceeding further.

❑ **Assess your sale options realistically.** If your company truly is a little gem with great growth potential, a loyal customer base, profit margins to die for, and a well-controlled market niche, you may be able to negotiate its sale yourself, by picking up the phone and approaching its short list of likely buyers. But if you know in your heart of hearts that the deal of your dreams will take some work (maybe because you don't know—or can't approach—all those possible corporate suitors), you'll need some help. It makes sense to proceed quickly to step #3.

❑ **Hire an investment banker.** Don't try to save money here by relying on a business broker instead. (True, they're cheaper—and they can do a great job in reaching out to the world of individual buyers. But most don't have the network of blue-chip contacts or the financial and legal expertise to negotiate a successful sale to a corporate buyer, especially if that buyer turns out to be a large or publicly traded corporation.) Rely on your network of advisers to generate good leads here; if you've followed my earlier suggestion and upgraded your accounting firm, it should be able to make some valuable introductions. Then, check out credentials carefully. You'll want to look for an investment banker who personally (as well as through his or her firm) has experience with your industry and strong ties to the types of corporations that might make a good fit.

❑ **Set some parameters.** Because these deals can take many different forms, it's essential to convey a clear sense of your financial objectives (see "Personal Planning," below) to your investment banker before he begins marketing your company. I'd also advise you to impose some boundaries—based in part on input from your team of advisers—since you won't want to pursue this option indefinitely if it turns out that your business really isn't a likely candidate for a corporate sale.

Be sure to guard against a situation in which the sales process continues for so long that your competitors or employees begin to sense instability, which could lead to business conditions starting to unravel. If you discover that a timely and profitable corporate-based sale isn't possible for your business, switch gears promptly and begin pursuing individual buyers instead.

Personal Planning

If there's one thing I want to stress to you right now, it's that all company sales are not the same. If you close a deal with an individual buyer, odds are overwhelmingly strong that you'll wind up with a pile of cash. It's a simple transaction that rewards you with financial liquidity, penalizes you with immediate tax consequences, and offers you a wide range of future spending and investment opportunities. If you sell your business to a corporation, your personal financial situation can be and probably will be much more complex.

First of all, these deals are seldom 100 percent cash based. In fact, it's not at all unheard-of for corporate suitors to present bids that involve little or no payment of cash; in those cases, what's offered is usually a swapping of stock. Basically, the seller goes from being the majority owner of his or her company to some type of minority ownership stake in the acquiring business.

Whether you're open to this kind of deal really depends on your personal situation (i.e., do you have immediate needs for some or all of that cash?) and the extent of your confidence in the acquiring company. After all, if those synergies really do deliver results, the stock you receive upon closing may eventually turn out to be much more valuable than it looks right now. There's one more benefit worth pointing out: Unlike a cash-based transaction, stock swaps do not incur a tax liability until those new shares are sold, which can give an owner more control over the personal tax planning process. Make sure to involve your accountant and attorney, however, so that you can qualify as a merger that will deserve this tax-advantaged treatment. These fees should also be tax deductible for the corporation.

But even if you do have a lot of confidence in the deal, I'd still advise you to stay away from stock-only transactions. During the 1990s, while the public stock market was booming, these deals abounded, because plenty of sellers convinced themselves that they weren't really risky at all. That's because the shares of publicly traded companies were liquid—and seemed capable of moving in only one direction, up—while options or warrants in a privately held company with plans for an IPO seemed like the next closest thing to a sure bet.

Regardless of what condition the stock market is in, I don't buy either of those arguments. There's always risk attached to an equity stake, and although entrepreneurs are, by their nature, risk takers, I try to warn sellers that it will feel very different for them to have their financial futures on the line when they're no longer the person in charge of the company whose stock or options they're betting on.

I also point out that equity-only deals don't help sellers achieve any of their important liquidity or investment diversification goals (since they basically just trade one stock stake for another). For all those owners whose fantasy boils down to a variation on the theme of "sell the company, buy a boat, and sail around the world," this strategy just won't get them from here to there.

My recommendation is that you tell your investment banker that you will only consider deals that include an up-front cash payment as well as an equity component. In order to increase your safety level, you might also want to insist on a higher cash-to-equity ratio if the bidder is a private company and there's more uncertainty about when (or even if) it will succeed in carrying out an initial public offering.

There's one more personal issue worth thinking about before you hire an investment banker to market your company to the wide world of business suitors. Do you want or not want to stay involved with your business after a sale? If you're willing, an employment or consulting contract can be a great source of continued income for you, which can help ease the transition from business ownership to early retirement. But I've heard enough complaints from disgruntled sellers to realize that this income sometimes comes at a heavy personal price. It's very difficult for many people to accept a secondary role within the company that they created and led. If you suspect you'd feel this way, that's another reason to think long and hard before pursuing a sale to another corporation, which might very well insist on your continued involvement after the deal closes.

Stage 3

Exiting through an Initial Public Offering

Although this strategy will be an option for only a select group of entrepreneurial companies, its rewards are well worth the careful planning it takes.

THERE'S NOTHING REALLY FAIR about initial public offerings.

For the owners of plenty of really great entrepreneurial ventures—I'd go so far as to say for most of them—there isn't a snowball's chance in hell that they'll be able to cash in some or all of their equity stakes by taking their companies public. This window of opportunity is simply too narrow for most privately held corporations to squeeze through. The dot-com mania of the late 1990s, extreme though it was, epitomized a reality that most small business experts know all too well: The only likely candidates for an IPO are those companies on a short list of hot industries—a list that shifts according to the whims of the stock market—and those that seem destined to grow fairly quickly to $100 million or more in revenues.

Regardless of what fantasies you may have had back in those early start-up days, by the time that you reach Stage Three of operations, you should be capable of assessing your real chances for carrying out this type of exit strategy. After having tracked the financial paths of entrepreneurs for more than a decade, I'm convinced that there are basically only two routes that will get you to an IPO:

❑ **Leap onto the fast track early.** If your start-up or early-stage business plan demonstrated enough accelerated-growth potential that you already have been able to bring in one or more rounds of venture capital money, you've very likely got the network of contacts and financial infrastructure in place to enable you to carry off an IPO at some early point in Stage Three. That assumes, of course, that you have been able to follow your business plan and basically achieve its targeted objectives. During the late 1990s, when this segment of the capital markets seemed to throw all caution aside, plenty of fast-track companies went public during Stage Two of development, when their business models were scarcely proven, let alone profitable. But given the failure of so many of those IPOs, that pattern isn't likely to repeat itself in the near future.

❑ **Shift gears.** At some point in a business venture's development, the owner may decide to diversify into an area that presents extraordinary growth potential or choose to change the company's plan, perhaps to pursue business on a national or international scale rather than simply a regional one. In some cases, after years of steady and profitable growth an entrepreneur's ambitions simply expand, seeking new and intensified challenges that may lead to the acquisition of competitors or the development of new business lines. Whatever the spark, it can ignite a new, turbocharged set of business plans and opportunities and attract venture capitalists, investment bankers, and

IPO underwriters to a Stage Three company that previously lacked their attentions.

If you find yourself in either of these two situations, this action plan should help you carry out a successful exit through an initial public offering:

Business Planning

Believe it or not, this part of your planning process is fairly simple, in part because if you truly are a likely candidate, you've got a team of advisers and professional investors already in place, ones who understand what's necessary to bring these deals to a profitable conclusion. That's the good news and the bad news. With this type of transaction, as opposed to exits through a sale to an individual or a corporate buyer, you won't be able to dictate this process.

Of course, this warning may not come as a surprise to you. Depending on how many rounds of venture capital money you've raised so far, you may no longer control a majority equity stake in the company you founded. You may not even be running the business anymore on a day-to-day basis.

But regardless of the particulars of your own situation, you'll need to come to terms quickly with the fact that IPOs are propelled by a momentum all their own.

❑ **Your company's choice of its investment banker and stock underwriter will very likely be determined by two factors:** your professional investors' network of contacts and your industry (because it will only make sense to choose firms with in-depth knowledge and transaction experience relating to your business niche). While you certainly should insist that you feel a personal rapport with any adviser hired at this stage, don't expect your vote alone to carry the choice.

❑ **Your company's timing in bringing its stock public may or may not be influenced by your personal timetable** (that is, unless you share your investors' goal of accomplishing this as quickly as possible). During the late 1990s, it became fairly common for venture capitalists to try to carry out an IPO within one or two years of an initial investment. Under less frenzied market conditions, most entrepreneurial companies can expect this to occur within two to four years of first-round financing by any type of private equity fund.

The biggest factor at play here will be the state of the IPO market itself. (Perverse, isn't it? It's the financing tactic, not the company, that sets the pace.) Your professional investors and their advisers will likely watch each week's roster of successful deals with close attention so that they'll be able to start the process going for you as soon as other candidates in your industry have concluded offerings at attractive multiples.

If this process strikes you as unpredictable and stressful, you're right. After the dot-com market collapsed in early 2000, nearly shutting down the IPO market along with it, I spoke to one entrepreneur in the health care market who told me that he was checking in with his underwriter several times each week to see if a window of opportunity was finally presenting itself. After some months, the answer was still no—and he was beginning to consider his other options.

❑ **Your company's pricing when its stock goes public will likewise be determined by the investor group's financial objectives** as well as current marketplace conditions. But although you can't set that price by yourself, there's one fairly big consolation: If you do successfully complete an initial public offering, you will almost certainly earn a significantly higher payment for your stock than from any other type of exit strategy.

One last point: Although you cannot control very much about the IPO process, you should have some room to maneuver when it comes to determining how much of your equity stake you want to sell or retain (see "Personal Planning," below). For most entrepreneurs, an initial public offering seldom represents the same clean break that a sale to an individual buyer would; even if you don't plan to remain involved in the day-to-day leadership of your newly public company, you'll probably want to retain a minority investment stake in order to give yourself some upside potential. And in fact, your underwriters will probably insist on this, since it would send negative vibrations to your potential investors if you tried to cash out entirely at this stage. Be prepared: You'll probably also face restrictions (sometimes known as a lockup clause) on how quickly you can begin to sell your post-IPO holdings. In most cases, your stock-sale options will be restricted for somewhere between twelve and eighteen months (although occasionally deals do include "windows" that permit small sales during very brief early opportunities).

The bottom line: If you choose to remain involved in your company's management while continuing to own a significant amount of its stock, your company's IPO will be more of a liquidity event than an exit strategy, at least for a while. But it's clearly a major step in the right direction, since post-IPO, it should be fairly simple for you to divest yourself of your equity holdings over time, as you desire to do so.

Personal Planning

For many people, this is the most challenging aspect of preparing for and carrying out an initial public offering. That's because there are so many different personal financial factors to weigh and, depending on your household's priorities, these can affect your pre- and post-IPO decisions in a wide variety of ways. Below, you'll find a checklist of questions that should help you begin to prioritize and plan.

Let me stress one point here: You'll face some tough decisions here. I urge you to involve not only your spouse but also your team of personal financial advisers (including your accountant and attorney and also, if you have them, an investment adviser and estate-planning professional).

❶ What short-term financial goals do you expect an IPO to help you achieve? If your family's financial position is already solid, your answer here may be fairly general: additional liquidity, which will permit you to further reduce personal risks by diversifying your investments. Or perhaps you desire sufficient funds to permit you to restructure your investment portfolio to support you during an early retirement. Or your financial goals may be quite specific. You may have a new set of entrepreneurial plans and want to raise enough cash to support the start-up of another growth-oriented venture. It may be time to concentrate on key family-oriented objectives (perhaps you've never been able to set aside enough for your children's college tuition bills, and this strikes you as a good way to raise those funds, as well as some others). Whatever the right answer is for you, that's a starting point in helping you begin to quantify how much cash you'd like to raise at the IPO stage.

❷ What long-term goals would you also like to achieve thanks to your public offering? When I ask them this question, many people focus on their future retirement security, even if they plan to continue to work, post-IPO, at their own companies or elsewhere. In an ideal situation, they'd be able to raise sufficient funds at the time of the public offering to prepare for this or other future-oriented goals, as well as their short-term objectives. Here again, it's helpful to try to quantify your financial target.

But whether it proves to be possible for you to achieve this now will depend on many factors, most especially how much of your personal stake you are willing to sell at the time of the IPO, how much stock your investors and underwriter will permit you to sell, and what kind of price it will

Post-IPO Strategy

AS YOU REDUCE YOUR PERSONAL stake in your company, during and after its IPO, you'll need to rethink your overall investment strategy. After all, the IPO sale process will drastically reduce your exposure to the stock market while significantly enhancing your liquidity and investment potential—quite a change from the position you've been in since you first bet your family's finances on your entrepreneurial brainstorm and launched your start-up.

If you don't plan to reinvest most of your IPO proceeds in a new business venture, I'd suggest that you spend some time familiarizing yourself with the wide range of equity options that may now make sense given your deep and diversified investment portfolio. Don't act too quickly. Many, many opportunities will now be open to you. It's important for you and your family to weigh their various advantages and disadvantages.

One caveat: Unless you're planning to make stock watching your new full-time job, I also recommend that you tap into the expertise of an investment adviser, whether you've chosen to do so in the past or not. You need someone who has experience in dealing with well-heeled entrepreneurs like you, preferably an adviser whose client list includes other post-IPO company founders. Depending on your personal needs and preferences, this person might be a fee-only financial planner, an investment broker, or a wealth-management consultant at a bank or some other financial services firm.

command. If there's a shortfall, aim to compensate for it through a gradual process of diminishing your post-IPO stake and investing or saving the proceeds.

❸ How will you handle the capital-gains-tax and estate-tax implications of the IPO? Don't try to answer this one on your own. You'll need input from your advisers and should have a set of financial plans in place pre-IPO if possible (which will at best allow you to minimize the negative tax consequences and at the very least make certain that you are prepared to handle the cost).

❹ How close to an exit do you really want to get? Don't underestimate the importance of this question. While it's not possible for you to walk away from your company the day you carry off your IPO, your answer here will determine how quickly or slowly you distance yourself from the business.

If you're not really looking for a way out the door, then it makes sense to hold on to as big an equity stake as you can afford to do. Your authority and experience as the company's founder, combined with your muscle as a significant minority shareholder, may be sufficient to keep you at the helm if that's where you desire to be. If you're convinced of your company's accelerated growth potential now that the public markets are behind it, then it's probably in your family's long-term financial interests to retain a significant exposure to its stock.

On the other hand, if you do have your sights set on an exit (whether because you're ready for an early retirement or because you know that you're not the best person to run a large, publicly traded company), then you should allow your answers to questions #1 and #2 to influence how much stock you sell now and over time.

Stage 3

Conclusion

VENTURE CAPITALISTS SOMETIMES JOKE that the financial projections on every entrepreneur's business plan look the same—basically, just like a check mark, meaning there's a small downward movement, suggestive of a few start-up challenges, and then the bold upstroke, representing sales growth or profitability, that soars into the stratosphere. Yet we all know that few, if any, companies wind up following that kind of pattern.

I'm also aware that the clearly ordered strategies spelled out in this book (attached as they are to three stages of corporate growth with a progressive pattern of development and achievement) may also seem a little utopian to a business owner who might find himself or herself in Stage Two today, back at square one tomorrow, and then faced with the prospect of selling the company to a competitor (or buying that competitor) by the end of next week.

But I don't expect you to carry out every one of the strategies in this book in exactly the same way that I've laid them out in these pages. For one thing, I'm very aware that once you—or any entrepreneur—actually start developing a personal financial plan, you'll probably find yourself amending it as frequently as you adjust your business model. So don't hesitate to leaf through these pages and to use this guide in whatever order works for you.

That's actually a very sensible approach to creating and carrying out a financial plan that will make the best sense for you, your family, and your company. Fortunately, successful entrepreneurs are masters of flexibility as well as ingenuity. Now that you have read through this guide, I hope that you'll pick and choose those strategies that seem most relevant and useful to your own situation. And may they help you flourish.

Index

Index

Index

About Bloomberg

BLOOMBERG L.P., FOUNDED IN 1981, is a global information services, news, and media company. Headquartered in New York, the company has nine sales offices, two data centers, and 85 news bureaus worldwide.

Bloomberg, serving customers in 126 countries around the world, holds a unique position within the financial services industry by providing an unparalleled range of features in a single package known as the BLOOMBERG PROFESSIONAL™ service. By addressing the demand for investment performance and efficiency through an exceptional combination of information, analytic, electronic trading, and Straight Through Processing tools, Bloomberg has built a worldwide customer base of corporations, issuers, financial intermediaries, and institutional investors.

BLOOMBERG NEWS℠, founded in 1990, provides stories and columns on business, general news, politics, and sports to leading newspapers and magazines throughout the world. BLOOMBERG TELEVISION®, a 24-hour business and financial news network, is produced and distributed globally in seven different languages. BLOOMBERG RADIO™ is an international radio network anchored by flagship station BLOOMBERG® WBBR 1130 in New York.

In addition to the BLOOMBERG PRESS® line of books, Bloomberg publishes *BLOOMBERG® MARKETS, BLOOMBERG PERSONAL FINANCE™,* and *BLOOMBERG® WEALTH MANAGER.* To learn more about Bloomberg, call a sales representative at:

Frankfurt: 49-69-92041-200	São Paulo:.........5511-3048-4500
Hong Kong:........85-2-2977-6600	Singapore: 65-212-1200
London: 44-20-7330-7500	Sydney: 61-2-9777-8601
New York: 1-212-318-2200	Tokyo:...............81-3-3201-8950
San Francisco:....1-415-912-2980	

For in-depth market information and news, visit the Bloomberg website at **www.bloomberg.com** which draws from the news and power of the BLOOMBERG PROFESSIONAL™ service and Bloomberg's host of media products to provide high-quality news and information in multiple languages on stocks, bonds, currencies, and commodities.

About the Author

JILL ANDRESKY FRASER, a professional journalist who has covered financial matters for two decades, is known and respected by entrepreneurs. She is finance editor at *Inc.* magazine, where she reports on corporate and personal financial strategies for the small business community, and is a general editor at *Bloomberg Personal Finance*. She has been a writer at *Forbes*, the Executive Life columnist for the Sunday Business section of the *New York Times*, and the Wall Street columnist for the *New York Observer*. She lives with her husband and two children in New York City and Montauk, New York.